GROWTH OF POPULATION
CONSEQUENCES AND CONTROLS

GROWTH OF POPULATION

Consequences and Controls

Proceedings of the First Conference on Population
held at Princeton, New Jersey, September 27 to 30, 1968

Edited by

M. C. SHELESNYAK
Professor of Biodynamics
Director, Interdisciplinary Communications Program
Smithsonian Institution
Washington, D. C.

GORDON AND BREACH, SCIENCE PUBLISHERS
New York • London • Paris

iv

FIRST CONFERENCE ON POPULATION

AGENDA AND
DISCUSSION
INITIATORS

First Conference on
Population

I. The Demographic Facts

A. What can be said with
assurance about the
numbers and charac-
teristics (e.g., age,
race, location, occu-
pation) of the present
population and of that
which will live on
Earth between now and
the year 2000 ?   Frank W. Notestein

B. What are the major
consequences of cur-
rent and expected pop-
ulation growth: for the
developed world? for
the developing world?

   1. Food   Theodore W. Schultz
   2. Resources: miner-
     als, water, air,
     space   Joseph L. Fisher
   3. The Cities   Kingsley Davis
   4. Political and
     social organization:
     individual liberty/
     national sover-
     eignty?   Merton C. Bernstein

FIRST CONFERENCE ON POPULATION
Princeton Inn, Princeton, New Jersey
September 27-30, 1968

Series Chairman:
O. Harkavy, Ph.D., Program Officer in Charge
International Division: Population
The Ford Foundation
320 East 43rd Street
New York, New York 10017

Merton C. Bernstein, AB., LLB.
Professor of Law
College of Law
Ohio State University
1659 North High Street
Columbus, Ohio 43210

Neil W. Chamberlain, Ph.D.
Professor of Economics
Graduate School of Business
Columbia University
Uris Hall
New York, New York 10027

Kingsley Davis, Ph.D.
Professor Sociology
Department of Sociology
Director of International Population and Urban
    Research

ix

University of California
Berkeley, California 94720

Paul R. Ehrlich, Ph. D.
Professor of Biology
Department of Systematic Biology
Stanford University
Stanford, California 94305

Joseph L. Fisher, Ph. D., President
Resources for the Future, Inc.
1755 Massachusetts Avenue, N. W.
Washington, D. C. 20036

Ronald Freedman, Ph. D.
Professor of Sociology
Director, Population Studies Center
University of Michigan
Ann Arbor, Michigan 48104

Frank Fremont-Smith, M. D., Director Emeritus
Interdisciplinary Communications Program
c/o 149 Brewster Road
Massapequa, New York 11758

Hudson Hoagland, Ph. S., Sc. D.
President, The Worcester Foundation for Experimental
    Biology
222 Maple Avenue
Shrewsbury, Massachusetts 01545

William T. Knox, M. S., Vice President
McGraw-Hill, Incorporated
330 West Forty-second Street
New York, New York 10036

George J. Marcus, Ph. D.
Visiting Associate Professor

Department of Population and Family Health
The Johns Hopkins University
615 North Wolfe Street
Baltimore, Maryland 21205

Michael Michaelis, B. Sc. (Eng), Manager,
Washington Office
Arthur D. Little, Incorporated
1735 Eye Street, N. W.
Washington, D. C. 20005

Frank W. Notestein, Ph. D. , President Emeritus
The Population Council
245 Park Avenue
New York, New York 10017

O. E. Reynolds, Ph. D. , Director,
Bioscience Program
Office of Space Science and Applications
National Aeronautics and Space Administration
Washington, D. C. 20546

Lord Ritchie-Calder, C. B. E. , M. A.
House of Lords
London, England

Sherman Ross*, Ph. D.
American Psychological Association
1200 Seventeenth Street, N. W.
Washington, D. C. 20036

---

*Present address:
Executive Secretary,
Committee on Basic Research in Education
National Research Council
2101 Constitution Avenue, N. W.
Washington, D. C. 20037

Lyle Saunders, Program Officer
Population, International Division
The Ford Foundation
320 East 43rd Street
New York, New York 10017

Theodore W. Schultz, Ph. D.
Professor of Economics
Department of Economics
University of Chicago
Chicago, Illinois 60637

Sheldon J. Segal, Ph. D., Director
Bio-Medical Division
The Population Council
The Rockefeller University
York Avenue & Sixty-sixth Street
New York, New York 10021

M. C. Shelesnyak, Ph. D.
Professor of Biodynamics
Director, Interdisciplinary Communications Program
Suite 700, 1025-15th Street, N. W.
Washington, D. C. 20005

Lawrence B. Slobodkin, Ph. D.
Professor Ecology
Department of Biology
State University of New York
Stony Brook, Long Island, New York 11790

Francis X. Sutton, Ph. D.
The Ford Foundation
320 East Forty-third Street
New York, New York 10017

Sol Tax, Ph. D.
Professor of Anthropology
Department of Anthropology
University of Chicago
Chicago, Illinois 60637

Gordon Rattray Taylor
The Hall
Freshford, Bath BA3 6 EJ
England

N. W. Weissman, Ph. D.
Office of Space Science and Applications
National Aeronautics and Space Administration
Washington, D. C. 20546

Sir Solly Zuckerman, O. M. , K. C. B. , F. R. S.
Chief Scientific Advisor
Cabinet Office
London, S. W. 1, England

ICP Hostesses

Mrs. Mary Aginar
Mrs. Virginia M. Balton
Mrs. Roslyn Shelesnyak

Stenotypist

Mrs. Floy Swanson

FOREWORD

This Conference was planned and organized col-
laboratively by Dr. O. Harkavy, Officer in Charge,
Population Program, Ford Foundation, and Dr. M. C.
Shelesnyak, Director, Interdisciplinary Communications Program, Smithsonian Institution.

The letter addressed to members of the conference following the acceptance of an invitation from
Dr. O. Harkavy, chairman of the conference, is
printed below to give the reader an idea of the objectives of the meeting and some picture of the conference process:

"We are delighted to hear from Dr. Harkavy,
chairman of the Conference Series on Population of
the Interdisciplinary Communications Program (ICP),
that you have accepted our invitation to the First Conference on Population, which will be held at the Princeton Inn, Princeton, New Jersey, beginning Friday
evening, September 27, and ending Monday noon,
September 30, 1968. The conference is sponsored,
under contract with The New York Academy of Sciences,
by the Smithsonian Institution with funds made available by the National Aeronautics and Space Administration.

"The major emphasis of this series will be on the
greater involvement of industry and technology, of the
physical and social sciences, and of arts and humanities, in the solution of problems generated by the

world population expansion. The impact on immediate
and current problems in developed, as well as developing, countries will be examined. We believe this conference will be a unique opportunity to enlist participation of the engineer, the communication specialist,
the physicist, the economist, the psychologist, the
sociologist and public servant, the moralist, as well
as the demographer, physician, and biologist, in
discussion of a topic of interest to them all.

"These conferences offer an unusual opportunity
for a group of twenty to twenty-five individuals repre-
senting the several fields of learning—science, technology, and the humanities—which bear upon a chosen
topic, to meet for an informal exchange of ideas, data
and methods, and suggestions for future research and
development. In contrast to the usual scientific
gathering, these interdisciplinary meetings are organized primarily for informal discussion, not for the
presentation of formal papers. Accordingly, the conferences may be looked upon as exercises in cross-
discipline communication, an essential means of
advancing a given field.

"Each session will be quided by a "discussion
initiator" whose function will be to evoke discussion
among the other participants. He will introduce the
assigned topic in such a way as to elicit comments
and questions, as well as disagreements. Participants
are encouraged to interrupt the initiator and each
other with queries, observations, and references to
relevant literature.

"Thus, the conference becomes a forum for lively
discussion in depth, for finding new areas of agreement, and more important, for specifying the nature
of residual areas of disagreement. Both theoretical

and practical aspects of the topic under consideration
shoud be brought out, and unsolved dilemmas should
receive special attention. This conference procedure
derives from the Macy Foundation type of conference
which was originated by Dr. Frank Fremont-Smith,
Director Emeritus of the ICP. The enclosed reprint
written by him will explain the ICP conference philos-
ophy and process in greater detail.

"In preparation for the publication of an edited
version of the proceedings, the discussion will be
recorded by a stenotypist. Each participant will receive a verbatim transcript and will have the responsibility for making revisions or deletions of his remarks, prior to publication. It is hoped that spon-
taneous and vigorous participation, therefore, will not
be inhibited by this commitment to publication.

"This conference will begin with dinner at 6:00 p. m.
on Friday, September 27. All participants are expected to be present then and throughout the conference proceedings, including meals. After the opening
dinner, the group will assemble for brief introductory
remarks, followed by self-introductions by the participants."

M. C. SHELESNYAK, PH. D.
Director, Interdisciplinary
Communications Program,
Washington, D. C.

GROWTH OF POPULATION
CONSEQUENCES AND CONTROLS

FRIDAY EVENING SESSION
September 27, 1968

The first conference on Population, organized by the Interdisciplinary Communications Program of the Smithsonian Institution and The New York Academy of Sciences, held at the Princeton Inn, Princeton, New Jersey, convened at eight thirty o'clock. Dr. O. Harkavy, Program Officer, International Division: Population, The Ford Foundation, presided.

Harkavy: Ladies and gentlemen, I am delighted that all of you have come to this meeting. Because I am a neophyte at these conferences, I would like to turn the festivities this evening over to Dr. Shelesnyak. He knows what one is supposed to do at this point.

Shelesnyak: Thank you. I will start by welcoming all in the name of the Interdisciplinary Communications Program. It is associated with the Smithsonian Institution and The New York Academy of Sciences. This particular conference is sponsored by the Biosciences Program of National Aeronautics and Space Administration.

Before I describe the nature of the Interdisciplinary Communications Program, I wish

1

to welcome Dr. Fremont-Smith, the father of
the program, and now emeritus. He will, I
trust, rectify any irregularities in my description of the program and its purpose.

The conference program has been developed
as a means of communication for people from
various, different disciplines who have common
interests in a common problem, but very often
have barriers of language and barriers of ideas.
To achieve frank discussion and communication,
to break down or overcome these barriers, the
standardized procedure has been as follows:
first a problem area is selected; then a chairman is invited and in this instance we asked Bud
Harkavy to be the chairman of the conference
series on population.

Among other things, we have learned from
the program that we have different practitioners
of many disciplines, so, it takes more than one conference to develop interaction and fuse relationships that become truly productive.

The chairman of a conference chairs the
entire series and is the managing director. He
plays the role of conductor of an orchestra.

He asks for a group of six or eight members
to join and stay with him for the five-year period.
This constitutes a core group with representa-
tives of different disciplines.

Then, at each conference we have structured
agenda around which we have free and hopefully
uninhibited discussion. The main ground rules:
No formal lectures; interruption for clarification
or confrontation during any discussion, and no
stacking up of queries, hostilities or frustrations
until a so-called discussion period.

It is pertinent to discuss the product of this type of conference when it is successful. We hope to open new vistas, develop new approaches and new ideas toward the solution of such problems that are basically multidisciplinary; of course, the immediate product is the actual participation by the members of the group. Although it is very satisfying in many instances for each person to go home and say to himself or his colleagues that he has had a wonderful, exciting experience, we have a second obligation, which is a public obligation. That obligation is to make the essence of our discussions available to a larger community of interested persons. For this, we have a publication of proceedings, proceedings that are based on the stenotypist transcript. This publication attempts to convey the spirit and substance of the conversations. It does not pretend to be a report of the state of the art.

So much for the general background, although it hardly does fairness to the program which has been going on for some thirty-five years, originally as a Josiah Macy conference series, later with the American Institute of Biological Sciences, and currently with The New York Academy of Sciences and the Smithsonian Institution.

Tonight's session has the following objective: As we are going to be a small, intimate conversational group. We begin with a special type of self-introduction. The self-introductions are not simply, "I am Professor So-and -so of the Department of Such-and-such; thank you very much." We would like to know who you are and especially how you developed your professional interests in relation to the subject which is under discussion. This will follow a few comments on what our objective is for this conference.

I shall ask the Chairman, who is really going to run the show, to present to us, the task of this conference.

Harkavy: Thank you, Shelly. I hope that in the course of the self-introductions each of us will say what we would hope to get out of this conference.

I undertook the assignment as chairman of this Conference—in preparation for which Shelly has done most of the hard work—in the hope that a distinguished interdisciplinary group of this kind will provide some clues for future foundation activity. What, for example, are the major issues arising from the consequences of population growth? Lyle Saunders, my colleague, points out that we can predict the size and the composition of the world's population for the next decade or two. But, are we realistically planning to accommodate such a population?

We are, of course, immediately concerned with what we can do to control population growth, which we believe is running a disaster course in many parts of the world. Some of the background papers that have been sent to you make the point that what is being done to control fertility is grossly inadequate. I hope we shall engage in some constructive discussion of these matters.

If what we are doing is not enough, then what should we be doing? Specifically, what should we be doing "beyond family planning"?

The question of the social control of fertility has become increasingly salient. The writings of Paul Ehrlich and Kingsley Davis have sounded a clanging bell that has caused all of us engaged in population work to sit up and take notice. I must say, just to be provacative at the outset, that I am highly skeptical as to the specific proposals, but the conference should offer an important opportunity to join some of these issues.

We will start our self-introductions with Hudson Hoagland.

Hoagland: I am President of the Worcester Foundation for Experimental Biology, an organization started by the late Gregory Pincus and me twenty-five years ago. It was an outgrowth of work that he and I had been doing at Clark University. As you know, his major interest was in mammalian reproduction. My field was that of neurophysiology and psychopharmacology; we teamed together in some research on stress in relation to responses of the adrenal cortex, and this got me interested in the question of the stress of crowding.

I have been concerned in recent years about biological phenomena in relation to human social problems and a major one of these, obviously, is the tremendous upsurge of populations that is polluting our environment and causing a great stress and social unrest. This, combined with Pincus' practical approach to the problem in developing the first effective, and probably still the best, oral contraceptive was the natural takeoff point for my increasing concern with questions of population control.

I am an amateur in this field and pleased to be here and hear what you are going to say. I have been interested in how animals control their populations and whether there is any carryover from what has been learned about animal populations to controls of human populations.

As many of you know, we have at the Foundation a number of people working on the physiology of reproduction and some are concerned with the problem of new and improved contraceptives.

Saunders: I am Lyle Saunders. I work with Bud Harkavy and I think my main function is probably to keep his desk clear of papers, because they end up on mine all the time.

I am a sociologist by background and I think it is honest to say that I don't have any particular training that fits me for the job I am doing, because as a sociologist, I was exposed to demography but certainly not of the kind that the professional demographers, such as those here, practice.

I am in population partly because I am frightened. I don't like the prospects that seem to be in store for us, and I am probably enough of a pessimist to have some reservations about the collective ability of the human race to solve some of the problems it faces, and I would hope to get from conference some optimistic reassurance that my pessimism is unjustified and that there are, in fact, good, workable ideas in prospect which we can do something with.

Chamberlain: I am Neil Chamberlain and I come from
the Graduate School of Business at Columbia University.

I probably have less reason for being here
than anyone else around the table, for I have had
no contact with population problems and my current interest is really one of a fortuitous nature.
My interests in the past have tended to center
around problems of bargaining power relationships, and it was really almost an accidental
experience that led me to question whether there
might be some "pay dirt" in exploring how population changes affect the distribution of power
within society. I have been trying to do a bit of
reading and exploration in this area for the past
few months. I must say I've not had a great deal
of success in terms of finding any analyses that
dig into this problem very deeply.

To be succinct, my interest lies in exploring how population changes within any particular
politics unit, whether aggregates as large as the
world or a nation or as small as a city, might
restructure the composition of this unit in such a
way as to redistribute power within that unit. It
is in those terms that I am particularly interested
in getting any leads that any of you may have come
across.

I am a newcomer and am trying to get ac-
quainted with the literature but would welcome
the expertise that you bring to the subject.

Shelesnyak: No one in this group should apologize for
not being a specialist in population. As a matter
of act, by design, a significant number are not

population specialists, but people with special professional skills whom we would like to see as participants in the efforts to solve the problem. Unfortunately, the engineers whom we hoped to have had to drop out. We want a much broader spectrum than the usual. The population people have not made the case clear enough for the total impact to fall on all of the disciplines, all the technologists, all the academicians, all the people who should be playing a positive and dynamic role at this moment, in seeking solutions.

Bernstein: I am Merton Bernstein. I am a lawyer. That ought to be confession enough for one recital. To show that I am reasonably honest, I am a law professor. I am also (and I should make my disclosures early in the game) the father of four children, making me something of an amateur expert on the pressures of overcrowding. In part, I am here due to a feeling of guilt.

My serious concerns with population have been lurking for a long time. Professionally, I have managed to avoid the practice of law, to my great enjoyment, and spent much of the 1950's working in the United States Senate as counsel to then Senator Humphrey's Subcommittee on Labor and Labor Management Relations. I have been concerned for a long time with the architectural uses of law, with law as a means of shaping and reshaping parts of private institutions as well as public institutions. In my teaching, I have been conderned with programs that fall under the broad category of social legislation, dealing primarily

with governmental responses to broad social
problems of the modern economy and the way we
organize our lives in an essentially urban, wage
and cash economy.

It would seem to me that the emerging or existing problems of population will require some
kinds of public intervention, and I am here to try
to find out what some of them might be.

Taylor: I am Gordon Rattray Taylor, a writer. I
started out to be a biologist and I came from the
University in the Great Depression. Although I
couldn't get a job as a biologist, I could support
myself by writing. I have written nine books,
most of them concerned with the nature of social
change.

I would like to get out of the conference some
information about optimum population density.
I was at one time in charge of a small social research organization and tried to set up a project
involving the concept of optimal population density.
This was very difficult.

Ehrlich: I am Paul Ehrlich; I am the clanging bell. I
am a population biologist by profession. In the
past, I worked mostly with populations of non-
human origin, but this inevitably leads one into
questions of what man is doing to his surroundings
and the system he is dependent on.

Over the past several decades, I have been
increasingly horrified by: (a) the rate of population growth and the deterioration of environment;
and (b) by the lack of interest in this problem on
the part of professional and non-professional

people. My colleagues and I over the years have
gotten more and more involved in public education and research. As a matter of fact, at Stanford we now have a program that is concerned
with the questions of optimum population. It is
amazing that the world goes on without asking the
overall question: How many people can the earth
support, under what conditions, with what boundary conditions, and so on? Preliminary conclusions would lead to the view that the United States
is already overpopulated.

One of the things that has puzzled me and a
number of my colleagues for some time, is why
many demographers, for instance, are unexcited
about the current situation and have not published
articles about how the population explosion in the
United States is to be overcome.

So, I am here to help inject a little biology
into the discussion and also to take home to those,
like Peter Raven and Ken Watt on the West Coast,
an opinion on the chance of getting help on the
population explosion problem from groups represented here like, the Population Council.

Slobodkin: I am Larry Slobodkin; I am an ecologist
who started out working with experimental population systems—putting organisms in containers
and letting them do what they want to do about
populating the containers or filling the container.
From this I have branched out into more general
field problems.

After fourteen years at the University of
Michigan, I am now heading up an ecology group
at the State University of New York at Stony

Brook. We will have about fifteen ecologists, all of whom are more or less interested in questions of population regulation, pollution, human influences, and so forth. Here I want to get some sense of how a group of this sort can integrate their activities with other people who are concerned with population research.

I am as frightened of the simplistic solutions that have been suggested for population problems as I am of the problem itself. This is why I immediately felt called on to come when invited.

Michaelis: I am Michael Michaelis, with Arthur D. Little, Incorporated. I am an unabashed generalist. I am most concerned with the very rapid growth in knowledge, technical and otherwise, and the equally slow application of that knowledge.

I am concerned with the growing needs of our society, many of which are based on sheer numbers of people. I would like to get a feeling in this conference of how one can change institutions that employ our resources in such a manner as to make it possible to apply knowledge beneficially rather than in an undirected and haphazard way.

Fremont-Smith: I am Frank Fremont-Smith. I was trained in neurology and psychiatry. I joined the staff of the Josiah Macy, Jr. Foundation in 1936.

My special interest has been in communication and in the obstructions to communication. It began while I was in the practice of psychiatry. I sometimes saw both husband and wife when there was an emotional problem and I would frequently get a very different description of the same episode from each and I was amazed to find how differently such an episode was remembered and/or interpreted by these two people. Such breakdowns in communication seemed related to the emotional tension between the husband and wife. I also found, as a physician, that when I would explain to a patient at the end of an examination, or the parent of a child after a careful study, the situation and what treatment was recommended, the patient, or the parent of the patient, didn't seem to hear what I was saying. So I got into the habit, and it became a very useful one, of asking the patient or parent, "Please tell me what I just said to you". I remember a dramatic example: a woman who had been very much concerned about whether her daughter should ever get married. I reassured the woman that there was no reason why her daughter shouldn't get married when she grew up. When I asked her to repeat what I had just said she replied, "And you tell me my daughter must never get married".

So, the factors that interfere with hearing or with the proper interpretation and the anxiety that influences the understanding of what has been said have been of real interest to me.

All of us are trying to get other people to do things in better ways than they are now doing them. But I think we make too little effort to examine the obstructions that interfere with what we want them to do. What are the obstructions hidden beneath the surface? One obstruction, that has had a great deal to do with conferences, is the mood or attitude of anxiety and hostility. We have found that if there are anxiety and hostility

in the group, there is much less likelihood of
people hearing each other accurately. The blind
spots as well as deaf spots that they bring to the
conference become enlarged. However, if you
can introduce the proper mood, these blind spots
tend to disappear.

I used to tell our groups that we had magic
aerosol that we would introduce into the group
and if people would only inhale deeply, they would
find that they could really understand one another.
Each would look at his neighbor— and the blind
spots would shrink. Suddenly he would look like
a decent person. This magic aerosol was called
"free floating security". This is the antithesis
of the psychiatrist's "free-floating anxiety". The
free-floating security was engendered in part by
our staff and by the informality of the group.
This interest in the difficulties in communication
was greatly accentuated in the Macy Foundation
Conferences where again I saw anxiety and hostility among scientists interfering with mutual understanding.

I am delighted to be here as Shelly (Shelesnyak)
takes over the Directorship of the Program.

Marcus: I am George Marcus. I am a displaced
Canadian and a displaced biochemist. I was
brainwashed into biodynamics by Dr. Shelesnyak
several years ago, and was associated with him
until recently. My main interest has been ovum
implantation and the mechanism of decidualization.

Ross: It is a pleasure to be here and to see again
some old friends who participate in these

conferences. Basically, my training is in history; I am however, an experimental psychologist, working with a wide variety of animals. In recent years, I have worked in the area of psychopharmacology.

Even more recently, I have become concerned with the issues of human affairs and society, both in our country and internationally—and the problems of human behavior. I am, I hope, about through with that particular phase of my life, as it has been a very difficult one, learning the issues and trying to be a representative for a newly emerging science, psychology. One line that I use frequently in public presentations about psychology is that it slices itself in at least three different ways: we talk about psychology as a science; we talk about it as a profession; and we talk about it as a discipline. There is argument about each one of these kinds of labels. Some don't think it is much of a science while others do. Some don't think it is much of a profession; others identify it as a profession. The only thing I am sure about it is that it is not very much of a discipline, and about that I am pretty confident, for it has been my domain in recent years.

All of the sciences are contributing to both the aggrevation and amelioration of problems confronting society. Information that evolves from new scientific knowledge and technical development affect the nature of human society and organization.

I am here as an optimist. I am optimistic that we are going to survive. I am skeptical in regard to those who ring the bells and tell me that tomorrow everything is going to collapse. I

believe the issue of the planet's population is one
of the important issues of our world and our society. Whether population is the central and the
most important is a complex issue interweaving
itself among the relationships to man's history,
to political history, to nations, to biological
issues, food supply and technology.

I am accustomed to making public confessions after I have committed the sins. Here I
am doing it before. Thank you very much.

Reynolds: I think I'll start off with a confession that
I think I am one of the people referred to who has
remained quite disinterested in what I recognize
as an important problem, and the reason I have
been so disinterested is that it seemed to be an
unattackable problem, which human beings are not
able to study objectively so as to apply the scientific method.

The one connection I have had with any kind
of population problem was with the blue crab
population of the Chesapeake Bay. After studying the fluctuations of population in the bay, it
seemed utterly unrelated to anything else occurring in the environment. This probably was not
true but at least we were not able to find any factor
that showed a consistent correlation with crab
population.

Certainly that is a less complex problem than
the problem of human population. So, I am inclined to agree with Sherman Ross, except that
I am more of a pessimist. I am inclined to think
that we will survive but that our population problems will not be solved by planning, mainly

because we don't know how to deal with the problem. I am ready and eager to agree that I might
be wrong, but that is the feeling I have about it.
    I don't know what I can contribute to the group.
I have had a feeling that it is not too fantastic to
think that human organisms will find ways of oc-
cupying the other planets, and I don't think the
technological problems are going to be insur-
mountable. I don't believe it will help the earth's
population problem but it may help the survival
of the species. I guess that is enough.

Schultz: Anybody who equates crabs with people
    ought to be pessimistic. There seems to be a bit
    of prestige here in claiming biological background.
        I came up through the agricultural sciences
    but shifted to economics. My main concern for a
    decade has been the human capital, the importance
    of the quality of human agents in modern society
    and modern economies. How do we acquire qual-
    ity and at what cost? What are the returns?
        I assume that we are here to discover what
    are the possibilities of altering the quantity and
    quality of people for the better. While I am not
    defining "better", it has to be in a context of the
    real choices of people and I shall argue strongly
    that the scientists, especially those a little re-
    moved from the social sciences, find it awfully
    easy to think that somehow you can cook up
    alternatives that people just ought to have sense
    enough to move on to.
        I want to see us clarify a process that will
    move us toward a population policy, in which we
    see public and private choices of many kinds.

This involves many things and where this conference can be valuable. We have not come very far
in understanding what is really involved in a population policy.

Fisher: I'm Joe Fisher. Like Ted Schultz, I am an
economist by profession. My avocation is politics in the practical sense, which helps me a
good deal more than my profession, perhaps, in
what you can get people to do.

I am associated with "Resources for the
Future", which is concerned with natural resources—the raw materials, the physical environment. My own work has been in studies that look
ahead to gauge the adequacy of raw materials (or
natural resources) to meet demands that may be
placed on them, but equally concerned with what
might happen to the quality of the environment as
time goes on.

What do I want to get out of this conference?
Well, in preparation for it, I asked our children,
who range from eight to sixteen years in age,
how many children they wanted to have. They all
answered something, and the average came out to
be a little over two and a half.

Fremont-Smith: What was the range?

Fisher: The range was from zero to six, and while
the sample is small, nowadays you can go a long
way with a small sample.

Anyway, the stopper of all this was the 16-
year-old who, after this had gone on a while,
settled back and said, "Why in the world did you
and Mother have so many of us?"

Schultz: What did you say?

Fisher: It stopped us completely. I opened my mouth four or five times to answer but each time I realized the answer wasn't going to do. So, I suppose I would like to get an answer to that question out of this conference, not only for myself but also for my children and for everybody else.

Ritchie-Calder: I will introduce myself as an expert on experts; it is my only qualification for being here. I spend my time studying experts, and I am here to study experts. I am also professor of international relations at the University of Edinburgh.

In that capacity, I have been with this population problem for a very long time. It goes back to the early 30's when I got involved largely through the food problem, nutrition, and so on; but, since then, I have had a wide and I think direct experience with this problem in traveling and in the curious role I have had since the war of being a consultant to various agencies in the United Nations. As a consultant, so far as the U.N. is concerned, I can look at problems and evaluate, not to provide the answers but to try to find the experts who can. That has given me wide experience. I think I have traveled something like two and a half million miles in the last fifteen years, and therefore, I have seen this problem at first hand.

It is the human element of this problem that concerns me and if I have one preoccupation here, it is with the problem of the developing countries, for this is something we cannot ignore, we cannot neglect. This is the basis of the great stresses we will confront in the next twenty years and we must find the solutions. Whether it is this conference or another conference, we must find the answers, because this situation is intolerable. It is not just a question of trying to work it out on paper or speculating about the unpredictables. As I see it, unless we find some way of attacking this problem in the best and most decent sense, the world is facing disaster, not just in the kinds of things I have read about the disaster of famine, and so forth, but really in the profound disruptive political sense.

In my opinion, there are only two big problems facing the world today: population and food. We may or may not have a nuclear war, but I am quite certain that the alternative to the population and food problems is as disastrous as anything we can conceive from a nuclear war.

Freedman: I have been listening to all these disclaimers about expertise with mounting concern. By my formal criterion, I am an expert. God help us if we must depend on people like me. I am a sociologist-demographer. I think it would be an error if any of you expected to come away with the view of the demographers as if there were one view. The presidential addresses of the Population Association for the last five or six years have almost all dealt with aspects of the population problem, and I think you will find that there is quite a wide range of opinion as to what

the situation is, and what the situation can be,
and I think this comes largely from lack of
knowledge.

Even though Kingsley Davis isn't with us as
yet, I think he and I would classify each other as
competent demographers, but with significant
difference of opinion on many policies. Most of
the demographers would not talk about the population problem as most of you have. Most of us
think it is much more complicated, that it is a
problem of the relation of human populations to
resources through a social organization in a
situation that is very complex. I don't mean to
say that we don't know anything or we can't do
anything about it. But, with all due respect to
the expertise that is represented from the other
disciplines here, my experience has been that the
people from the natural sciences, in particular,
when they work on the social aspects of this
problem, present solutions that are incredibly
naive. I come prepared to be shown that mine
is a wrong perception. I would like to have the
answer to the problem if it comes from elsewhere.

I have been doing research for some ten or
fifteen years on what happens to human fertility
under various conditions. What are some of the
factors that affect levels of human fertility under
those conditions? One of the reasons we don't
have any solutions, in my judgment, is that we
have done incredibly little work on these problems.
I am amazed that I am an expert. I have become
an expert in the last three or four years on this
subject because there are very few of us around.

I have been studying this problem with re-spect to human population since about 1950, and since 1961 I have been increasingly concerned with a new phenomenon–organized large-scale programs, trying to change national birth rates. This is a new phenomenon in the social environ-ment which we have only begun to study.

I came to the field of the study of human fertility about 1949, when I was asked to help analyze the data from "The Indianapolis Fertility Study," which some of you may know. This was the first really intensive study of the social as-pects of human fertility in one American city, Indianapolis.

In 1955, a group of us, through the Survey Research Center at the University of Michigan, did what I think was the first national study of fertility in relation to the use of contraception–showing what strata of the population were using contraceptives in relation to what values, and things of that sort. That was as recently as 1955.

When we undertook that study, there was a lot of discussion about whether this could or should be done; there was a lot of criticism, and we felt a little like heroes in undertaking this be-cause we were warned that you just don't do that kind of thing. Please keep in mind the date, 1955.

In 1960, Frank Notestein subverted me by sending me to India there for two months of ob-servation. Since that time, I have been con-cerned about the problems of high fertility in poor countries.

In 1962, I was subverted by the Population Council to go to Taiwan to help on the social science statistical aspects of a small-scale study they were starting in one city, and again I would like to remind you of the date. These dates are important. That was 1962; that was not long ago.

As many of you probably know, the birth rate has come down considerably in Taiwan since 1962, but it was then quite high. I remember the discussions we had at that time and none of us who were involved predicted that the birth rate was going to fall as rapidly as it has. I don't know of anybody else that had predicted it.

I make this point because since that time, many have said, "Of course it was going to fall in Taiwan." After the fact, that is easy to say. We think we are just beginning to understand some of the things that are going on in Taiwan. There are very few populations where you have had such a study in detail of what actually happens in the life history of people getting married, having children at certain intervals, and so forth, in relation to social and economic factors, with the introduction of a family planning program.

Since then there have been other programs that have gotten under way. There were some that began earlier. This was, I think, one of the first things that was really pushed intensively, and I have observed some of this work in India, Pakistan, Korea, Hong Kong, Singapore, and Malaysia.

I have put quite a lot into this and I admit I know very little. I am anxious to hear what we ought to be doing.

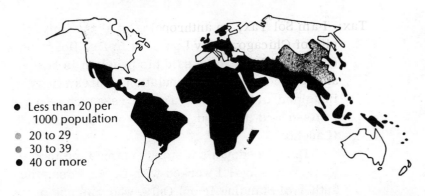

- Less than 20 per
  1000 population
- 20 to 29
- 30 to 39
- 40 or more

Birth rates are highest among the underdeveloped regions of the world:
Birth Rate, 1960-66.

- Less than 1.0%
- 1.0 to 1.9%
- 2.0 to 2.9%
- 3.0% or more

Population has grown most rapidly in Latin America, least rapidly
in Europe: Annual Rate of population increase, 1958-66. Source:
United Nations.

- Less than 20
- 20 to 59
- 60 to 99
- 100 or more

People are packed most densely in Europe and Asia: Density population
per km². Source: United Nations.

Tax: I am Sol Tax, an anthropologist at the University of Chicago. May I go back to Dr. Hoagland's comments? When he said his problem is how animals control their population, I dreamingly imagined an interesting area of research because I mis-heard the word "animals" as "cannibals." (Laughter)

   Dr. Freedman's history reminds me that forty years ago, I worked with E. A. Ross, the author of Standing Room Only, who was one of the original worriers about this.

Notestein: Ross' book came out the same year as The Twilight of Parenthood by Enid Charles.

Tax: I worry why people behave as they do, especially communities of people of one culture and background, who are planned for by people of another cultural background who, in turn, wonder why the obvious improvements imposed do not have the good effects they planned. As the years go by, I realize that one can bypass most of the problems of understanding and misunderstanding cultures by simply providing alternatives for people. Some of the alternatives will sprout and spread; what might be weeds in one place turn out to be very useful in another place; and more solutions are provided than by the planning that we do from scratch.

   It is difficult to change institutions by deliberate manipulation. If we let new institutions expand to wherever they will "take", and if we provide new technological devices, watching them play out their unforeseen consequences, we will

get more answers than the anthropologist will
provide. On the other hand, what I might contribute here, if anything at all, are some absolute rules of some things you can't expect to
work.

If you violate somebody's values or percep-
tions, he is unable to behave as you assume
every "normal" human ought to behave. If you
threaten his identity when his identity is important to him (as in many communities today)
and if you're giving him a "tie-in" deal, then you
are simply telling him, "If you become like us,
then this and that will happen." This won't work.
These are a few of the obvious things we ought to
think of when we plan. We might usefully talk
about them occasionally during our time here.

Harkavy: I am Bud Harkavy, an economist by training. I was involved in economics and business
administration in the Ford Foundation for some
years. In fact, the first grants made by the
Foundation in the population field were under the
Behavioral Sciences Program headed by Bernard
Berelson, now president of the Population Council.
When the Behavioral Sciences Program was
phased out, I found myself in population work,
and I am now responsible for the Foundation's
Population Office.

Since 1952, the Ford Foundation has committed more funds for population work than any
agency, public or private—about $100 million.

Shelesnyak: I am called Shelly. We may have a
problem here because there are two of us called
Shelly. Sheldon Segal and I.

I was a student of the late Earl Engle, in
anatomy, but actually in the physiology of reproduction. How many of you recall a journal,
The Journal of Contraception? In 1934, I published a paper in that journal. It was about a
gadget I designed—a slide rule to aid women in
calculating the menstrual period and the so-
called safe period.

In 1950 I went to Israel and became rein-
volved in studies of reproduction. I formulated
a concept of biodynamics in which we tried to
achieve an inter- and multidisciplinary approach
for solving problems in reproductive processes.
My researches and facilities were greatly aided
by the Population Council and the Ford Foundation. Last year, after setting up a laboratory
and developing a group of investigators, I turned
everything over to a younger person.

Now I have been back in the United States,
associated with The Smithsonian on the Interdisciplinary Communications Program. As I see
it, there are two fundamental problems confronting mankind. (It is odd that all of us tend to put
aside the nuclear problem because it either will
or will not happen.) They are both explosive.
One has to do with the explosive increase in numbers of people and the other has to do with the
increase in information. I am trying now to
achieve better utilization of information for the
solution of problems—not only scientific, but
societal problems. I couldn't think of a more
beautiful union than having my first conference
dealing with the relationship of information and
population. I would like to see come out of this

conference series a greater involvement of people
who have a role to play in the solution of population problems, yet who are not deeply aware of
the population problem; that this group and de-
rivative groups bring greater participation of all
technologists and professionals. There is a
tremendous amount of latent talent that has not
been tapped. If, indeed, we can energize this
talent, we may be able to accelerate the solution.
In this respect, it is vital for us to solve
problems which are the consequences of the impact of the population increase during the past
twenty years. Such solutions may give us patterns that may help deal with problems of the
next twenty years. Let us not limit ourselves to
what will happen in 1985, in 1990, and 2000.
Perhaps we can start wrestling with what has happened and what is happening now.

Harkavy: Thank you. Sir Solly.

Zuckerman: On the biographical note, which is the
prelude to a statement of my hopes and wishes, I
am a biologist. One of my continuing interests
over at least forty years has been the physiology
of reproduction. I published my first paper,
"Comparative Physiology of the Menstrual Cycle,"
forty years ago. Also, I was responsible, in
the early 30's for the first demonstration on how
to suppress a primate ovary with one of the steroids; that work is still going on. It is well supported by the Ford Foundation and I hope happily
so.

About the same time that the precursor body to "Resources for the Future," the Paley Commission, was set up, I was made chairman of a corresponding body in the United Kingdom, the "Natural Resources Committee". At first that body was concerned with the same range of problems as was the Paley Commission, but as the immediate crisis in hard resources started to diminish, it focused on food problems.

In that capacity I attended the first of the conferences called by the United Nations on the resources problem, which led to the Population Conference in Rome. I also attended that.

I have attended many meetings in the United States (as well as other countries) dealing with control of population or, control of conception, I should say. That interest, with my interest in the physiology of reproduction is, as it were, my credential for being here.

I am also concerned with the world of politics and I was pleased to hear (I think it was Professor Freedman) that we don't want any simplistic views to come out of this meeting. I must be a politician because I am concerned with action, and so far as this conference is concerned, I would like to know that I am going to leave with a clearer conception of what we are talking about, whether we are talking about a global population problem or about a series of population problems depending upon the particular circumstances of the people to whom we are going to address our remarks.

I think I heard somebody say, in these Oxford Group confessions which we have heard, that

England is possibly overpopulated, or that the
United States is. That may be, but there is also
a major labor shortage. There are other population problems in England with which we can't
deal, for example, labor mobility. We have got differential fertility rates. We know little, as
Professor Freedman said, about the background
of variations in fertility levels. There have been
several studies in which old parish records have
been analyzed, going back into the distant past.
Repeated post mortems have been made of the
social changes that took place in Ireland in the
earlier half of the nineteenth century, which influenced fertility rates. So I first want to know what
we are talking about: Are we talking about a
global population problem or are we talking about
the real issues which control variations in fertility rates?

Secondly, I would like to learn, as a biologist, whether we know enough about the genetic
structure of society, enough about its breeding
habits and all the rest of it, to "impose" general methods of birth control, as though we were
a deity who could decide what the genetic structure of tomorrow's society should be. It is conceivable that some human authority might one
day be in a position to do this. I would like to
know if he will have the background of information to do it safely.

The third thing I would like to know, again
from the biological point of view, is whether or
not we are going to focus (as I believe the agenda
suggests) in our discussion of the technology of
birth control on methods that could reduce fertility

levels in general, that will probably be safer
from the point of view of the structure of society,
or whether we are going to focus specific methods
on specific groups of human beings. Also I want to leave this meeting assured
that the realities and limitations of political con-
trol are understood by those who speak about the
subject of birth control in its relation to population control.

Knox: My name is Bill Knox. I have recently joined
McGraw-Hill, a publishing company in New York.
I am a chemist, somewhat of a chemical engineer,
and after a number of years with ESSO Research,
I became interested in the communications problems within the chemical community. This was
followed by several years with Don Horning in
the Office of Science and Technology in Washington. I then became so convinced that one of
the major problems of our time was communication and information, I decided to forego the relatively quiescent energy front, Joe Fisher having
assured us that there are enough energy resources
for the rest of my life, anyway. On the other
hand, there may be too much information and too
many people for my comfort during that period of
time. So, I have become a professional (not an
expert but a professional, I guess) in the general
area of communications and information technology and information science.

I am working with Shelly, involving The Smithsonian, on another project, the Council on Communications. This has a different focus from this
conference as it is concerned with the impact of new

technologies of information processing in communication on society, people, our social institutions, our philosophies, our guidelines, and
our policies.

In this conference, I am equally interested
in the effect of population growth, or lack of it,
on that same general area, communications. If
we have more people, they, of course, create the
need for acculturation, using the conventional
information transfer mechanisms such as con-
versation books, TV, schools, radio, newspapers, movies, and periodicals. The pressures of these people will create a need, obviously, for these mechanisms to satisfy their demands for culture and for information, and as
several have already mentioned, certainly these
same people will be generating a great deal more
information for potential dissemination and exploitation. These are problems for the information mechanism.

Since there is a greater need for solution of
some age-old problems of human society simply
because there are more people today, and these
people can no longer avoid these problems or
minimize them by going away to new lands, and
since the solution of these social problems depends rather heavily on communication between
people, I am interested in what you have to say
about what communication devices, technology
and institutions can do to cope with this problem.
Notice that I don't say roll back the times. I
don't say that we must go into a negative population growth. I am of the opinion that there are
many factors about this we do not understand.

Perhaps I would trust an elected official to make
a decision about population policy; but I doubt
if I would trust an appointed official solely. But
we are going to have to concern ourselves with
the mechanisms by which some of these decisions
are made, and in the process communications
will obviously play a very great role.

I have a great hope that the fantastic, revo-
lutionary new information processing and communication technology will be a great help to individuals and to the institutions of our society in
coping with the very problems that we are creating by these additional people. I don't know that
I can place a finger now on specific ways in which
these can help. I have already been stimulated
by the wonderously divergent viewpoints and approaches that are brought to this conference
table. I could quit now and be ahead, but I am
looking forward to the remainder of the session.

Notestein: I am Frank Notestein, since about 1925 an
unabashed demographer. I worked first at the
Millbank Fund on differential fertility and the
problems of contraception, and for twenty-three
years at Princeton University, where I directed
the Office of Population Research, I set up the
Population Division of the United Nations during
1946-1948 and went, as President, to the Population Council in 1959, from which I retired in
April of this year.

I am now worrying with among others, Dr.
Harkavy about a Training Institute for the Pakistan Family Planning Organization, doing some
writing, and teaching in the Woodrow Wilson
School at Princeton University.

Why am I here? I suppose because I live
here and the subject is relevant.

What do I want to get out of this conference?
I am always fascinated and often irritated to hear
people who have not been concerned with population pontificate on the subject. It is better to do
one's own pontificating. For example, I am bored
with the problem of the optimum size of population and you would be, too, if you paid much attention to it. I think it is an utterly useless concept. Nevertheless, I am always fascinated to
hear what the people who are coming at it from a
completely different direction are saying.

At the moment, I am somewhat shocked at
the strength of the proposals that are made for
the control of population in view of the state of
our ignorance. The proposals that I hear tend
to go far beyond anything that we have a right to
consider. I hope this gets developed because one
of the great issues of the time will be what the
role of coercion and the role of consent are—
fundamental. They are coming up anew in a
terribly important way and this is what I would
like to hear about most.

Harkavy: Shelly Segal?

Segal: The secret is out. I am the other Shelly you
have been expecting. I am a biologist but that
term doesn't tell you very much. There are
seven biologists around this table and they all
represent completely different but important fields.

I would like to take the occasion of this conference to give you a report from the working

reproductive physiologists, the physiologists
who have made a commitment to devote their
work, their careers to a better understanding of
reproductive processes and, among them (and I
include myself in the group) some who have made
the further commitment that there is nothing in-
tellectually or morally wrong working within this
field on new means to control fertility.

This is not a small group. There are literally thousands in the broader definition, and perhaps hundreds in the more narrow definition.
These are people who are approaching the problem from what seems to me to be the most logical
attack points—by doing the things for which they
are properly trained at basic levels, intermediate
levels and applied levels, with the expectation
that this new information in the bank of scientific
facts will fall in place and lead to technological
advance.

I think, in fact, it is plagiarism from Ritchie-
Calder that I use frequently: basic science is,
after all, the prior condition of methodologic advance.

There are some faults in this argument,
and I think considering the urgency of the problem, it would be a mistake to expect that in the
natural course of events these technological advances will take place rapidly. I believe
there is a need for some type of behind-the-
scenes catalytic activity to see to it that advances
at the basic front, having the most likely chance
to lead to applied methodologic advance, will in
fact, get that opportunity.

Through the fifteen years or so that I have been involved in this problem, it has been apparent to me that we cannot leave this role, this catalytic role, to private enterprise. The traditional view has been that, given the profit motive, as new facts become available, the pharmaceutical industry and the like will certainly take advantage of them and produce for the world new contraceptive methods or other fertility control methods. This is not the way things are going to work. Such organizations are interested, quite properly, in new products but not necessarily in new methods.

One of the roles we have tried to play at the Population Council is exactly this; to try to keep an eye on developments that can be advanced more rapidly and play a role through our own intramural research program as well as our grant program in bringing this about as rapidly as possible. We have had successes and disappointments, but on balance, I think we have a right to be proud of what we have contributed to this field and are in the process of contributing.

I would like to mention a problem that speaks somewhat in modulation of my praise for the biological sciences in the role that they are playing. I think it is best exemplified by a true incident that occurred in our august university. My laboratories are at the Rockefeller University, as some of you know, where we have an unusual graduate student training program. In this program, the faculty-student ratio (and remember that sequence) is roughly 6 to 1, so that students are rather rare and highly sought after. When

one student decided to do his work under my
direction, I assigned him the topic, which was of
interest to him. That topic was on the mechanism, the biological mechanism of action of the
intrauterine device. He worked on this for a
year and a half, hitting a few snags but making
some progress. One day at the Faculty Club bar
one of the influential members of the faculty,
particularly interested in the graduate training
program, said to me, "You know, I think Earl is
doing a fine job in your lab but why don't you take
him off that problem and put him on your RNA
problem?"

Well, this is one of the difficulties we have
in this field. There is still an unwillingness on
the part of many scientists to acknowledge the
role that they can play to understand the importance of the problem in terms of the need for
the contribution of biological knowledge.

One other word of warning that harks back to
comments made by Sir Solly and Ron Freedman,
among others. One of the things that we have
worked on—and I take pride of authorship only because it is necessary to establish a certain authority for the fate of this example—is the development of an implant that could potentially give
contraceptive effect for at least three to five
years, and possibly longer; perhaps for an entire
reproductive life span of a woman, but right now
that is only theoretical. When word of this leaked
into the lay press, suddenly there were the most
fantastic proposals as to how this development in
contraceptive methodology could change the entire
pattern of reproductive behavior of the species.

Now we had a way, according to these, of reversing the entire process so that to have a child, a woman would have to make a positive decision rather than the reverse; that female newborns shortly after birth could have an implant secreted away in some computerized location that only the computer would know, and that sometime in the future if she were selected, she could have it removed and start to reproduce — which is a very nice postulate except that it is completely fantastic in terms of the biological activity of the implant.

To carry it further, what the implant can do in a woman of the productive age group is quite different from its potential hazardous effects in the newborn or in the pre-adolescent, and so forth. So there is a certain amount of unreality attached to some of the interpretations of the potential use of biological weapons.

I am sorry this has gone on longer than I thought but I cannot close, Bud, without referring to Frank Fremont-Smith's concern for the communications issue and the breaking of barriers. In addition to being able to carry out the work that I think was important in my years at the Population Council, also I have been associated with demographers, a species I had hardly heard about while I was an embryologist, and a little of this exposure has taken affect. To prove it, I have done some calculation. The last interdisciplinary conference that I attended, Frank, the one on fetal homeostasis, had thirteen participants. I have counted that this one has twenty-six. If this rate of growth continues for

just another ten years, we are going to have to
use Palmer Stadium.

Sutton: I am Frank Sutton, from the Ford Foundation.
I began an abortive phase of my adult life in
Princeton, studying pure mathematics. I de-
scended then to the denser and more obscure
realms of sociology at Harvard for some years,
and later plunged into the Ford Foundation, which
I suppose is still another depth.

I have been concerned for more than ten
years with the international side of our activities,
particularly our concern with aid to development
around the world, most particularly, with Africa.
I am now broadly concerned with the full
range of the Foundation's international activities,
including population. I came to this subject through
a long-time interest in total development process
and the problems of the developing nations, and
I am particularly interested in getting a clearer
understanding of the consequences of population
growth and population pressure in the developing
countries. I share the anxious concern about
population growth that seems to be common at
the present time, but I think it is important to get
a clearer conception of some of its consequences
than we have. A lot of the effects are bound to be
diffuse ones, and it may be the difficulty of trac-
ing them which explains why we don't often follow
them far. I have been particularly concerned,
for example, with the problems of transition
from predominantly rural subsistence societies
to societies that are built around wage employment and moving toward being industrialized

societies. One quickly comes upon the fact that
population growth is a serious brake upon the
rate at which this sort of transition can occur,
and one discovers that a great lot of the tensions
and difficulties which characterize the underdeveloped world arise precisely from the sluggish-
ness and difficulty of this transition.

Here is a kind of diffuse effect of the rate of
population growth that seems to have something
to do with the political instability, over much of
the developing world, and hence presumably with
the concern we have for better international
order.

These efforts, as I say, are diffuse things
and difficult to appreciate, but I think it is important for us because of the influence that analysis of these questions can have upon the policies
of many governments around the world, and also
as a kind of general guide to the attention that
we should give to population problems in various
places.

Obviously, we have many questions in trying to understand the relative importance of efforts at population control in the total corpus of
activities of an organization like the Ford Foundation. But, at the moment, I find my own attention particularly focused on the question of the
causative relationship of population growth to
other problems of development. I am happy to
see that the first part of this conference is directed toward these consequences and I hope to
learn something about them.

Weissman: I am Norman Weissman of the National
    Aeronautics and Space Administration in the Be-
    havioral Biology Program. My training was
    originally in zoology and later in psychology. I
    consider myself a behavioral engineer, that is,
    somebody who thinks about the ways in which
    one can change the environment to change be-
    havior.

    Most of my work in the laboratory has been
    with animals, with the goal of setting up an
    environment in which the behavior would be pre-
    dictable, that is, by manipulating both the en-
    vironmental conditions and the contingencies for
    certain kinds of behavior. It seems to me that
    the problems of population are greatly related
    to other problems which psychologists face:
    problems of aggressive societies, crime, even
    mental health. My interest would be in the
    technology developed to control these problems.
    Although my training and knowledge are not in
    the population problems per se, they have po-
    tential application to the problems of population
    control.

SATURDAY MORNING SESSION
September 28, 1968

The conference reconvened at nine-ten o'clock,
Dr. O. Harkavy, Chairman, presiding.

Shelesnyak: I am happy to see that Kingsley Davis
    has reached the territory. I would appreciate
    his just picking up the self-introductions we
    started at the onset of the sessions. However,
    he may have had word of it and preferred that we
    start otherwise.
        Bud asked me to make a few remarks, to
    elaborate a little bit on, what was the phrase you
    used ?

Harkavy: Conversatus interruptus.

Shelesnyak: At any rate, Bud put it this way, "How
    do I indicate who shall speak ?" and I said,
    "That is the game we play here. No one indicates
    anything. Occasionally, somebody will plead,
    "Let me finish a sentence before you attach me,"
    but the concept is essentially that this a collec-
    tive conversation and, among other things, what
    Bud has to do is to try to keep, at most, only
    two conversations going at once; three are hard

41

to follow. Nevertheless, please don't jot down
questions; ask them of the person who is speaking or anyone else, loud enough so that we can
hear. Don't address your questions, or even
your critical or caustic remarks, to your neighbors alone. It is unfair to the rest of us.

Welcome, Dr. Davis. We are sorry we
missed you last night.

Davis: I was sorry not to be here.

Shelesnyak: Well, you have a surprise. You are to
pick up the threads of last night's meeting. Last
night's meeting was essentially a mass confes-
sional. Everyone introduced himself, not simply by statement of name, title, and organization, but also, by brief comments stating how he
became involved in the subject of this conference
and what he expects to get out of this meeting.

Davis: It would, unfortunately, take too long to give
a full account of that.

Segal: That didn't stop the rest of us. (Laughter)

Davis: I first became interested in population by an
interest in the family, because it seemed that
population policy had something to do with the
family. As a matter of fact, the first thing I
did in the field of population was to write a paper
on population policies. The prevailing policies
at the time were policies designed to raise the
birth rate; I attempted to show that these policies were not adequately taking account of the

relevance of the family to reproduction. Like
many people here, I am sure I continue to have
the same point of view I had then. I am still
coming to the question of population policy with
an appreciation of the role of the family with
reference to reproduction.

Harkavy: A word about the agenda I prepared for the
conference. First of all, one of the distinguished
demographers with us will say something about
the demographic "facts of life." Let's start off
with some hard data. Then we shall take up the
consequences of expected population growth for
the several geographic sectors of the world for
food supplies, resources, the cities, and for
broad questions of ecology and the quality of life.
There should be major points of difference under
this heading which should be brought into the
open. Then we discuss the control of population
growth. First, family planning, then, "beyond
family planning."
Frank Notestein, would you please give us
a short lesson in elementary demography?

Notestein: This is, in a way, an easy assignment
because I ritualistically have to say what I know
already. It has only one complication: What can
be said with assurance? Of course, not too much
can be said with assurance if we have to play
around with the possibility of a major nuclear or
other worldwide-devastating event. I, personally, am little interested in seeing what the consequences of such difficulties would be, so I am
going to suppose they won't happen.

That being the case, then, what can one say? You can say that the world population is probably 3.4 billion but you should add plus or minus 100 million. In fact, I am not sure we know China's population within a 100 million. If I were to guess, I would say the current figures were a little too high, but I am not quite clear about this.

On race, the figures perhaps are not too important because of the matter of definition. We know that the white race increased more rapidly than the others for a considerable period of time, and now it is increasing more slowly than the others, because it entered the modernization period earlier.

The age differences are very sharp, indeed. As you probably all know, age is mainly determined by the birth rate. Where birth rates are high, populations tend to be young, so that in the underdeveloped world, the youth load is very heavy. Any country with a birth rate of 40 over a sustained period will have over 40 percent of its total population under 15 years of age, and in the less-developed areas, birth rates range in general from 40 to 55. So, the proportion of people in the working years of life is small. The proportion of people in the ages of youth dependency, where the educational burden comes, is very large in the poorest nations.

As for population density, there is nothing to say that this group doesn't know except to call attention to the fact that of the two most densely settled continents one is the most wealthy, Europe; the poorest Asia. One can't say that there is a gross and immediate relationship of density without qualifications.

As for other characteristics, marriage, in
the less developed countries, tends to occur at
a younger age and marriage is nearly universal,
but recently there has been a strong trend
throughout the more modernized nations for
marriage ages to drop.

What can be said with reasonable assurance
about prospects for growth? Let's try to bracket
it. If from today onward all of the people entering the child-bearing period in all parts of the
world were to reproduce at rates that just reproduce themselves, by the year 2000 the world's
population would be more than 4.5 billion. That
seems to me, barring a nuclear event, a conservative prediction. It is incredible, really to
suppose that when very few countries are reproducing only at the replacement level, that as of
tomorrow, the new cohorts entering the child-
bearing period would drop to that replacement
level everywhere in the world, so the prospect
of getting as low as 4.5 billion seems very small.

On the other hand, if fertility didn't change
at all and there was some reasonable decrease in
mortality, the world population could get to 7.5
billion, and the truth, barring catastrophe, will
lie somewhere within those margins. The
United Nations' median for the year 2000 is 6.1
billion. I don't like that figure because it seems
to me that mainland China has been peculiarly
handled, giving it a very small growth potential.
I would be happier with the kind of calculus that
poses some drops in the birth rate. I think
drastic efforts to reduce birth rates by 2000
might get us 5.5, but that would be a very drastic change—or anything between that and 6.

As for rates of growth, these median rates of growth involved in the U.N. presuppose that the population of the world will grow at about 2 percent per year between 1960 and 2000. At least, the figure as I have adjusted it for mainland China would. The formal U.N. figure is 1.8. Although these projections of population for the future are made following the component method of working on births, deaths, and assumptions about migration, you would be off only a little if you take the exponential rate of 2 and put it against your figures. You never depart by as much as 5 percent—in most cases not by as much as 2 percent from the figures.

In the projection systems of the U.N., Latin America grows the most rapidly—that is projected to 2.9 percent, an average rate between 1960 and 2000. Africa is next at 2.6 with very little fertility drop assumed. The more-developed nations are assumed to grow at about 1 percent, on the average, the range being between 1.6 for Australia and New Zealand (where there is a good deal of migration) and temperate Latin America is a little less, down to half a percent for Europe, with North America and Russia about equal at 1.3 and 1.4, respectfully.

So, the gist of the foreseeable growth patterns is that growth will be substantial; the difficulties will come heavily in the poorest areas of the earth where with the rate for the less developed countries at 2.4, the proportion is projected to double in 29 years. This is pretty difficult array of problems of economic development and education are concerned.

I only want to make one other point which bothers me, and it bothers Professor Schultz, that is to the extent that there is a problem of food, there seems little chance of absorbing massive amounts of new labor in agricultural production. The problem of food for the world is <u>total</u> production, not production per man, and if one thing is more clear than another, it is that in the underdeveloped countries agriculture will have to be increased by inputs other than human labor, and so all of these areas face the tremendous task of transferring labor to nonagricultural pursuits.

In countries of the underdeveloped world, the proportion of the labor force engaged in the production of food and fiber ranges from 60 percent to, I guess, 80 percent. In the United States it is 7 percent. It might be a little lower than that. In Russia I think it is still almost 50 percent. There is going to be need for a tremendous transfer and I am afraid there will be a large amount of concealed and overt unemployment and a very large move to urban centers. What frightens me, frankly, is the risk of losing political coherence in the face of this enormous problem. What do such large numbers of people do if they can't farm and if they don't have the alternatives to farming?

I am not discussing whether they have any margin of productivity. This seems to me irrelevant. What I am saying is that they have nothing very fruitful to do, or it looks that way.

This seems to me to be one of the major problems. It certainly has been a problem in

the United States. Half of our counties lost
population between 1950 and 1960, and, by and
large, they lost population because agriculture
was being handled more and more efficiently by
fewer and fewer people. When this trend is
more world-wide, it will have greater complications, starting from gross poverty–instead of
starting with substantial wealth, as in the United
States.
     Doesn't that set your stage enough?

Harkavy: Very nicely done. Thank you.

Ehrlich: Is it time to start disagreeing now? I don't
     really disagree with anything Dr. Notestein has
     said, but I think what has been ignored in this
     situation and what is classically ignored, is the
     death rate. I realize it hasn't been ignored in the
     calculations, but we have all the emphasis on
     projecting birth rates. The assumption is made,
     which I tend to agree with, that you can't calculate
     thermonuclear war into these equations, although
     I think a very good case could be made for every
     additional increment of growth increasing the
     chances there dramatically.
          You must put in this class the possibilities of
     worldwide plague which worries a lot of biologists,
     including Josh Lederberg and Macfarlane Burnet
     and me. We are building up to a situation for
     such a possibility, but I think we have to shove
     that aside with the consideration that you can't
     calculate from that a potential death rate and put
     it into your projections. I think the figures just
     given indicate a doubling of the population, plus

or minus, by the end of the century. This means
that all of the facilities we have created for taking care of human beings, miserably as we do
the job today, must be duplicated to maintain a
status quo. I don't think we need to get into the
rising "expectation" situation, which gives us
estimates of needing to quadruple food production
to keep the lid on, politically speaking.

I frankly think that these projections are all
high for the reason that we are not going to be
able to keep a lid on the death rate. I realize that
Orville Freeman likes to spread around his fine
little stories about "green revolutions," but there
is no sign whatsoever that we can come close,
even with fertilizers and better grains, such as
IR-8 rice, and so on, to feeding this number of
people. In fact we are not doing the job today
and this is one of the reaons I am perhaps thought
of as being a fanatic on this subject. That is why
I am not satisfied with attempts to cut the birth
rate, bringing it down from 40 to 21, with the
death rate still down at 10, and so on. That is
why it is necessary that we move toward a reduction in the total number of people.

I will just add one more comment at this point.
A manuscript went across my desk the other day
from the Center for Advanced Studies in the Behavioral Sciences at Stanford which made a very
strong case for the maximum number of people
that can be maintained, not in an exploitative
economy, but in an equilibrium type of economy
where we use only renewable resources instead of
non-renewable ones. It put the maximum carrying capacity of the earth at 500 million people.

That is obviously, in very large degree, a guess,
but if that is the case, we are already seven times
beyond the carrying capacity as of the hundred
years from now, when we are out of all these
fossil fuels. In this context, talking about 7.5
billion people in the year 2000 is extreme folly.
I think we must do something now dramatically
to make sure that we are nowhere near that, but
closer to the estimated 4.5-5.5 billion, if that is
at all possible. I realize there are tremendous
difficulties of achieving that.

Notestein: Of course, estimates range widely. Brown
said 50 billion.

Ehrlich: You are not interested in the problem of the
optimum population, but this is where I think it is
critical. In other words, we have to know what the
boundary conditions are before we know whether
there is any point in talking about 7.5 billion people.

Notestein: I think we can get into a discussion about
the optimum, but I would think it would be useful
a little later. My objection is that I would talk
about optimum rate of change rather than the
optimum size of population.

Zuckerman: What is Dr. Erhlich saying, Mr. Chairman ?

Ehrlich: I am saying we are in tough situation. There
is a very small chance of getting through what is
coming in the next twenty years and no chance at
all unless, instead of concentrating on getting

scientists operating slowly within the realms of political reality, we manage to affect the politicians enough that they start to operate within the bounds of scientific reality.

Zuckerman: What does this mean? I am not trying to be obtuse. At this hour of the morning, I am usually alert, but I still don't understand what the politician is supposed to do. I heard you say there must be a reduction.

Ehrlich: I said we must start moving toward a reduction.

Zuckerman: How do you achieve this reduction? How do you do this?

Ehrlich: Then we will be getting into Part II immediately.

Shelesnyak: That is all right.

Zuckerman: How do you achieve the reduction? Who is the "we"; who is the "you"; and who is reduced?

Ehrlich: Do we want to enter this area now?

Chamberlain: Could I raise the same question in a slightly different way? We had the projections of population increase based upon likely fertility rates, but without getting into the whole area that Paul Ehrlich was talking about here, I am curious whether any consideration was given to the

environmental possibilities—the economic possibilities of sustaining that kind of growth. This
is purely a projection of numbers without respect to the environmental circumstances; is
that correct?

Notestein: Except that in doing this sort of thing, one
is projecting from some past trends, and implicit
in past trends is certainly the economic part of
it, though in this particular set of figures there
has been a further drop in mortality projected.

By the way, if I may, there is one point on
which we agree but which I would like to get attention. I personally don't think the relation is
food versus growth. This seems to me nonsense,
but I do not think that the possibility of maintaining political coherence is very encouraging in
these circumstances, partly because of the move
out of agriculture and tremendous unemployment.
The margins of protection are thin. It wouldn't
take very much disorganization to freeze trans-
portation and to block control of disease and you
would then have a major catastrophe. In the
orderly sequence, that will happen a long time
before people begin to get hungry.

Ehrlich: Why do you say before people start to get
hungry? The U.N. says that between 1 and 2
billion are hungry by some standard today.

Notestein: All right, use another word.

Harkavy: Hold that for Dr. Schultz.

Chamberlain: Do these projections, for example,
    take into account possible location, the degree
    of urbanization that might be envisaged by this
    and how that might tie in with your political
    stability?

Notestein: Following the projections, there is a book
    put out by the U.N. dealing with that. If it is
    difficult to handle total population, and that is a
    little bit of crystal ball gazing, then urbanization
    is a much more difficult field.

Slobodkin: I think Sir Solly was pointing toward a
    ground rule that we might establish now, that is
    we cannot advocate solutions, which bring on or
    in themselves constitute the political upheavals
    that Dr. Notestein was discussing. If I under-
    stood it correctly, this was Dr. Zuckerman's
    agrument with Dr. Ehrlich, that if we had dicta-
    torial power, God forbid, we could perhaps do
    things we cannot now do, but we do not have
    dictatorial power and we do not want dictatorial
    power, therefore, any attempts at solution must
    be within either political realities as they now
    exist or, at the very least, not beyond the limits
    of normal political morality.

Ehrlich: Normal political morality where?

Chamberlain: And what do you mean by that, what
    dictatorial power?

Ehrlich: First of all, I wouldn't want any ground

rule like that. I think that is a naive set of ground rules to set up.

Harkavy: We have among us some of the most distinguished demographers in the world. Does any one of them wish to challenge the population projections presented by Dr. Notestein? Or do we have general agreement on these?

Slobodkin: They are characteristically, if I understand them, linear projections. That is, nonlinear effects are not generally included.

Notestein: That is right.

Slobodkin: This has to be because of the way the data come.

Notestein: Yes.

Slobodkin: Yes, but the possibilities of complex interactions have not in general been included in the projections, nor are they included in normal econometric models. I think that is a fair statement. If it isn't, correct me.

Notestein: That is right.

Fisher: Except, since they are based on historical trends, whatever complexities and interactions that have been operating in the historical period are built into the projections. This is one of the difficulties. You don't know exactly what it is that you are projecting, but it seems to me that

the complications of the base period are built
into the projections, whatever the drift of those
complications may be.

Slobodkin: If the complications remain linear.

Sutton: A population projection is never linear. It is
always exponential.

Notestein: But he is talking not so much about linearity. He doesn't care whether it is curvilinear;
he doesn't want a sudden shift.

Davis: What is the alternative? How else would you
proceed?

Slobodkin: Dr. Ehrlich mentioned some alternatives.
It is conceivable to imagine (this is not my area
so I am imagining) a set of boundary conditions,
the transcending of which would violently alter
the kinds of projections we make.

Davis: Whatever the conditions assumed, they are
contingent. In making realistic projections, one
has to state the most probable conditions. One
has to face the question of how likely are they.

Slobodkin: Fair enough.

Davis: Again, I don't see that the logic is any different from one set of assumptions to another.
To judge extreme assumptions, one judges on
the basis of past knowledge. If it is a matter of
warfare, how many people in the past died

because of wars and can you then project future losses on the assumption of warfare?

Slobodkin: What you are saying is that quantitative predictions are legitimate predictions, with which I agree, but I am saying that the legitimate predictions occasionally get into difficult problems.

Davis: Practically all predictions of population have been wrong and it is a good question to ask: Why have they been wrong? Lately, they have been mainly wrong in developed countries because of fertility, which I presume is one of our topics of discussion. So the way is open to an attack on the projections, not on the basis of linearity versus non-linearity, which is a metaphysical proposition, it seems to me, but in terms of the assumptions behind the past predictions. Can we learn anything by examining those past assumptions?

Slobodkin: I have to answer that if I can. The possibility of plague, one of the non-linear possibilities, was mentioned by Dr. Ehrlich. I have not looked into the possibilities of plague but these are presumably, at least in principle, stateable: What are the possibilities of a plague outbreak, given such-and-such living conditions, given such-and-such number of people? This kind of outbreak has a probability which forms a kind of nimbus or halo around the predicted value that Dr. Notestein presented.

I am asking what, in a sense, is the probability of various terms from the straight-line predictions, given various contingencies.

Schultz: That is what Kingsley is saying. You approach it systematically, reexamining every assumption that has gone into the calculations.

Zuckerman: We are playing with predictions that are wrong and have always been wrong.

Davis: They have always been too conservative. People have been unwilling to believe that population growth would be as fast as it turned out to be.

Notestein: The projection on fertility has been the weak part in the modernized world. I guess the prediction on the drop in mortality would be the big weakness in the underdeveloped world, being too conservative. The death rate in some of the underdeveloped countries is lower than it is in the developed countries because the population is young. Taiwan has an expectation of an average age of sixty, as I recall.

Ehrlich: I think Dr. Slobodkin is indicating to us—at least to me—that the death rate has not had built into it the proper contingencies; in other words, it is basically a linear extension of the death rate for which there are all kinds of reasons for not making that kind of projection.

Notestein: It is monotonic. It isn't linear.

Freedman: I think Dr. Ehrlich is correct; the death
     rate in these calculations has not had the ex-
     amination it merits. On the other hand, I think
     there is an implicit assumption here that if you
     have gone back any period of time, Dr. Ehrlich
     could have made this speech; and in fact, a great
     many of the predictions of catastrophe are based
     on extrapolating the demographic trends with
     the assumption that social organization, technol-
     ogy, and so forth, do not change.

         I would like to hear from him in the course
     of the meeting why he is so certain that we have
     reached that critical point at 3.2 billion instead
     of at 2.2 billion where we were before. This
     same speech could have been made many times
     before.

Ehrlich: I was putting it at 2.7, too.

Freedman: O.K. There is one other point I would
     like to make on a demographic side. There were
     references yesterday, I think, to some of the
     things that demographers have said and I indi-
     cated that demographers don't agree, but some
     of the statements that were quoted I think were
     the statements of our colleague, Donald Bogue of
     the University of Chicago, who has been in the
     press prominently in asserting that the rate of
     growth, if we really knew what it was, is not
     going down, and that we have turned the corner,
     and so forth. I just want to say that I don't know
     any demographer who agrees with him or has an
     explanation of what his rationale is for this.

Ehrlich: I really ought to apologize for that, but one of the troubles is that since I became a part-time propagandist, the newspapers and media in general are very anxious to pick up the slightest sign of anything like that. One of my Stanford colleagues recently put out a press release with regard to food research, saying that there were too few people in the world and what we needed were more people so that we could have more farmers. This hit the AP wire and was all over the country, just like Bogue's stuff, whereas the responsible replies to this (there were a number made by the demographers) appear on page 27 in the Woman's Section of the newspaper, if they are anywhere. So I probably should not have quoted Bogue in that context.

Notestein: On the subject of these discontinuities, the worry about sharp discontinuities, one can say something in principle: if the productive technique and the social organization get extraordinarily complicated, if we go to higher levels of complexity and interdependence without being able to have reasonably high levels of living, the risks that something will go wrong will have been enhanced. If there is a lot of subsistence farming, there can be a lot of local catastrophes but it is a little harder to get a big one. If, on the other hand, we have complicated techniques with worldwide interdependence and keep living levels terribly low, then when some political disorganization comes, the margins for retrenchment are not there and I think one can build a sort of model for castastrophe. But, you can't predict it. You

can say that the risks of a discontinuity become
higher under that kind of circumstance.

Slobodkin: Can't you push it even a little bit further,
stating that the probability of catastrophe is
simply proportional to the complexity of the system and not necessarily to the low standard of
living level? For example, the electricity
blackout in New York City was a curious thing,
Think of the effect of tugboat strikes in New York.

Notestein: Oh, that doesn't matter in terms of---

Slobodkin: But it matters to people living there.

Notestein: But the margins for retrenchment are so
great.

Slobodkin: A tugboat strike does affect the quality
of food in New York.

Freedman: You can make the same point the other
way around, that the complex system has more
resources for meeting problems. The risks and
the potentials are great, but it is not a one-way
business.

Slobodkin: Can you give any estimate of the relative
risks in potential?

Freedman: No.

Zuckerman: Isn't the risk that you are concerned
about more likely to occur in countries such

as the United States, as opposed to countries made up of scattered subsistence farmers?

Ehrlich: I think plague possibilities are much more amenable to direct analysis that does not necessarily involve a cutoff point. After all, there is every reason to believe that as population density increases, both the probability of getting a mutant virus that would have the proper characteristics, including transmissibility, and the condition of the public health situation in general, can be projected with relative ease. I think this is the kind of thing you can project more easily than the kind of death rate solution that a thermonuclear war would involve. Of course, the political instability counts there because on it depends in part the size of biological warfare laboratories. Biologists are afraid one of our "beautiful" creations will escape. You can look into the probability of accidents in virus laboratories, which tend to be rather high. There is a relatively high mortality rate among virus researchers. Macfarlane Burnet quit the whole game because of the chance of one of the viruses getting away, which theoretically could be so rugged that there would be no resistance against it at all; or one of the new drug-resistant strains of anthrax that we are breeding in our biological warfare laboratories could escape. We have two sets of probabilities: a natural mutation of a virus into a killer, a super-1918 sort of strain; or the probability of escape from biological warfare laboratories. I think you could put these into your estimates.

Notestein: They would have to be before 1918 to be effective.

Ehrlich: Oh, absolutely, but you see, we have jet transporation today, besides the very dense and very much weakened population. We will be able to carry any sort of thing that develops around the world very rapidly. The possibilities are enough to scare the wits out of people like Lederberg.

Shelesnyak: I wanted to ask what is probably a naive but important question. What is the validity of the values upon which you make your projections, in relationship to the data-collecting for vital statistics and actual knowledge about things that are happening in various places? Are these significant factors?

Notestein: I am not sure I understand you.

Shelesnyak: If you have a good census program, you are in better position to count what is happening and project into the future. I am asking if you consider the entire range of real situations, from where the existence of villages and communities is unknown to a government to a highly advances statistical program, does the quality data-collecting play a significant role? Is it a critical factor?

Notestein: I think the inadequancies of the data are great but not so great as to really change the overall diagnosis of the problem. The big

lacunae, of course, are Africa and China (the
biggest). You can work out the demographic
situation if you have a couple of censuses, some
age distributions. It is nice to have more than
that but, by and large, this can be done in areas
where fertility hasn't changed much, and these
are areas where the data are bad. The techniques
of using, on the one hand, sample surveys and,
on the other, quasi-stable analytical techniques
enable you to work out the heart of the story.

We don't know, for example, India's birth
rate. Well, it is not as low as 40 and probably
not as high as 45. That is quite a margin of
error; but Pakistan's is not as low as 45 and is
doubtfully over 55. (It might be a bit higher.)
This is a bigger margin of error. But you are
in the same house insofar as the sorts of things
we are talking about here are concerned. Always we need better data, but at the level of our
discourse we are not going to have too much
trouble.

Shelesnyak: The critical point in my question is:
Being aware of the fact that data could be improved, nevertheless, are not the projections
influenced by the lack of superb preciseness?

Notestein: The number of people in the world, yes,
but the changing patterns is the most important
thing. The actual number is not so important.

There is a way in which the improvement of
data is highly important. People don't worry
about population until the facts are obvious and
understood, and it is no good telling them that

the facts are real because of your inference
based on information from another country. It
is a reasonably good generalization that every
group knows it is different. It isn't all that different, but every group thinks it is. Few are
impressed until you can somehow get evidence
directly from that group about its own behavior.
In that sense, having better data that can be
written about and talked about to the community
leaders–this is important in getting any firm
action with budgetary impact.

Shelesnyak: That leads to my next question. Since
data and projection are important for operational
purposes for population control, policy, development of societal and political points of view, is
there any concerted effort being made to improve
the technology beyond just the current, standard
ones? Are we trying to evolve new technologies,
new information techniques, new professional
skills in improving our counting, so to speak?

Notestein: I am sure we are, and then the question
is, are we doing it enough or imaginatively
enough? Everyone has his own answers. Techniques have gotten pretty good on survey work,
on sample work. Aerial photography has been
played with but not very much in detail. I suppose every demographer is going to say: no, we
are not doing nearly enough. That is probably
true but, some progress has been made.

Ritchie-Calder: What happens when you get a community like Afghanistan where the census-taker

finds that the head of the household discloses
the number of his cattle and goats but not the
number of wives?

Notestein: You get some very peculiar sex ratios.
(Laughter)
   You look around to see what's what. This
happens all the time. In Moslem communities,
unmarried girls of marriageable age are rather
rare. Some is sheer omission and some distortion.

Ritchie-Calder: Am I right in saying that the recent
census in Kenya made the citizens aware that
they had a problem that they didn't realize before?

Notestein: It did. I think the analysis of that pointed
up, for instance, a 3 percent rate of growth in
population. They are very proud of their educational program there. A continuation of their
growth would mean that with their wonderful
educational program, twenty years from now they
would have more illiterates than they have now.
This was very impressive.

Freedman: I think we ought to add, Frank, that while
our knowledge is pretty good with reference to
these gross projections of the kind you are making, we are very, very weak, when it comes to
data on some preliminary obvious things with
reference to why the trends are that way. This
data would permit you to answer questions
whether the birth rate or death rate is likely to

move in certain ways toward the end of the century, and whether changes are going to take place. So, it seems to me, your answer is correct with reference to a very gross level. When it comes to analyzing what has happened and what is likely to change, and so forth, we are in real trouble.

Notestein: I agree.

Michaelis: I was about to ask not why is it so, but can one naively pose the question to historians or the psychologists here? I am reminded of Joe Fisher's remark last night: Why are we putting these people into the world, as many as we are? Why are we content with death rates one way or another? Are there any historical insights?

Tax: May I ask, who are we?

Michaelis: We, the people; we, the earth, the population that exists, mankind.

Tax: Why is mankind having children?

Michaelis: As many? Why does mankind want to expand the life span? Why does mankind want to multiply?

Freedman: Answering that question does require the kind of data I have just mentioned. A few people are beginning to work on it.

Michaelis: What kind of work is being done?

Ehrlich: There is a very strong biological component to this. The game of evolution is played by
natural selection and that is purely differential
reproduction.

Michaelis: What is differential reproduction?

Ehrlich: For the last 60 million years any organism
which had managed to produce more viable offspring was the kind of organism that made up
the next generation. Similarly avoiding death
obviously is part of differential reproduction. I
am giving the genetic point of view, understanding there is a large cultural component. Basically mankind has been selected and always will be
selected for maximum reproduction, so that you
have a strong biological component which has
been strongly reinforced culturally as well.

Segal: I think there is another side to that argument,
Dr. Ehrlich. I think you would agree that you
can also look at the total pattern of evolution
and establish there has been a natural reduction
in the reproductive rate for its survival value.
If you look at some of the evolutionary changes
that have occurred in the natural process of reproduction, the curious thing is that they are frequently, if not always, in the direction of reducing natural reproduction.

Ehrlich: You misunderstand what I said.

Segal: I didn't misunderstand but I was just trying to expand it.

Ehrlich: But that is not right. Evolution has not moved toward minimal reproduction. It may have moved toward laying fewer eggs, if that was more reproductively efficient.

Segal: It is more than having fewer eggs–it is increasing their opportunity for survival.

Ehrlich: That is what I said; it is the transmittal of genes to the next generation which is the thing that counts. The more gametes you donate to individuals of the next generation, the further you have gone evolutionarily. Some organisms do this with very few offspring and with great maternal and paternal care. Others do it with monstrous production of eggs, and so on, and no care. But the name of the game, whether you are a bird or a mammal or a fish, is maximum number of offspring.

Notestein: On mortality, I guess, if people preferred dying to living, we wouldn't be here, discussing population.

Davis: Maybe that's the first "value" we should change.

Ehrlich: It has been suggested to me, Kingsley, that "instead of being so much for birth control, why don't you kill yourself?" (Laughter)

Slobodkin: There are a couple of other complexities
    underlying what Dr. Michaelis and Dr. Segal
    were agreeing on. One is that it is a rather
    complex problem in evolutionary theory to de-
    velop a small population as the descendants of a
    large one. I think this is where the two points
    of view meet. It can be done, but you have to go
    around Robin Hood's barn, theoretically, and
    there is a great question about parts of the theory.
    That is Item 1. Item 2, equally curious, is
    there are many species that are very rare and
    always have been but are still with us; and there
    are species that have been enormously abundant
    became extinct quite rapidly. Apparently the
    process of extinction is not necessarily related
    to absolute abundance, as the whooping crane
    said to the passenger pigeon. It may even be an
    inverse relationship, so that this is sufficient to
    indicate that the question, biologically, is a very
    delicate one, and the question why people want
    children, while in a very long sense a conse-
    quence of the evolutionary process, can't in any
    practical way be explained by the evolutionary
    process.

Freedman: I would like to hear the biologists some-
    time during the day say something about what
    biological explanations there are for differential
    reproduction between countries or major strata,
    and so forth, because I think most social de-
    mographers now would say that all of the large
    differentials that we know about are cultural
    and social—not biological in origin.

Slobodkin: I think Dr. Freeman has just opened a tremendous trap which I would like to close so that no one falls in. You started by saying, "I wish the biologists would explain to us why there is differential reproduction in"---

Freedman: I don't think you can, but I thought Dr. Ehrlich was talking as if he could.

Ehrlich: Let me make it absolutely clear that I agree with Larry and you that this cannot be explained. What I was trying to indicate was the form of the infant's face, the shape of the baby's head probably has been selected into the human population to stimulate certain reactions in human females. They just like babies and this is very important. Actually, Dr. Notestein summed it up very well: people don't like to die and they like kids. That is what I was saying in a complex way, and I apologize.

Zuckerman: So many generalizations are being shot out so fast, and some are so sweeping, that my head has become more or less empty. We heard, quite correctly, about the evolutionary process whereby certain species, containing very few individuals, have managed to survive.

Slobodkin: That the species itself is rare.

Zuckerman: Yes, that the species is rare, but manages to survive.
   I won't ask you the reason for that. We also know of cases where species have survived almost

as long as there is information about the geological record. You said that some species become extinct and, within the context of what you were saying, extremely rapidly. Are you talking about species that became extinct because of human intervention, or species that became extinct because of environmental change?
If so, the latter does not concern us in the con-text of our discussion about human population and its control, and about the difficulties of adjusting population growth to what is being called political stability. The other does.

I am saying, which species have become extinct very rapidly—and by "rapidly" I mean within a time scale that is relative to the discussion before us—as a result of natural environmental changes and which have become extinct as a result of human intervention?

Slobodkin: The human is biggest geological and biological force operating on the world today. In general, a species becomes extinct due to environmental change. I think almost every curator in the Smithsonian was present when I asked if any of them knew of any case of an extinct species as the result of becoming rare and not becoming violently rare as the result of being on its way to extinction. The distinction here is one of a sort of a Schopenhauerian decline of a species on the one hand and an environment having shifted from under a species on the other, and the thing is no longer adapted and just wiped out. There is no case that where a

species simply declines and goes to extinction
in the absence of rather good reason to believe
that the environment has changed rapidly. Man
is the major agent for changing rapidly the
environment at the moment. Does that answer
your question?

Zuckerman: This answers my question and disposes
of the question of the elimination of animal
species so far as our discussion is concerned.

Ehrlich: Not at all. As a matter of fact, quite the
contrary. Man is living in the environment that
he is changing.

Zuckerman: Exactly, but I don't wish to delve into
what I understand is the latter part of the question. I don't quite understand some of the talk
about nuclear warfare. I understand less some
of the things about biological warfare. Equally,
I know little of plague. I would prefer, from the
point of view of focusing our discussion, to consider changes in human population and trends in
the light of the projections which Professor
Notestein was talking about. We are talking about
a period of twenty years, thirty years; we are
not talking about geological time.

Ehrlich: So are we, and the kinds of changes, caused
by man, that are going on now are much more
dramatic than many of the geological changes that
took place over millions of years. They are

much more dramatic and much more critical to our possible survival as a species.

Hoagland: Man changed his environment profoundly in 1945 when we atom-bombed Hiroshima, and this change is with us to say. It seems to me that history might sometime record, if there should be any history, that man became extinct because his great cerebral cortex turned out to have been a phylogenetic tumor, capable of producing destructive weapons which his ancient limbic brain was unable to control from the point of view of his hates and fears, involving his fellows as a part of his environment.

Michaelis: I would like to come back to the remark that if we would rather be dead, we wouldn't be here. As a lay reader, one has the impression that certain cultures, Eastern and others, seem to be content (is that the word?) with a fairly rapid death rate in the past. One used to say that the value of life seemed to be different from that in the Western world. I know it is a generalization that I shouldn't be making.

Tax: I guess these statements were always made by people in the Western world.

Michaelis: If it is a misstatement, I shouldn't continue, but let me just---

Tax: No—in any village I have ever been where people cry that a baby died it is painful, even though they know that this is the way of the world—easy come, easy go, so to speak.

Michaelis: I was leading to the question, What motivates those, who had presumably power in the village, to embrace medical or other techniques that were offered in order to extend life? Is it just as simple an answer as you have given, as human an answer—if you can, you do—right?

Harkavy: I think we ought to go on. It is interesting the way groups are sort of forming: the biologists, as such, interacting with the social demographer. And the question as to whether they all might be out of order as Sir Solly suggests. I don't know.

Zuckerman: I didn't mean to do that. What I am trying to get at is this. Density-dependent factors help determine the size of animal groups and do apply in certain human societies. If, for example, you go to New Guinea, where I have been recently, and go to some of the recently-discovered little groups, you find they have their territories properly laid out in relation to their numbers and in relation to the numbers of people on adjacent territory, and we know about the disturbances which occur at the boundary zones. Equally, I was born in a country in an area of South Africa at a time when certain of the native peoples were affected by the same sort of natural biological controls of population-size as apply to most of those surviving species that have not so far been dealt with by human beings. There is an extremely interesting account about southwest Africa of what is occurring with the bushmen in that region.

We know that what I shall call simple biological control of population still applies to some groups of human beings. But the moment these people become transformed into the kinds of societies with which we are mainly concerned (societies which we are helping to transform, and which we are encouraging, like China and India, to follow the path of the USSR and the U.S.A.) we get a different set of factors operating the control of population.

All I was trying to do was clarify in my mind—and I think that the discussion this morning has clarified the issue—that the biological factors that used to be called density, if I remember correctly, density-dependent factors, are not the ones with which we are concerned.

You might say, so far as evolution is concerned, that since no animal should ever be looked upon in isolation, its particular environment is always a fourth dimension that should be taken into account when one considers its natural selection.

Slobodkin: You may be quite right about people, but people even now are living in a biological context and to a large extent the quality of their life depends upon that biological context—even in New Jersey or New York or London. Later I will come back to that.

Zuckerman: That is the part I would like to have explained to me.

Ross: May I go back to what we said in the initial
       remarks, for I am concerned very much about
       the stance that we take in consideration of a
       problem and the opening description which pre-
       sumably, to clarify, had to do with population
       estimates, but the stance that I think is the
       critical one we are taking, and we haven't ver-
       balized it, it may be useful to do.
            The scope is the entire planet. Am I cor-
       rect that when the demographers were talking,
       they were talking about the whole planet? We
       should not think that on this planet, our task is to
       achieve homogeneity. Its surface is not homo-
       geneous and it varies below its surface. There
       are other differences, including social, organi-
       zational, and political differences. So if we just
       start with the primitive reality and the total
       number, we had better keep remembering a lot
       of critical things that determine the nature of
       human behavior. That is my only point and I
       will go no further.

Harkavy: Can we get back to the more mundane
       question of food and population? I won't antici-
       pate Ted Schultz, other than to note that some
       writers assert that a large part of the world will
       surely starve. Others feel the world will manage
       to find enough food. They point to the develop-
       ment of such miracle grains as IR-8, rice de-
       veloped at the International Rice Research Insti-
       tute in the Philippines. Thus, other authorities
       feel that insufficient food isn't the most crucial
       consequence of world population growth. I hope
       Professor Schultz will tell us what the truth is
       on the food and population issue.

Schultz: Let me start by saying I am a little worried.
We talk biology in connection with human behavior and leave it out where biologists have introduced such extraordinary change in plants and
animals that alter the food supply. There is a
good deal to be said, when you operate within a
period of twenty-five years, for the advances in
biological knowledge in the production of food.

I grant that you just don't want to restrict
yourselves to twenty-five years, but if you al- ·
low that constraint of time in your thinking,
then I argue that the modernization of agriculture
(primarily advances in biological techniques for
food production) is such that production will stay
abreast of Dr. Notestein's figures—maybe "unfortunately" in that this might not discourage
population growth.

I turn to the supply of food in different parts
of the world, on timing for the next ten years
the Soviet Union, the satellite countries, Europe,
Latin America and Southern Asia. In each the
process of growth is now rather clear. You can
talk, of course, about catastrophes occurring
in Southern Asia, if the modernization in agriculture were to be brought to a halt. It could
happen for one or two reasons, or both. One,
there might suddenly come a pest, disease, or
rust that would wipe out the superior biological
stuff. It has happened to us. The new varieties
of wheat that were introduced into the Plains
States a number of times have been "wiped out"
by rust spores and so on. The pathologists

are worried about this, particularly with the
rapid expansion of the superior wheats in Pakistan and India. Conceivably, this could hit very
suddenly.

I suspect the rapidity with which the biologists today can develop new strains, as they
have done in the Western world when something
like this happens, would cause me to say that the
second reason for a catastrophe is perhaps the
more serious: if these countries were to go back
to a cheap food policy, which they followed until
six or seven years ago, then indeed they could
stop this whole process. There are disquieting
developments, now that they have had a couple
of good crops; things look a lot better in terms
of surplus supplies, and might result in a return to a cheap food policy. This is popping up
in Southern Asia at several places, so there is
some pressure on the Asian Development Bank
to not emphasize agricultural loans. In fact,
the bank has already put in some resources in
loans to facilitate the agricultural thrust, and
several countries have already begun to protest,
saying this is the colonialization process and they
don't want to see it go into agriculture; and this
view could mean once again a cheap food policy.

Harkavy: Ted, may I interrupt you at this point for
a clarification? Would you please explain about
th A, B, C's of a "cheap food policy."

Schultz: A cheap food policy is a policy with which
a country embarks, through its public process,
public policy, on a plan to price food to consumers

below the cost of producing it at the margins in its own agriculture. It is that simple. The countries that we are talking about, in Southern Asia, notably, and in Africa have priced their agriculture into stagnation by simply beating down the price. About three or four years ago there was a reversal. The reversal occurred in Russia a little earlier. There is a reversal going on in Eastern Europe.

This is a conscious economic policy of the past. It was a postwar policy until a few years ago, and the reason why agriculture has come to life in these parts of the world is that there have been the superior biological varieties and a pricing policy which provided the economic incentive.

Tax: How did they come to change their economy?

Schultz: Russia was forced by circumstances of drought. China has been forced to change. Eastern Europe has been forced by shortages. Czechoslovakia, which used to be an exporter, has been importing large amounts of food. In India and Pakistan it was drought.

Latin American, by and large, has not been forced to change. As a generalization, Mexico is an exception throughout. Argentine, the Pampas, is coming to life but it must be said that throughout a good deal of Latin America it is essentially stagnant, for reasons of public policy. There is plenty of biological knowledge in Chile and Peru and throughout these countries,

but policy has persisted to underprice foods,
and the results are the obvious ones.

I would like to take a few minutes, under
the assumption of the modernization of agriculture,
to proceed to these poor countries, looking at the
implications of modernization.

Slobodkin: Pardon me, I am still confused. When
you say "underpriced," you mean that the
farmer is getting less or the consumer is paying
less, or both, or something in between?

Schultz: Both.

Slobodkin: Where does the food come from and where
does the money come from?

Schultz: In India, for example, in Madras, where
I spent some time last summer, and where they
were not hit quite so hard by the drought, they
were buying food there at about 25 percent below the market price and most consumers were
acquiring food at this "low" price.

Slobodkin: "You" being the government? The
government is purchasing the food at below cost?

Schultz: The government is purchasing the food.
These are essentially forced deliveries at the
"low" price. There is no other market for it
in an open market sense. Thus, the food to the
consumer is that much cheaper and it is that
much lower in price at the farm level.

Nigeria is another example. The government of Nigeria, before the Civil War, actually collected about one-half of the value of the major export, oil, and used it as public revenue. They sold the palm fruit in the world market at a price twice as high as the farmer was getting and thus acquired public revenue. This "export tax" greatly depressed industries. Producers were simply letting the trees go bad, not keeping them up. This is what you would expect.

Let me turn to several consequences of some success in agricultural modernization. These are results of the economic dynamics of modernization of agriculture in India but you can see them in our society in recent history; we don't have to go back very far. Also, you can see them in Europe. One of the consequences is that an advanced technical, highly productive agriculture (and here you can include all of our own and that of Europe) is not sufficient to eliminate hunger. I remind you that we have hunger in some counties and we obviously have a highly productive biological agriculture. There is no reason to believe that just creating and succeeding with the modernization of agriculture in itself will eliminate hunger. You will quickly say that it will reduce it. I am not going to argue that, but I suggest that we don't want to draw the inference that a modern agriculture will eliminate hunger.

The other consequence is that if one looks only at hunger, from the economist's point of view, one simply misses the contributions that a modern agriculture can make to the real income

of the country. Consider Mexico, with large
increases in agricultural production in the last
decade. The Mexicans have transformed this
production into real income. But, I suspect
that India is going to find it difficult to transform
her larger food production into real income. The
Philippines is getting into trouble now and is
wanting to subsidize exports of rice, not knowing how to transform the additional rice into income within her own society.

For those of you who think in terms of nutrition, we have had a lot of work on a nutritional
budget and we have reasonably good knowledge
going into this. This approach has been adopted
by FAO. I think it is absolutely true from an
economic point of view that the modernization of
agriculture cannot be administered, has never
been administered, in such a way that what it
produces is the optimum mix of nutritious foods.
People, the consumers, demanding food, do not
demand nutritious food as it is rated by nutri-
tionists. So the farmer is responding to what the
consumer is telling him through the price system.
So you get something else than what is called
for in any nutrition budget.

The next proposition is even more important.
Some of you talk about space; the modernization
of agriculture is a process which reduces the importance of land in agriculture. It is a process
in which you find and use other inputs. The other
inputs are largely these new imputs that biologists
have come up with. They cannot be produced in
agriculture. They are purchased by farmers and
they substitute for land. This, essentially, is

the reason why the Ricardian-Malthusian predictions or the so-called diminishing returns
from land, with capital and labor pressing
against it, have not held in a secular, historical
sense, and we see it clearly in current history.

The point is a simple one: agricultural land
is no longer the classical limitation factor in
producing the food supply. This is one of the
major consequences of the modernization of
agriculture. It is in the cards that India, (God
forbid that it gets to 1.5 billion people), can
actually reduce the amount of land it will need to
produce enough food.

Reynolds: Even if that land is considered as water-
shed?

Schultz: I don't know what that means. India may well
be giving up scores of millions of acres of land
for agricultural purposes made possible by agricultural modernization, which will start within
the next two or three decades if this modernization thrust is allowed to continue.

The next proposition that I argue is that the
opportunity to modernize agriculture is, as a
rule, very unequal spatially with a country loca-
tionwise. This again is a fact of the environment,
natural endowment plus the knowledge of modern
science coming together, and this is clearly true
in large countries. There are exceptions in some
small countries, for example, Denmark.

The comparative advantage of one part of
the country is greater relative to other parts as
the consequence of modernization. Our own

history shows this clearly. Parts of agriculture
in France are seriously depressed. We have our
Appalachia. In Italy, compare the Po Valley
and South Italy. It is the same in Russia. The
one country that is escaping this problem in
large part seems to be Japan. It is hard to explain this but in Japan, of all the countries, there
has been a substantial modernization of agriculture, and yet Japan has avoided the depressed
areas problem within agriculture to a much
greater extent than the European and Western
countries, Canada and our own.

Now, back to Mexico. Mexico has been very
successful in this modernization process for two
to three decades. The northern part and the
central part have been the beneficiaries, but not
the southern part. Today Mexico is rightly becoming very much concerned about the income
inequalities throughout the country in the sense
that the south is falling behind in real income
relative to the middle and north.

As you look into what Mexico has to face in
the next several decades, the migration implications of these inequalities, inside Mexico,
are tremendous for public policy. By comparison, the Appalachia of the United States is a
much smaller problem.

The modernization of agriculture in India
implies that the north, the Ganges Plain, and
the big rice bowls in the south have a marked
comparative advantage to profit, to benefit, to
move ahead as the consequence of what I am
talking about, whereas that large triangle in the
Deccan toward the south, in which scores of

millions of people live, simply cannot benefit
proportionately from agricultural modernization.
The reasons are simple: rainfall and water differences. The water supply is unequal to that
of the north and the rice bowls. The results of
this are already showing up in India.

Last year and this year it is becoming clear
that you can generalize about countries such as
India and Mexico. In the short-run, the first
five years, the area that is modernizing and expanding production requires additional labor in
agriculture. This is one of the first effects. It
is reported that the wage rate for hired farm
workers in India has gone up 40 percent, real,
in the last three years in the northern part of
the Punjab. They are short of labor because
they have gone to much higher yielding varieties
of crops, much higher outputs, and additional
double-cropping. In the longer run, which is
my twenty years, these areas also, as they proceed in the modernization process, will begin to
get along with less labor.

The profound policy problem India faces in
the modernization of agriculture over the next
three or four decades is the relocation, the redistribution of a human population which involves
scores of millions of people in the Deccan area.
No one has really considered what is happening
here and how you cope with it. I have alluded to
Japan. I don't know whether there are lessons
from Japan that are relevant to India. I have
some guesses about why Japan is more successful
than Britain or France or Italy or we are.

I could go on, but the key part of what I
want to emphasize in terms of population implication in this redistribution of gigantic populations like those in settled areas of Southern Asia,
Pakistan, particularly India, parts of the Philippines, and so on, on which I have been putting
the major emphasis. If there is a theme in this,
it is simply: by means of the biological sciences
it is now possible, not only in the West but
rapidly and at hand in developing countries, that
the food supply, as a consequence of a given
policy, will stay ahead of population for ten years,
fifteen years, twenty years, without much difficulty. But this process has profound implications in a particular economic sense and here
I have stressed largely the redistribution of the
population. But, don't expect it to eliminate
hunger; don't expect it to fulfill the requirements
of the nutritional budget which I stressed in passing.

Harkavy: Some people may want to raise questions
     on the economic aspects of Professor Schultz's
     talk. But keeping certain risks in mind, Mr.
     Schultz is relatively optimistic with regard to
     the food-population equation for the next ten or
     twenty years.
          Joe, did you have some point you wanted to
     raise with regard to this?

Fisher: I did, but perhaps Sol Tax would be the better
     one to raise the point we were discussing, since
     he originated it.

Tax: You seemed to bring the United States into the
      same context with others, saying that we have
      had a cheap food problem also, and yet to many
      of us it would seem that we have had an opposite
      policy, paying farmers, raising the...

Schultz: Oh, yes; United States policy is high-support
      prices.

Tax: The other question I had was this (and you
      might want to answer them together): the eco-
      nomics of it is a little hard to understand be-
      cause when there was a cheap food policy, say,
      in India, the government kept the price down so
      that consumers would be able to buy. As soon
      as the lid was off because the production had
      gone up, and the food must be sold to somebody,
      consumers seemed to be able to buy more at
      higher prices than they were buying at lower
      prices, and this also seems a little confusing to
      me.

Schultz: I agree. We have indeed manipulated farm
      prices. Ours is not a cheap food policy; it is the
      contrary. Rich countries can afford a dear food
      policy.
          In the case of India they did keep food prices
      down as a matter of public policy to the benefit of
      the masses of poor people who are consumers in
      this context. In a larger context, in the public
      policy, they thus could keep wages down and
      thereby induce more industrial growth.
          The consumer price picture is very mixed
      from city to city. In some, it is still subsidized;

food is still cheap. In others, it has shifted over quite substantially to becoming high, with great burdens on the poor, compared to the better off.

Let me be a little harsh and rigorous on the economic side. Unless one of following two things holds, no country can afford a cheap food policy and get by with it. One is that it has an export surplus which it can run down. The U.S.S.R. did this in its earlier period. There are countries that have that situation, they have surplus food in terms of export and they can then afford a cheap food policy until they consume that export surplus. This is obvious.

The second is food by aid. India could actually administer a cheap food policy and get by with it for so long because there were large amounts of food-aid. You asked what is happening now. The consumer is, in fact, paying more. Thus food takes a little more of the income of the lower half of consumers.

Zuckerman: Does that mean, in your view, one cannot anticipate that any country will be able to enjoy the circumstances that have permitted the United Kingdom to develop—in spite of the political difficulties which have arisen from so doing—the kind of cheap food policy we enjoy? Neither the issue of export food surplus nor aid—unless by "aid" one means loans of the kind we are now repaying in manufactured exports—applies.

Schultz: I would describe the U. K. as follows: The U. K. has, in fact, subsidized its agriculture very substantially, and to that extent (to the

extent that it is a part of the prices to consumers)
it is an expensive or a high food-price policy.
Meanwhile, the U. K. is still an importer of
considerable amounts of food stuffs (wheat, sugar,
and so forth) and is benefiting from the stupid
policies of exporters producing surpluses and
selling them below cost. You are buying sugar
below cost and you are buying wheat below cost
in the world, and England is still one of the few
countries that continues to benefit from this.

  When you add these up, it is not clear but I
suspect that England has a food price policy that
is high relative to real cost in the aggregate, a
little closer to ours. This is a rough guess.

Zuckerman: The major political issue we face at the
    moment is our exclusion from the Common
    Market; in comparison with food prices there,
    ours are very low.

Shelesnyak: That is, food prices as distinct from
    food costs ?

Zuckerman: Yes, the price paid by the consumer.
    The farmer is getting about $1 billion a year in
    direct support at the present moment.

Shelesnyak: I am saying that there are a psychologi-
    cal cost and a real cost—of a sort. The man who
    goes in the shop and picks up something at a
    specific price forgets that part of his taxes are
    used for subsidy and he is actually paying more.

Schultz: Let's keep it in terms of the context here and be quite specific. In the United States this fall wheat is selling off the farm for about $1.20. This is close to a world price. The farmer, however, is receiving in the way of a total program about $1.80 a bushel. So, this is a high price in terms of what goes to the farmer, although so far as wheat that goes into consumption is concerned, it is at world price because the mills are buying it for flour at $1.20.

In Japan, the rice price is set at about $225 a ton, which is just twice the world price. For the last twelve to eighteen months, the world price of rice has been about $100 a ton. Japan is subsidizing her agriculture handsomely, so consumers in Japan are paying a high price for rice.

In Thailand, the farmer has been getting about $65-$70 a ton for rice. The government takes the rest as a tax. The farmer in this case doesn't get the $100, which is the world price, but gets about two-thirds of that. Thailand has a cheap food policy, both for public revenue purposes and to subsidize consumers in Bangkok. It is well known and it has been a long-standing policy, and the poor countries by and large have followed that policy.

The rich countries have gotten so concerned about their agriculture that they have tended, in this dramatic adjustment period, to subsidize agriculture, and this has led to a high food price policy.

Freedman: Professor Schultz: As I understood you, your optimism is based on two technical

considerations: (a) that the agricultural inputs
on the biological and mechanical side are good;
and (b) that we know what kind of economic incentives or organization there ought to be in
order to produce this. I would like to ask whether
you are also optimistic that the political decisions
that need to be made to use those technical facts
are likely to be positive in the next twenty years.

Schultz: I think in a general sense the trial-and-error
experience of the postwar period has so sharply
jarred the poor countries that, for five to ten
years they are likely not to drift back to the extreme cheap food policy of the previous fifteen
years. That is pretty safe to say. Political
processes learn from their own difficulties and
experiences. We learn, they learn, and when you
get into the kind of box Russia got in, it reversed
its policy substantially. So did China.

It doesn't matter what type of government you
have; supply-and-demand forces become so powerful they bring about an adjustment. In India it was
the drought that forced the change. There were
drastic changes in economic policy through the
government at all levels. Pakistan preceded India
in this. Argentine was simply stagnate until four
years ago, when there was a shift in price policy,
and now the Pampas is beginning to produce.

Will these countries swing as far back as
they were seven years ago? I doubt that this is
likely to happen. Some of them may swing back
somewhat and make somewhat the same mistakes
as before, especially if they are not successful
in converting the larger production into income.

As I noted earlier, the Philippines is already worried about what to do with their surplus rice! The Philippines has been an importer for twenty years and now, suddenly, she is confronted with what looks like substantial exports of rice.

Thus, the picture is complex; very different from country to country.

Ehrlich: Could a biologist who tends to feel the rational point of view in this kind of situation take the pessimistic estimates rather than the optimistic ones and interject just a few points on this? I agree with virtually everything that Dr. Schultz has said. I think he has pointed out a lot of the difficulties that make the "green revolution" a little bit more doubtful in some of our minds as to how far it can or will go, but I think there are others that ought to be brought out.

I think most biologists agree that the best way to increase the world's food production, if it can be done, is by increasing yields on land already under cultivation and by revolutionizing agriculture. These varieties, for instance, will require very high fertilizer inputs. I had correspondence with Ray Ewell, who was India's fertilizer consultant for a number of years, and he has a very dim picture of the likelihood that India is going to move in the fertilizer area far enough to permit the yields to continue, partly an economic problem.

Schultz: How recent was this?

Ehrlich: Three or four days ago.

Segal: We keep getting these invocations of the higher spirits. Ray Ewell predicted in 1965, in the height of the drought, that there would be 20 million deaths by starvation. I am not just talking about deaths by attrition, which still maybe occurring, but mass epidemic starvation by the end of 1967. We have to put his views in some perspective.

Ehrlich: I was going to ask Dr. Schultz to comment on this. I am not an expert on fertilizers and Ewell may be wrong. For instance, if we want to go back to wrong predictions of how many people can be fed, I think we can all just dredge up, for whichever side we choose, all the wrong predictions we want, but there is no question that they require high fertilizer inputs and this is going to be a factor.

Schultz: Let's hold on this for just a moment because this is important. Ray Ewell and I were together on this quite recently and I owe a good deal of what I am about to say to him because, as a chemical engineer, he is closer to the technology than I am or can be ever.

To see the development in fertilizer in better perspective, we came out of World War II with a technical advance in the production of nitrogen, which reduced the cost by half. By 1950 the cost to farmers, relative to consumer price or to farm product prices, had dropped 50 percent. The other fertilizers did not drop quite as much. The explosion in the use of fertilizer in Western Europe, in this country, Canada, and in Japan is in substantial part a response to the much cheaper fertilizer.

In 1962-63 there occurred another major technological advance. This was the "rotary" compressor, using the high compression principle of the jet engine. This has cut the cost of nitrogen production by another half. Meanwhile, potash, because of the Canadian resources, has also dropped by half. The price of better fertilizer, paid by U.S. farmers, began to drop quite substantially this year.

Actually, Europeans are starting to dump some fertilizer via exports, because many of their modern plants are coming on stream. We have thirty-seven on stream; Japan has four; Canada has two; but Europe must have between twelve and fifteen. They are mainly one-thousand-tons-a-day nitrogen plants.

Whether all of the poor countries will supply farmers with this cheap fertilizer is an important matter. India is trying to keep the price of fertilizer from declining inside India; the government wants to make a profit on it for public revenue. The belief is that fertilizer is cheap enough to the farmer as it was, and now that it can be imported at a lower price, the government can take this difference. According to word a couple of weeks ago, India appears to be collecting revenue rather than letting the farm price of fertilizer decline. The South American countries, except for Mexico, haven't moved, as yet, on the cheap fertilizer.

To go back, there is an extraordinary changes in commercial fertilizer prices. If you accept the view that this sets the stage for higher crop yields, the cheap fertilizer becomes most important for the highly populated countries where, as I have emphasized, the biological advance means the new varieties that will respond to this fertilizer.

Ehrlich: I agree with that. Let me go on just a little bit because one of the big questions involved is whether the fertilizer will come in, whether a plant will be produced. As for the phosphate situation, I understand, at least in relatively long-term prospect, if we move into these high yield grades, the phosphate supply in the world as a whole looks rather serious.

Schultz: Watch it. You are wrong, but let me be careful. The phosphate prices have not broken, though this year they are down a little bit. There has been a real gain from the increasing scale of production. But sulfur is required to free the phosphate from the rock. The price of sulfur has risen, it has gotten in short supply all over the world, so for five years now the price of sulfur has been rising, offsetting the gains in scale in the production of phosphate. But the price of sulfur is starting to break, and is going to break substantially. The reason simply is that it has become technically possible and profitable to use all the so-called stinky gas. Western Canada is full of gas that is full of sulfur, and the big companies are now taking out the sulfur, putting the gas back in the ground. The sulfur is valuable and Canada becomes a big exporter of sulfur.

They are doing this now in the Middle East,
so the increasing supplies of sulfur are going
to beat down the price. It is already in the cards,
in terms of what we can see, in terms of plant
conversion–to get sulfur out of gas.

When that happens, then the scale plus the
lower sulfur prices will decrease the price of
sulfur for fertilizer substantially.

Ehrlich: Let's move on to another point. What concerns me about revolutionizing agriculture in the
tropical areas of the world is the necessity for
increased pesticide input. I am thinking of Japan's
experience. We now face a very large protein
deficit. Certainly a very big aspect of the nutritional question that you raised is the potential for
getting animal protein, high-grade protein out of
the sea.

Schultz: No, no; stay with the pesticides.

Ehrlich: The pesticide usage is adding to polution of
the sea, which, combined with the race to over-
fish the sea, has a lot of biologists very depressed
about the prospects of maintaining today's protein
yields from the sea.

Schultz: You are too heroic, actually, but this is because I have said twenty years, twenty-five years.
You may be right in that first statement on the
pesticides, and let me put it in economic terms.
In the Philippines, the evidence is now good, and
I am sure it is going to stand up similarly in India,
that if you put in $7 an acre of fertilizer, $4 an

acre has to be spent on pesticides before the
marginal return from the pesticide will be down
to normal returns. You must have the pesticides
and a lot. The $4 is quite large, really, and as
we see it here, climbing upto the fertilizer figure.
Pesticides are really a very important part of
the story in the context that I am trying to present.

Taylor: May I put in here? Hugh Nicholl has asserted
that the intensification of agriculture will bear
heavily on some other resources, notably metal.
I believe the amount of metal tied up in farm
fencing greatly exceeds the amount tied up in
railroad tracks in countries like this one and
Britain. He has argued, therefore, all depends
on fossil fuels; agricultural machinery, metal,
fuels for transporting fertilizer, ships; that the
real limiting factor is the availability of fuels on
which to base the intensification.

Ehrlich: That was my next question, particularly
since the petrochemicals are involved in the
pesticides and in the fertilizers, and in their
shipment, and so on. In other words, we are
building toward a cropping system which is totally dependent on our fossil fuel supplies that are
running out.

Notestein: In three hundred years.

Ehrlich: One hundred, three hundred, it depends.
The plasma boys think about a hundred, but maybe they have a built-in bias.

Schultz: Let me not take this on. I have my own
    judgments.
        If we can hold you to twenty years, then what
    you say, I think, must be sharply qualified. But
    let Joe Fisher take this on.

Zuckerman: I wonder whether Professor Schultz has
    finished the statement he was making. You said
    if in the Philippines you put in $7 of fertilizer and
    $4 of pesticide, that—and then you were interrupted.
    I don't know what the consequences were.

Schultz: The economic test is that you push each of
    these inputs to the point at the margin that each
    input per dollar earns as much as the other in-
    puts. This is the optimum concept in allocating
    resources, and what this shows is that you have
    to go up to $4 in pesticides before you have enough
    pesticides to be at an optimum, which suggests
    to me a very large figure, because if you gen-
    eralize, it means a large pesticide importing
    industry or producing industry, and this has not
    been sufficiently in the picture in the discussions.

Ehrlich: The pesticide situation, in the view of most
    biologists, is desperate today.

Schultz: Not supplies.

Ehrlich: No, I meant the effects. The picture of
    converting world agriculture to the kind of pesti-
    cide inputs we have, say, in the United States,
    which are not as high as in Japan—the consequences
    of this, in my view, I think may be potentially

worse than having half the people in the world
die of famine. It depends on how far you go.

Schultz: Just to keep you a minute, don't forget we
    are spending in terms of purchase inputs, largely
    fertilizer and pesticides in this country, around
    $40 an acre. This is the United States figure, and
    maybe we are going to the dogs in your sense in
    twenty-five years. There are problems, but let's
    not get them out of proportion.

Ehrlich: All right, we can discuss later whether they
    are in proportion or not. Let me have one final
    comment on this point.
        I heard at the Freedom-from-Hunger Confer-
    ence, when the Ambassador from the Philippines,
    accepting an award for their substantial achieve-
    ments in IRI-8 rice, say that, "This proves that
    any country that wants to can feed itself and we
    can now have all the babies we want." This
    above all, I think, is the attitude that has to be
    avoided. As you point out, you can always "feed
    up" any amount of food that is available, and very
    rapidly.

Davis: Mr. Chairman, I am sorry I missed last night's
    session because that is where I assume you defined
    what the problem is.

Harkavy: No.

Davis: I am lost here. I am very interested in what
    Ted has to say, but I don't see that it bears much
    on what I think the problem of the conference is.

All I want is to ask him a question. Let us assume that our problem here is how to control
population growth. It seems to me that what Ted
has been saying is how much of a problem that
will be because it looks as though, from an agricultural point of view, we will facilitate a great
deal of population growth.

But I want to press him now and ask, as an
agricultural expert, what are the agricultural
policies that you believe would operate most
effectively to control population growth?

Schultz: I can't, really. I am out of water now. I
am willing to make some guesses, but I don't put
much weight on these.

Let me pull out one guess that I suspect I
could argue with favorable results. A country
that is successful in getting rather rigorous elementary schooling into the population has developed
a factor which seems to have positive influences in
reducing the net reproduction rate. You feel the
truth of this strongly in Japan moving around on
farms and seeing what they have achieved in terms
of the quality of their schooling in the farm population relative to Western countries and compared
now with some of the poorer countries.

I would also say that finding off-job work for
women, such as schoolteaching, would help mar-
ginally. But you see how far I am out of my depth
here, Kingsley.

Davis: Actually, the second one is partly an agricultural policy, I suppose, because it would com-
bine other work with agriculture. The first
alternative one is not really an agricultural policy,
it is an education policy.

Schultz: Oh, sure, sure.

Davis: I was thinking from the point of view of agriculture itself.

Schultz: I don't think I can think this way. I do believe that if you look strictly at agriculture, any farm people who have gotten sophisticated enough to understand modern biology have a small plus in understanding their own biology. This, I suspect is true, although I don't know of any evidence I can cite. The other, education is outside and I think there is evidence on this one. I think there is some evidence that I can tie in, women working today.

Davis: How do you judge a fair question from an unfair question? It is a question growing out of the relation of a given body of material to what the conference is about and, therefore, it is a fair question.

Slobodkin: Can I give an answer in an agricultural sense immediately? In one sense, it is as fair as the question itself. If they worked it out on a unicorn-based agriculture, everyone knows that unicorns are only happy in the presence of virgins. This might do. Would you buy this as an hypothetical reply?

Davis: I am out of my depth. (Laughter)

Tax: I think one could make a little presentation on what is complementary to what Ted said. I will

try.   It requires us to change our perspective a
bit, but I think we can tie in what he is saying
very easily to the problem of the conference.

Since it is masses of individuals who make
population decisions, it is worthwhile to ask the
basis on which they make any decisions.   We tend
to assume that we are the only rational people;
we know what is good for everybody, and something is wrong with those who don't do what we
think is good.   Of course, we at this table know
that this is a foolish view.

It is fortunate that most of the people of the
world who we are worrying about are peasants
and not hunters.   The North American Indian
tribes that I know very well, or the Kalahari bushmen or the Australian aborgines, are people who
have these odd cultures that are not at all like
ours. They are a small minority and could never
over-populate the earth.   That problem is brought
about by people who are food producers, have gone
through the peasant tradition, and are what I
would call economically oriented.   This is true of
all the populous peoples of Asia, Africa and
America.

They are rationally oriented people.   They
will do in the family what is economically useful
for them to do.   For the most part, they have the
notions that we have, but have not had the facilities for what we call progress.   In their situation
it has not been to their evident advantage, from
their point of view, to do what we may think they
should have done.   I said last night that there are
two things that one shouldn't expect them to do:
to make a change which violates their own values,

or which threatens their identity. The more obvious thing I am saying only now: they will make
a change which is evident to them as having an
economic, a utilitarian advantage—provided it
doesn't violate these other things. When their
own interests become evident to them, and they
are left free to pursue them in their own ways,
they will upset all your pessimistic predictions.
All people can think for themselves and, fortunately for our purposes, the populous ones are economically, or in this sense rationally, oriented.

What is the reason then why they have been so
foolish as to have more children? It may well be
a matter of timing on the one hand, and on the
other of the absolute level of poverty. In a set
of 12 villages in Guatemala where I have been
working (contiguous villages of the same culture),
the average birth rate over 15 years runs from
41 to 61, from village to neighboring village.
The causes are complex and we still have to dig
them out. In part, it seems to be a difference
between being so poor that it doesn't make any
difference and being just rich enough to have some
hope of getting somewhere. These are exceedingly economically oriented Indian people, maybe
more so than in many other cases. But it is a
good case to study, since it is fairly clear that
as soon as it looks as though fewer children will
make an economic difference, they have fewer.

One of these towns has a high birth rate despite the fact that it is economically on the rise.
This is a critical case. It turns out that here
the children are economically useful. It is a

rope-twisting town, and children, as soon as they can toddle are put at one end of a line.

Ehrlich: You were talking about the immediate situation.

Tax: I am talking about the immediate economic situation, and I'll bet (I don't know) that you would find the same differences within the towns, the birth rate between the very poor and those on the upgrade. If you are on the economic upgrade, you become interested in stopping drinking and in stopping fiestas because you want to make that advantage a little bit better; but if you are very poor, you drink and you waste your money on fireworks for fiestas.

In one of the poorest towns they had some hope (at least this is our hunch what happened) and imported a priest to enforce a Protestant ethic: "You live here and keep us sober; we are going to have a school and we are going to get our kids educated and we are going to get somewhere." In contrast to the close-by, neighboring town, they become progressive in orientation.

Ehrlich: Consider the situation in Japan today. Here is a progressive people. You can see, in the long run, their present growth rate is suicidal. They had a governmental policy which tried to cut it. Now a little economics comes into the picture and ---

Tax: I am talking about the decision-making process variable according to whether you are very poor or whether you are somewhat ---

Ehrlich: And you are saying that the very poor ones
    can't but the ones who have a chance ---

Tax: I am trying to explain why we have had this
    population explosion with economically oriented
    peasant peoples and the difference it will make
    suddenly to have much more opportunity for
    economic advancement. That is the point I am
    trying to make. I am trying to tie the two things
    together.

Hoagland: Dr. Tax, I wonder if you would comment
    on the change of the attitude of the Soviet Union
    on population problems. I remember in 1961
    I was involved in trying to work out an agenda
    for a Pugwash Conference and a representative
    of biology, Vice President of the Soviet Academy,
    was very much interested in having world food
    problems discussed and we agreed this was a
    good idea, but I said you can't really get anywhere
    unless you talk about the problems of overpopu-
    lation, but he replied, "Oh, we can't discuss
    population problems." The Russians felt it was
    all very simple. The communist system would
    completely eliminate overpopulation problems
    since there would be no limitations on the food
    supply or anything else. Within the capitalist
    system, they believed starvation and misery from
    crowding to be inevitable.
        Well, we didn't discuss it. We talked about
    food and not about population. That has changed,
    I think quite dramatically, in the last few years.
    Have you any idea as to why?

Tax: No. There are other people who must know
       more about the Soviet Union than I do.

Harkavy: I am torn between two things: following
       lines that to my way of thinking are a bit remote
       and recognizing people who have sputtered a
       start but just can't get themselves to interrupt the
       next guy. I am going to go back a bit. We will
       vary in this thing. First Frank and then Neil.

Sutton: I really wanted to follow up on Kingsley Davis
       (and I think also on Sol Tax), and underscore the
       importance of the question Kingsley raised. It
       seems to me that policies of rural development
       that may have beneficial effect on population con-
       trol are extremely important to consider over the
       next years. If you take the next twenty years that
       we have been talking about, countries that are 80
       percent rural now are going to be at most 60 per-
       cent rural at the end of those twenty years. When
       we talk of the rural population, we are talking
       about a major part of the population.
           We know from history that there have been
       policies of the handling of rural areas that have
       had a major effect on population. Impartible
       inheritance is one outstanding example and is a
       policy that has been pushed in some rural areas
       in recent years.

Harkavy: Frank, define that, would you please?

Sutton: The land has to pass to one son. I am think-
       ing of the famous French policy which surely had
       an important effect on the course of French

population.   A modern example occurs in Kenya
in the famous land consolidation movement in the
Central Province.   It is pretty hard to judge the
effects of population because nobody has studied
them carefully, but it does look like the right
kind of thing to do.

Schultz: Frank, to generalize your point, I think it
is a very strong hypothesis to test, to look for,
and I think the evidence would be strong that
opening up of opportunity for rural people leads
to smaller families. I interpret the Irish experience in this fashion.   When the British laws
finally opened up land ownership to the Irish and
an opportunity for people to go to school, to go
into law and to go into the professions, this seems
to be just what happened, as shown by the Connell
study at Oxford.

There are also other pieces of evidence that
seem to go in this direction. The opportunity to
own land and hold it is one. The opportunity for
your children to get ahead and for the parents to
sacrifice to help them acquire a schooling is
another. This, I think, is not inconsistent with
what you are saying, Sol, and yet I would like to
see this evolve from people who know something
of family behavior as such, because it is a family
decision, the formation of having kids and bringing them up, that really becomes the relevant
decision. But the point can be generalized; i.e.,
anything that opens up real opportunities will
start this kind of process.

Sutton: If I can underscore the logical place of these

remarks in the context of what we are talking about, we are all thinking now beyond family planning to what kinds of measures may affect population growth that are not strictly of a birth control character. It seems to me many of the things of a more diffuse institutional sort hold out more attractive prospects than the kinds of specifics that Barnie Berelson has reviewed in his paper which was circulated to us as background to this conference.

Ritchie-Calder: I would like to say that the most depressing part of Professor Schultz' paper was the idea that modernization meant that more people must migrate to other parts of India, for example, because I thought one of the advantages that was going to come from the modernization of agriculture was that people would recognize they needed fewer hands on the land, and this surely is the case in India. You can find in the Ganges Delta that on neighboring holdings one family is living on a quarter of an acre with seven children, and on the next, the people living on ten acres, which is a big holding, have four children and they are just as illiterate, but the fact is that they have bullocks, and so on, and the thing has changed and they have a new factor.

I was hoping that out of the modernization of agriculture we would begin to make people in India and elsewhere realize they don't need so many hands on the farm and this, I think, would be one of the biggest population factors.

I have always hoped, as a result of farm improvement, and so on, that this would be,

coming back to Kingsley Davis' point of view,
one of the factors that would operate.

Tax: I was arguing that it will, given a year or two.

Ritchie-Calder: One of the things I would like to say,
one of the positive contributions I can make, is
to suggest that we convince people to keep
children alive. If you could convince people that
children are not going to die, they wouldn't have
so many children.

Zuckerman: It does, though, Ritchie-Calder, mean
providing opportunities within many areas. You
are against migration of population?

Ritchie-Calder: I was taking up the point that with the
improvement and modernization of agriculture in
the Ganges, now you are going to have a migration, which to me meant you have to have more
hands.

Zuckerman: You have precisely this problem in the
country from which you come but on a much
smaller scale, and it is an extremely difficult
political problem. You have it in the northern
part of East Anglia; you have it in Scotland.
That is to say, as you require fewer hands on the
farms, if there isn't the capital to provide industrial plants which might provide the opportunities for the employment of people who otherwise would be gathering the wheat with their
hands, they move away.

Ritchie-Calder: I know, and that is fine.

Zuckerman: And you don't want that, you say?

Ritchie-Calder: I am sorry, sir. I am trying to pick up Professor Schultz on the one point where he said that in the Deccan there would be a change and you would have the migration of the Deccan planter to the south or to the Ganges because they needed more hands.

Schultz: No, no. That is the short run. The Deccan Plains will have too many people relative to other areas as modernization succeeds.

Ritchie-Calder: You are going to have more people in the Deccan Plains?

Schultz: Modernization will just take less labor.

Zuckerman: To me, that is the longer-term problem, which is the more important.

Schultz: That is going to show up in two decades.

Freedman: Professor Schultz, your generalization of Dr. Davis' remarks emphasizing that if people feel there are opportunities for themselves and their children to get ahead, that's a move in the right direction. Doesn't this involve another thing that seems to come out of what you said. Those opportunities to get ahead involve these people in much larger "systems of interchange" like those you described for agriculture. The

opportunities to get ahead and the opportunities
for their children, and so forth, are not things
that they get as rewards from the activities of
their own family and local community. It seems
that is very important because if you simply increase the opportunities within the family context,
so to speak, I don't think that is going to happen.

Schultz: You are right.

Freedman: This is the critical diffuse process both
you and Frank have been referring to.   The
modernization of agriculture is putting the peasant and his family into a completely different
framework. This is a framework in which the
things that they regard as worth having in life
come from different institutions and exchanges
than have existed in the past. This will affect
both migration and fertility.

Chamberlain: Rather than Ted Schultz's paper being
away from the main interest of the conference, it
seems to me that it is squarely within the purview
and it highlights some of the major points for
discussion, because I take it that what Ted has
been saying, with an element or an air of prediction about it, is that there is a good possibility
for supporting, by food (the nutritional question
laid aside), a very much larger population than
now exists, perhaps even doubling it by the end
of the century.

     If this is the case, then it seems that we are
back with the title, the question that is posed to
us as the title of our conference, "The Growth

of Population. " Consequently, we do face this
very significant question: What are the consequences of that much larger population—facili-
tated, permitted, and made possible by this spectacular increase in agricultural possibilties?
Here we face, with others, the kinds of questions
that Ted himself has raised: What happens to
those sections within particular countries that are
left out of that kind of agricultural revolution?
What happens to economies like the Philippines
that are having difficulty in monetizing their increase in food supply, of including it within the
framework of their economy?

These become, in my opinion, critical kinds
of questions, and instead of simply leaving it at
the aggregate level, saying that we can have and
support a population of 6 - 7 billion people on a
worldwide basis, that we must break down these
overwhelming aggregates and see how this affects
various countries. What does it do to the structure of the economy, the structure of the government, and the way the food supplies get taken in?
What happens to those people who are left aside?
These are the kind of questions which should be
at the heart of many issues involved with the
growth of population.

Slobodkin: I want to turn back to what Dr. Davis said
because I think one of the most important questions
we can ask now is whether Dr. Davis feels he has
received an answer. Otherwise, we have a communication problem that is very interesting.

Davis: You know, our subject is consequences and

and cures, and I want to understand clearly what
we are curing here.

It is very difficult to separate a presentation of facts from an analysis of the implications
of those facts for the issues that we are considering. I wasn't accusing Ted of irrelevance.
I wanted to hear what he had to say about specific agricultural policies. As a matter of fact,
the inheritance mechanism is one I had in mind.

Secondly, as between the peasants today in
Guatemala and those in Poland in the past, there
is pretty good evidence that in Poland if a couple
didn't have any land, the children of that couple
didn't get married very early, or not at all. The
average age at marriage for women would go up
to 29. It was precisely because those peasants
felt they did not have an opportunity that they
refrained from founding a family. That is quite
a different reaction from what Sol Tax says
about the Guatemalans, and it seems that there is
some kind of community or institutional factor
there. If the local controls are firm enough so
that given kinds of demographic behavior wind
one up in a lower status, (it isn't just a matter
of going up in status, it is also a matter of going
down) then the system of rewards and punish-
ments may be such that reproductive behavior is
lowered or postponed because of lack of opportunity. That seems to me to be a sort of ideal
institutional arrangement if it can be worked out,
but exactly what the mechanics are, I don't think
anybody at the present time can say, and it
would require a good bit of research.

Schultz: Kingsley, again I think this point ought to be generalized. I would say that, to the extent that anything is done, or can be done, by public decision which would increase the burden of children explicitly, or improve the benefit to the family of fewer children, which is quite different, you get the consequences that we are talking about.

    We should allow ourselves the assumption that underneath parents in this context are behaving quite rationally in assessing how these forces, social, economic, and others, play on them in terms of burdens. The difficulty is to give it content. You are giving it some content.

Tax: One word about the difference between the Polish peasants and the Guatemalan Indian: there is a traditional difference in absolute level of living. The poorest Polish peasant was much richer than a middle-rich Guatemalan Indian. Compare the way country people live in Europe, in Japan, in Java, or, for that matter, even in Thailand, with the way they live in India or South America. You will see that difference. Europe had moved to a very different level of material life a long time ago and now the people say, "In order to maintain my social position in this society, I can't have children because I must keep this high level of material culture." Japanese country people similarly have a very high level of living and high standards who want to be able to serve tea formally, and so on.

    I was thinking, rather, of the very poor

peasants in India and South America where the
level is so low that you will just have children
because you haven't got anything else, anyway.

Davis: That may be a part of it but I don't believe
that it is a very important part because even the
lowest level of living, any level of living that
permits a community to live if it is going to be
there for any length of time, can be accompanied
by a pretty tight social organization, so that the
degree of control over individual reproductive
and family behavior in terms of the community
is not just a function of the level of living. There
are other elements, especially on the agrarian
side, and some of those elements can be figured
out.

Tax: There are differences in cultures and one of the
characteristics here is that these families in
Southern Mexico and Guatemala, where I have
worked, and many other places, are exceedingly
individualistic. There is relatively little social
control of the kind that you are talking about,
though sorcery from the envious is feared. At
the poor level there isn't the kind of pride which
says "I must keep up with the Joneses," or, "I
must do something or other." Each person is
at a low level where he simply has to get barely
enough to live and to divide among his children
when he dies. It is the absolute low level and the
atomistic form of society that I think are significantly different from the place you are thinking
of.

Ehrlich: I was trying to make a somewhat different point with Japan and wasn't really trying to disagree with you, but here you have a country where everything should be on the side of people going for more affluence, and I believe they do make family-size decisions in part on an economic basis, but at the same time they haven't managed to push their rate of growth down far enough.

Tax: Neither have we. That is because it is to our advantage.

Ehrlich: Our individual advantage at the moment, but the question is: How can you get people to take this larger societal view of what the advantage is? In Japan if they lose out on the fishing race, they will disappear.

Schultz: Oh, no.

Freedman: We are talking about the late Robert Kennedy and his family and you are going to say, "You should take a larger view. You shouldn't have so many children."

Ehrlich: And it is a very difficult way to get anybody to act, unquestionably. Ten generations of Robert Kennedy and you get 10 billion descendants. Excuse me, he had eleven. I can't calculate that.

Harkavy: Dr. Hoagland left a question dangling.

Hoagland: I wanted to say that sometime we may look

forward to the day when any politician who brags
that he has ten children would automatically not
be elected because he would be regarded as
socially irresponsible. His opponent might
bring that out but perhaps it would be something
he wouldn't like to advertise too much. I am
afraid we are very far from that state of affairs.

Harkavy: I wonder whether we have said enough about
the consequences of the growth of population for
food supply. Mr. Ehrlich raised the question as
to whether the entire agricultural revolution on
which we put so much hopes rests on fossil fuels
that might run out. I wonder whether Joe Fisher
can at least start the discussion. Would you,
Joe, say something about minerals, water and
such.

Fisher: To some extent, I will work along the line
that Ted Schultz has worked in connection with
food and come out with a fairly comforting view
of things, At least so far as most of the hard
resources are concerned. Looking ahead for
the United States, one can't find a very compelling reason for controlling or limiting population.
I am aware that this is only a narrow sector.
There are several ways of approaching this.
One is to look at the resources: minerals, water,
air, fuel, space. But one of the difficulties in
looking ahead is that you don't know what will
turn up on the scientific and technological side.
Within categories these things, and even across
categories, substitute for one another. Within
the fuels component, for instance, there are four

or five main sources of energy that overlap and substitute quite easily, depending upon technological changes as these work themselves out in terms of relative costs and prices. So if you see a problem or a shortage or a cramp on development in one of them, you have to look at all the others.

Or, one can approach the matter by looking at different regions. One can look at the United States, the western world, the less developed two-thirds, or in other ways. Here, of course, one gets into difficulty because trade can move within and between regions so that, for example, the problem of oil supply in Western Europe can be met with imports from the Middle East, or discoveries in North Africa, or with imports from elsewhere, or in other ways. Therefore different regions or countries become quite concerned that ready access from other parts of the world is maintained.

The third approach is in terms of time periods. The businessman typically will take a look that isn't too much longer than the amortization period for his investment. Probably governments should be able to take a longer look but frequently don't. The politician is interested primarily in the length of his term or political career. The ecologist frequently will be able to take a longer view. Economists have now stretched themselves out to several decades. Of course, the prophets can look much further ahead, but they don't instruct us too well on the difficulties of policy.

One has to look at the different resource

categories in terms not only of the resources but
also of region and the time period, and play back
and forth between these. My organization has
spent some time looking ahead on these matters
for the United States, making reasonable assumptions and qualifications. I don't see indicators of
increasing scarcity in the economic sense for
several decades ahead. For certain things, certain times, and certain places, yes; but in a general way I cannot see the economic growth or a
likely population increase in the United States
much cramped by inadequacy or high cost of fuels,
most of the minerals, water, or space. I think
that new discoveries, new technology, economic
adaptations, substitutions, and so on, should be
able to handle incipient shortages moderately
well--at least for several decades.

Taylor: This is just in the United States?

Fisher: I am for the moment talking about the United
    States. Of course, this optimism won't hold
    if scientific-technical-economic progress suddenly
    stops, and if there is a breakdown of world trade
    and investment.

Ehrlich: What technology do you expect to take care
    of the water problem?

Fisher: Let's look at the arid West in the United
    States where the sheer quantitative problem of
    not enough water would be most severe. About
    ninety percent of the water there is used in irriga-
    tion agriculture, and used rather inefficiently in

terms of canal leakages, wastage to support useless plants, and so on. Great gains could be made
by preventing these losses.

Ehrlich: By cutting down this plant growth that isn't
used?

Fisher: Yes, or by trying to check loss from evapora-
tion, loss of storage capacity through sedimenta-
tion, and similar problems. Also, there are new
prospects for long-distance transfer of water from
surplus to shortage regions, such as the Columbia
River system to the Colorado system.

Ehrlich: But you are talking about public works there
that, even started now, would take fantastic
amounts of time.

Fisher: We are already making interbasin transfers
on a big scale, say from the Colorado system into
the Missouri system and the Arkansas system.
The whole giant California Water Plan ($1-$2
billion worth of it is underway) involves massive
transfer from the northern Sacramento River into
the south.

Ehrlich: We are running into fantastic dilution
problems to keep from other consequences that are
going to require more water. What about the cost
of roofing over all those miles of canals? I get
an air of unreality. You are the first person I
have seen who thinks that the California water
problem really could be written off this way.

Schultz: Of course, Joe Fisher projects this correctly.
   You missed one point. Joe said a moment ago
   that 90 percent of the water in the West goes into
   agriculture. If this is a fantastically inefficient use
   relative to its value for urban purposes, that part
   of the world might have extraordinary abundance
   if, through public or private allocations, 15 or 20
   percent of this water were transferred for better
   uses.

Ehrlich: What about the agriculture?

Fisher: This was going to be my last reason.

Ehrlich: I need to be educated. It takes a lot of water
   to grow plants and there's no way to get around
   that.

Fisher: If five of the ninety percentage points of the
   water in the arid West, now going into agriculture,
   were shifted to a mix of industrial and municipal
   uses, the population there could be doubled and the
   industry tripled--at least.

Ehrlich: But it is going to quadruple in the next twenty
   years; that's the problem.

Fisher: Much of the agricultural water, of course,
   goes into the production of crops that we haven't
   needed during much of the last couple of decades
   and could have gotten more cheaply elsewhere.
      A similar story could be told in oil. If the
   cost of conventional underground oil in Texas and
   the Southwest really starts to increase steeply,

(which it hasn't because of lacking technological improvements, better pumping, secondary and tertiary recovery, and so forth) then we have waiting more potential imports and a vast reserve in oil shale. In addition, large reserves of oil are available in Alberta. Also, there is the possibility of liquefaction of coal. These alternative sources are probably within 5 or 10 percent of the cost of gasoline from conventional sources.

Finally, there are new discoveries. For example, a major field has been found in northern Alaska. Once the pipelines are put in, as much as 10 to 20 percent of the present U. S. consumption could be met from this source. For the next couple of decades, the story of substitution and new sources will be an immensely rich one, especially for a country like the United States which has a large diversified scientific-technological-economic base. This assumes, of course, that nothing seriously erodes our technical capacity to make use of these possibilities.

(The conference recessed at twelve-twenty o'clock.)

SATURDAY AFTERNOON SESSION
September 28, 1968

The Conference reconvened at two o'clock, Dr. Harkavy presiding.

Harkavy: I think that we should continue with Joe Fisher.

Knox: Mr. Chairman, before he starts, I wonder if his comments and those of his hecklers might be better focused if we knew whether they are thinking about one hundred years from now or thirty years or two hundred years.

Shelesnyak: Also, there is a possibility that we think about the next twenty years as testing time to develop methods for handling the next one hundred.

Fisher: I have said already that the time horizon is very important in these discussions, and in terms of my work and discipline, I couldn't say much beyond the next twenty or thirty years.

Reynolds: If we don't make it through the next thirty, the rest becomes academic.

Fisher: I share that, but looking beyond that time, I

123

am perfectly willing to speculate with the best of
you.   But I insist that much of this is speculation.

Fremont-Smith: The dictionary meaning of speculation
is to speak about or ponder upon.

Fisher: Then, I am perfectly willing to speculate.
But I am talking about up to 2000, unless I say
otherwise.

At any rate, I would like to talk briefly about
the resources (listed on the outline as "minerals,
water, air, space") on a world scale, because it
would be a mistake and misleading simply to
carry the much narrower U. S. view into the world
scale.

On a world scale, I can't speak as definitely
as I can about the U.S. situation because of the
unknowns.   But I believe that the outlook in general is more hopeful for meeting likely demands
for minerals, fuels, and water than it is for food,
even though Professor Schultz has said that over
a time span of a couple of decades the world's
outlook for food is by no means hopeless.   In my
mind the prospect for food is uncertain.

First, I will talk about the energy commodities, because they are probably second in interest
to food when people think in terms of running short
or running out, or running into severe trouble in
the next few decades.   On a world scale I see
numerous possibilities for new discoveries of
conventional energy commodities, plus the whole
story of nuclear energy that is rapidly unfold-
ing before us, especially if we succeed in developing economical breeder reactors in the next ten
years.

Rapid increases in population must be placed against this and an even more rapid increase in requirements for energy. Considering that the economy of the less-developed part of the world is at a stage similar to U.S. some time ago, it can be seen that increases in energy consumption will have to be greater than increases in population and even in gross national product. Estimates for a period to 2000 indicate that on a global basis the amount of energy produced and consumed altogether might have to increase fivefold. Checking that against the possibilities of supply, discovery, and the opening up of new energy sources, as far as quantity is concerned, the amount should quintuple.

Obviously, you can't indefinitely produce and consume increasing quantities of something when there is limit on total supply, but scarcity can be deferred for many years, depending on what science and technology can turn up. When you consider peacetime uses of nuclear energy and the development of other new sources such as solar energy, you are in a different ball park. As for the next few years, the most interesting energy material is petroleum. About seventy percent of the total consumption of energy in this country comes from oil, natural gas, and gas liquids. In Western Europe the trend is also toward greater use of petroleum. Petroleum, I think, will be the giant among the energy commodities for a while.

When it comes to the non-fuel metals, the picture becomes quite cloudy. I don't see shortages or cost increases for iron ore. Ore is to be

had, in many places in the world, and if you consider steel, undoubtedly there will be technical
improvements along such lines as direct reduction.

There could indeed be problems of adequacy
of supply for some of the other major metals like
copper, lead, zinc, and the best hope lies in substitution: light metals in many uses and transfers
from the mineral categories into wood products or
plastics. Plastics, of course, come principally
from petroleum, but the amount used is quite
small. That amount could be doubled and trebled
without putting a severe bite on the total petroleum
consumed. Without any doubt there could be
difficulty here. We may have to reach deeper into our bag of substitution tricks which could cause
trouble. But, if the technical-economic base is
sufficiently diversified and resourceful, one can
redesign around specific problems even by reshaping the end-use product.

Unlike minerals, we cannot tell the water
story on a world-wide basis. Water isn't freely
shipped all over the world. It is located in place
and it goes downhill unless you spend a lot of
money to make it do otherwise. But you can ship
the products of industry and agriculture that use
water. In fact, the amount of water for human
consumption is small in the total—probably less
than 5 percent in this country.

Bernstein: Is that percentage consumed or percentage
used?

Fisher: The term used is "withdrawn and depleted."
Maybe through the cycle it gets back into the

system eventually, but not quickly. I will return
to the water problems when I talk about environmental quality.

    Space is a localized difficulty. Cities get
crowded. My own view is that the use of space
in cities is always subject to much better planning,
management, organization development and use
than we yet have seen in most cities. We are
only beginning to use the vertical dimension, up
into the air and down into the ground. This is
coming fast; even now there is quite a market for
air rights over various properties in cities: I
am not sure where the limits are.

    I think the phenomenon of crowdedness, with
all its social, behavioral, and biological implications, has to be seen in the context of how space
is organized and used by people. For example, it
should be possible to organize urban or park space
in such a way that density of use could increase
several times without a feeling of crowdedness.

Slobodkin: Could you be a little bit more specific.

Fisher: Yes, perhaps. To condition the atmosphere
    to get an effect of isolation is not confined to the
    space within a room or a building. It is possible
    out in the parks, by placement of roads, trails,
    and camping grounds, to increase the use of most
    of our outdoor parks without people feeling that
    they are being interfered with by other people.
    This is a job chiefly for the landscape architect.
    For example, in the summer there are forty
    thousand people in Yosemite Valley; but Yosemite
    Valley is probably less than 1 percent of the land

area of the park. It is the most spectacular, to
be sure, but there could be ways by which people
might do their camping outside the valley and
come in during the day. The main idea is that we
should apply the possibilities of design, planning,
and management to the uses of space. I am an
outdoor type but I think we have a long way to go
in this direction before we conclude that just
having more people in a land area will result in
the kind of crowding that sets up psychological,
biological, and behavioral problems. There is a
factor in this equation that has hardly been examined.

Of course, if you freeze the management-
planning-design adaptation side of the population
resources equation, then you quickly get overcrowding. The arithmetic of population projection is easier, frankly, than the arithmetic of
projection on this other side.

I am somewhat overstating the optimistic
view of the case but I think it needs to be kept in
mind because it does indicate that there are
possibilities for coping with more and more
people that have to be worked on before concluding
that we are just not going to make it.

I think, for example, that the compelling
argument for population limitation and control
(still in the perspective of two or three decades)
is not to be found in the exhaustion or the inadequacy of resources—and raw materials generally.
That could happen, but I wouldn't expect it to
happen, and I believe it need not happen if the
scientists, the engineers, and the planners,
among others, do their jobs. As I see it, there

are more compelling, pressing, and valid reasons for population control. I think that environmental damage brought about by crowding may be a compelling reason for population limitation. By this I mean air pollution and other kinds of pollution, landscape spoliation, and so forth. These largely aesthetic factors offer better argument for population control than the depletion of water. In fact, you know, in this country, it is hard to justify most of the water investments in terms of the need for cleaner water for human consumption, industrial use, and irrigation. For industrial uses, even the cleanest natural water has to be treated because it is not the quality required. The investments in facilities must be made anyhow, even if the stream used is what you might call very clean.

Water has to meet certain standards for drinking, but if you will accept a certain deterioration of taste, this can be done through water treatment plants that don't cost so very much. The big reason we spend money on cleaning up streams is aesthetic, affecting sports, recreation, and visual amenity. For example, in the Potomac River system, there is a plan for about $400 million for improvements; and about half of that has to be justified in terms of cleaning the river for aesthetic or recreational reasons, not in terms of industry, human consumption, or electric power. For these purposes it is not the sheer supply of water that is involved so much as the quality.

Hoagland: When you referred to the consumption of

water, you said something like 5 percent was used for human consumption. Did you include power and industrial uses in that, too?

Fisher: No, but there is some industrial because that gets into the domestic water systems.

Hoagland: But aren't these domestic water systems you are talking about?

Fisher: They are. The big users over the country and the world are, first, agriculture and, second, industry for the process of cooling. The big users among the industries are steel, electric power, chemicals, pulp, and a few others.

It seems to me that the whole thrust of the last few centuries, at least in Western history, has been to understand natural and social phenomena and trends with an eye to exercising a degree of control and direction over them. In some basic sense, this may be the best reason of all for wanting to control and direct the sheer numbers of people.

Slobodkin: You seem to be saying that the reason for controlling population growth is that the population is growing, and that is the only reason—or maybe I missed the sequence.

Fisher: No, just the idea or the faith, if you like, that people and society can be "better" in some sense if it understands the major trends that are moving within it and is in a position to exercise direction and guidance over them.

Slobodkin: Does this follow from what you said previously? I missed the transition.

Fisher: It is an assertion. I have tried to indicate that I think the sheer exhaustion of raw materials in the time horizon of a few decades is not a compelling reason for population control. Other reasons seem to be more compelling. I have been listing them, and this last, if you prefer, I assert as a value.

Slobodkin: That controlling things is good?

Fisher: No, that to understand them so that you can guide and influence them, if you wish to, is good.

Ehrlich: I certainly would agree with virtually everything that you said about depletion not being a major problem in the next few decades, with the possible exception of the water situation. If we have other kinds of breakdown, we might find ourselves in difficulty with the distribution problems in this country.

Perhaps we should be asking ourselves (and maybe this isn't too pertinent to this conference) whether we have the right to continue to extract the high-grade stuff during our time without some really serious planning toward what follows at the end of a generally extracting economy; but that may be a side issue.

One interesting thing that I have come across in energy is: I have gotten in touch with the plasma people because I am interested in seeing what the chances of fusion, and so on, are. The thing

seems to be in doubt, but the response from them
was that basically it doesn't make any difference.
We have a limit, anyway, because even if we perfect fusion, which is essentially the be-all and
end-all of the energy resource problem, we still
have the thermal problem it creates and, therefore, we are going to be limited anyway. It has
been pointed out that the inversion layer over
Los Angeles has been pushed up by just the thermal output from the city so that the smog has remained even but has spread over a greater area.
Now they report tree killings almost to the Grand
Canyon from it, and a very large group of biologists and M.D.s recently published a notice in
Los Angeles advising anybody who didn't have a
compelling reason for staying there to leave for
purposes of health. Two days before I came here
I got a clipping from the Manchester Guardian,
reporting on a UNESCO meeting in Geneva. It
reported that "within the next two decades life on
our planet will be showing the first signs of
succumbing to industrial pollution. The atmosphere will become unbreathable for men and animals; all life will cease in rivers and lakes; plants
will wither from poisoning."

Let me finally ask you one question: What do
you think about moving now into more effort toward
recycling?

Fisher: My feeling is that we should. We should take
as a kind of working principle that we'd do well
to confine the waste throw-off of industry and
hold it as close to the source as we possibly
can—rather than throwing it into the atmosphere

or the streams. Benefits and costs being unknown or equal, I would confine the waste and
recycle it—hold it close in so that it doesn't get
out into a bigger system. One of my rules of
thumb would be to put lots of money, effort, and
scientific work into this.

Zuckerman: You were referring to the thermal
    problem in respect to nuclear reactors. Is there
    no question in your mind about the disposal of
    irradiated material?
        How is that being dealt with? You have indi-
    cated that between now and the year 2000 you saw,
    if I remember correctly, a five-time increase in
    the power consumption of the world, and the
    distribution of that power consumption (that in-
    creased consumption) is unfortunately going to be
    heavily weighted in favor of the advanced societies.

Fisher: It is going to be growing faster in the under-
    developed areas and is already growing faster.

Zuckerman: But in absolute terms, I don't know how
    many thousand tons of enriched uranium you're
    thinking about. Between now and 2000 you must
    certainly have in your mind at least some
    thousands of tons per annum. The bulk of that
    increase, if I understand correctly, will be con-
    centrated in this country, possibly the USSR, and
    Western Europe. What is going to happen in
    those countries so far as the disposal of irradiated
    material is concerned, as opposed to the thermal
    issue, which to me seems less relevant? Surely
    advanced technology will look after that with our

heat exchangers and better uses of waste heat. But radioactive waste is persistent and what are you going to do about it?

Fisher: This is a severe problem, there is no doubt about that. I don't think I am the best person here to answer it.

Slobodkin: I was at a meeting of CRAM. It is a group sponsored by the National Academy, dealing with this kind of problem—waste disposal, and so forth—and the representative of the Geological Survey said that the proper handling of radioactive waste permits you to form the waste into a glass block, and if it is done right the glass is (a) safe to handle, and (b) very compact. He reported that the total energy usage of the United States would produce no more than one or two tons of this glass per year.

Zuckerman: I don't believe it. I'm sorry. Was it made by the United States Government or was it made by an enthusiast?

Ehrlich: No, it was made by the United States Government. I have heard it many times.

Zuckerman: It is not for me to comment on United States politics. (Laughter)

Slobodkin: Let me back away from this.

Michaelis: The obvious answer is that you ask this particular authoritative source to substantiate the statement.

Zuckerman: Let us go back. We know, roughly
     speaking, what is the present power consumption
     of the world. We know what world demands are
     likely to be; I don't know anything about the year
     2000--yours is the first figure I have heard. I
     do happen to know some demand figures up to
     about 1980 for Western Europe. Those figures
     vary enormously. There are two particular
     estimates I have in mind, and both are related
     to real demand as now envisaged; they are not just
     a prediction of loose claims, but a statement of
     capital investment programs.
          I can see what your figures would mean in
     enriched uranium on the basis of European demand.
     Your figures are very much higher and take us to
     the year 2000. We are told here that there is
     already a problem in the disposal of thermal
     waste, but, as I say, heat exchangers can be
     improved, and in any event one can always use
     waste heat if one knows how and if one invests
     appropriately.

Ehrlich: Sir, you are mistaken. Don't write that off,
     because it is not just the heat from the reactors.
     All work that is done produces heat: every time
     you put on a brake in a car that is the source
     of the thermal problem.

Zuckerman: But you are not talking about the world.
     Every time we breathe in this room, everyone of
     us produces 40 watts, or whatever--I have heard
     that figure. I am not worrying about that.
          I am talking now about the very restricted
     problem of the generation of electric power, and

the issue was raised on thermal waste. I wanted
to know, apart from questions of investment, is
there any limiting factor on the development of
electric power?

Fisher: I think the more serious part of the problem
is the environmental damage that may be caused.
Since I am no expert on this, I don't like to talk
too much about it, but there are conventional
ways of handling this waste: burying it in the ocean
or underground, and sluicing it down rivers that
have a big volume flow. Then there are other
things that you read about, like the glass thing.

Zuckerman: May I remind the meeting that there are
already political problems involved in this particular issue in a minor way. I am not talking about
reactor accidents, such as a relatively trivial
one we had in the United Kingdom some years
ago, but am referring to the movement of nuclear-
powered ships. At the present we know, from the
newspapers, that the Japanese Government is
protesting the free movement of ships from this
country. The Brussels Convention, the convention relating to the movement of nuclear-powered
vessels, has not been ratified by the United States
nor by one or two other countries. We have here
an existing political restriction on the potential
use of a source of power to which you are referring
as the major source to the year 2000.

Fisher: No, I didn't say that was the major source.

Zuckerman: If you take the world at large, it could
turn out to be major source.

Fisher: I think in terms of electric power by the year
     2000, just power.   That is a minor part of the
     total energy.

Zuckerman: Is it not conceivable that in some parts
     of the developing world, and regardless of other
     factors which could influence the agricultural
     revolution, the need for small power units could
     confine the use of oil—mainly imported oil—for
     agricultural purposes.   So while it would be
     possible to have oil-fired power stations, you may
     not be able to use oil for that purpose because of
     its selective end use in agriculture, and so forth,
     which will put greater pressure on the nuclear
     fuel.
          We are facing a major problem, and facing
     it now.

Schultz: You lost me on two points here.   It is a
     major problem entirely because of the disposal
     of waste, is that the one point?

Zuckerman: Yes.

Schultz: Nothing else?

Zuckerman: At the present moment, to the best of
     my knowledge, quite apart from the economics.
     I will come to that.

Schultz: Let me enter a small piece of evidence,
     because I shared your judgement completely until
     some months ago when I was in company with a
     Mr. Haywood of Canada, a physicist, who has

been associated with atomic developments and a
vice president of the Chalk River Nuclear Laboratories. There were two issues: running out of
the supply of fuel itself and disposal. His position was that the disposal problem was as close
to solution as was the problem, five years ago,
of getting economic use of atomic energy for the
production of electricity.

Zuckerman: May I make my position quite clear?
I have no views on the subject. I am only asking
questions. Unfortunately, I happen to sit officially
in a chair where I occasionally have to risk a
view, but I don't know what the answer is. I was
merely asking, and you have introduced another
question. Did your Canadian friend inform you
of the economics?

Schultz: No, no; that is not his field.

Zuckerman: There are a lot of people who believe
that we don't know all about the economics of
nuclear generation, and I want to bring this down
to what is a critical issue at the present in the
United Kingdom. I am sure Ritchie-Calder can
complement what I say. We have a major problem
now because we have a big coal-mining population that is being run down because it is assumed
that the economics of our investment over the
years in nuclear power justifies a transfer.
    Four years ago we started getting natural gas
from the North Sea. Now, using your time scale,
the next ten or twenty or thirty years (for me,
the year 2000) the investments we are going to

make today are the investments that are going to
apply to the economy in 2000. Decisions must be
made now.

We'll have to make social investments that
could be enormous if we move one or the other
way. We have to see to displaced coal miners.
We may not be able to bring alternate forms of
occupation to the coal villages and towns, because
people won't accept them. We have the whole
business of building up new places to which their
children will go, at the same time as they are
being supported. That is one aspect. But at the
same time we may be making the wrong decision
about the economics of nuclear power versus gas.
These are present issues; yet, we are talking
about a five-time increase in power consumption
by 2000. In the United Kingdom we have a small
laboratory experiment of the kind of political
issues that have got to be dealt with as we look
forward and project ourselves into a world of
demand and use with a population of 7 billion
people.

Ritchie-Calder: This is something to which I have
     given some attention and where I might be able
     to contribute. The problem of the disposal of
     waste is, without any question, one of the biggest
     problems we have. It has already cost the United
     States considerably to bury live atoms, and the
     whole question of the accumulation of waste is
     fantastic. Think of the costs of getting live
     atoms—waste to their burial grounds by
     2000—just here in the United States.
     The other problem, as far as I know, not

satisfactorily solved, is that, first of all, I don't
accept the glass solution. We have been over this
a lot, but the other thing is, as they have done at
Oak Ridge, to try to dispose of it by hydrolytic
fraction, which is the only way you can guarantee
it won't be upset by earthquakes. Even then, you
have got a very big problem.

But just to extend it to the other one, how do
you get rid of massive waste by trying to dispose
of it at sea? The amount of reticence about this
is alarming, because we don't know. On one
occasion I remember when we were talking about
disposal of atomic waste in the Atlantic, the
British boasted that they were putting it down
safely somewhere in solid form. Professor
Revelle pointed out that there was a 50 m. p. h.
river that ran through this particular canyon which
would just smash up the whole thing.

We are running into this problem constantly
and I would say that just as we have done it in
terms of the hydrocarbons and the fossil fuels,
this would change climatic conditions progressively. So now you are introducing a completely
supplementary factor into the natural environment
by the use of radioactive materials, because they
have never been there before, and I have not seen,
apart from a few pious people like myself, anyone stopping to think about its total effect. Everybody gives a partial answer which is satisfactory
to them, but this, to me, is one of the really
serious problems.

We must go back to the point about the fossil
fuels; there is no question in my mind that the
addition of carbon to the atmosphere is altering

radically the nature of our environment. When
we come to Princeton and find a sunny day when
we don't expect one, or when we get torrential
rains and floods in the south of England when we
don't expect them; a good deal of this, I maintain, is the alteration that is happening in the
total environment, and this is going to accumu-
late in the next twenty years. (Let's just
restrict it to the next twenty years.)

The estimate is that by 2000, the mean temperature of the earth will have risen by 3. 6
degrees. No one stops to think what the effect of
this is going to be. This will mean the breaking
of the ice dams of the Himalayas; it will mean
this and that, but absolutely unpredictable. At
this stage, according to Dr. Fisher, I do think
that what we should seriously consider is not just
the idea of it but, what it is going to do to us in
the next twenty years if it happens.

Ehrlich: May I please set the record straight? I
did not say nor did I imply that the problem of
cooling reactions, although that does present
serious thermal pollution problems, was the
limiting problem. The thermal problem is all the
electricity you generate by the reactors or whatever, which eventually turns up someplace in
this same ecosphere as heat. This with the
CO_2 problem, plus the contrails that are being
laid down now and apparently are building the
"greenhouse effect" further, are the serious
limiting factors as far as I can see on the entire
world ecosystem. What you do as you keep
humping the temperature up is ---

Shelesnyak: But I think Sir Solly was talking about
the impact of the nuclear source of energy, and
that the thermal problem with that is not the most
serious.

Ehrlich: That is not what I am saying. We were
talking about two different problems.

Zuckerman: I know there are all these other aspects
of the disposal of waste problem. I know about
the CO_2 and the increase in heat. I was trying
to take one specific problem which has to be dealt
with now, not tomorrow, if we are going to get
ready for the year 2000. I don't know how these
things are done in the United States. I know a
little about how they are done in the United
Kingdom and in Western Europe, as a whole. But
investment plans are being made and are being put
into effect now that will be determining the nature
of one part of the environment (I am not going to
discuss the risk), by 1980.

Ehrlich: There is a great deal of difficulty in finding
out about this waste problem in the United States.
I have tried and others tried, after hearing this
glass routine, and I have never seen a single
technological question with more extreme answers
given, depending whom you are talking to. Some
people say "a few lumps of glass," and other
people say, as they are apparently doing now, that
there is this fantastic disposal problem. I
wonder where one goes to get a definitive statement from the government on this.

Harkavy: Joe, is this something that your people are
working on?

Fisher: Some are. I am sympathic to this line. My
point was to try somewhat to remove the argument
that it is scarcity of resources that justifies
population control. I am with you on the seriousness of the waste disposal problem. If what you
say is true (and I am inclined to think that if it is
in Britain, it is probably elsewhere), you should
thank your stars that gas came from the North
Sea and that they discovered oil in North Africa,
your side of the Middle East, and that they may
discover that much (and more again) in northern
Canada. It seems to me you should shape policy
so as to slow down and discourage nuclear power
production in favor of these other sources. In
the meantime—in the breather—do everything you
can to deal more adequately with the radioactive
throw-off.

The situation also shows the importance of a
diversification within the energy sector of an
economy: that you can, with only marginal differences of cost, turn for a period of years to
something elso while you work with this other
problem. This is a dangerous kind of tightrope-
walking but people have been doing it since the
beginning of time.

Zuckerman: You say it is dangerous tightrope-walking.
The difficulty is that those people who can draw up
the balance sheet and who could turn to action
can't really get onto the tightrope. The decisions
in these matters are not taken by some grand body

of people sitting around a table like this. In the
United Kingdom we have nationalized energy
companies. They fight between each other as to
what the National investment program should be.
In the case of Western Germany, the federal
government has no power over new investment
by the utility companies so far as the generation
of power is concerned. The situation is extremely
difficult.

Whenever we look at institutions, it becomes
very difficult to say, "We ought now to define a
clear policy about what is what." It would take
about ten years of major political discussion,
one or two revolutions, at least, to get to the
point where you could say you have made the right
decisions. Ten years may be an understatement.

Schultz: Joe, will you say something about the recovery process of lead and zinc—perhaps even
copper, as one moves through time?

Fisher: Since you have given me a choice, I will
choose copper. Over a period of about fifty years,
the deflated cost/price trend for copper has been
about level. As we have had to go to leaner and
leaner ores, deeper and farther away, and therefore having to spend more to get it, this has been
offset by technological improvements, from the
mining down to finished products. This is the
record of copper. In the economic sense, it
hasn't become more scarce.

Schultz: I had a different point. I had the story that
came out about the time of the Paley Report,

saying lead could, in fact, be recovered. Lead goes into a product, the product serves its purpose; most of the lead is there, so in some sense it isn't lost but can in fact re-enter again. And zinc, too. Is that economic? I don't know the state of the art here.

Fisher: Again, I am not an expert on this, but there is the lead-zinc anomaly, as geologists call it. Does somebody know more about that? The evidence is that you just can't march off into the country or dig down deeper to find more of this stuff, though not so rich. You seem to reach a discontinuity of some sort on a global scale, and this would be a danger signal. You really might run out of these things in any meaningful sense, and the geologists talk about this. I don't know if this is responding to your question.

Ritchie-Calder: You are talking about reconstitution.

Ehrlich: You can get the lead back from our bodies, because the concentration is building up toward that dangerous level where we all suffer from chronic poisoning. Tetraethyl lead is being spewed out on the landscape by automobiles, and lead pollution from other sources is common.

Fisher: All I know about that is that if there is this discontinuity and limitation of supply, then we must focus attention upon the reclaiming of lead wherever we can, or substituting other materials or redesigning such things as batteries and gutter flashings so as not to require lead. I am sure that as the price pressure increases, the people in the business will work on these things with great concentration and fixity of purpose.

Slobodkin: We seem to be in a position that is much more difficult than I thought when I entered the room. There is much expert opinion and a great deal of actual political power and authority in this room, and the solutions for the problems seem fairly obvious. I think they were obvious to everybody before they came, in a sense. We discover horrendous details here and there that we didn't know about.

The attempts at solving the problems are strange. We will allow natural law or economic law to solve them for us, in a sense, and if natural and economic law will not solve them for us, then there is almost no solution to be had, at least with reference to the metals. I understand other things will happen with reference to fertility, and so forth. With reference to the actual fertility problem, there are programs and we have received documents about them and the story is known.

In Dr. Fisher's talk, and in Sir Solly's comments on it, you saw these two sides of a peculiar problem. I don't know if I can say this as clearly as I would like. I am aiming at a question that I want to ask. That is, Dr. Fisher takes the approach that as problems of this sort have arisen in the past, there have been technological advances that have by and large tended to resolve them, and there is no compelling reason to believe that these technical mechanisms of finding solutions will stop operating in the next ten or twenty years. Is that a fair statement?

Fisher: The presumption is that this will continue. There is too much history of it having happened to abandon it for any short-term period ahead.

Knox: I would like to support that.

Zuckerman: There is no technological limitation at the present moment in this discussion, so far as I can see.

Slobodkin: Then I quoted a statement which I understood as a factual statement from the American Government, which turned out to be quite false, and for very good political reasons. Sir Solly, who says he is in a position to say this is false, can do nothing about it; this makes sense. Then Sir Solly said that there are profound political and organizational problems for doing anything about the disposal problems and planning problems that one knows exist. So on one side we have: natural law has done it and we must assume will do it again. On the other side we have: there are real problems but there are organizational and political reasons why we can't "get there," starting from here.

Schultz: I wonder if I could shift to what I think is a main thrust that we perhaps arrived at here this morning: looking at the real cost of population increase in the short run of two or three decades. Then take what I said and build on to it what

Fisher has called the hard resources, including
water, and it shifts the constraints on the resource side that are required due to population
growth (it seems rather substantially) and this
part of the discussion was not clarified, although
Fisher says that crowding, environmental damage,
and risk are helpful in knowing how to control
population.

Another set of resources produces services
for people, requiring high skills and abilities--
and in relatively short supply. These services
are important in improving the population in terms
of quality. Today this set of resources in the
United States represents about 80 percent of all
inputs.

Slobodkin: Are you referring to skill as a resource?

Schultz: I am talking about human beings, and particularly their skills, as the resource that counts.
We make a mistake, I think, in trying always
to fix costs, which are becoming prohibitively
high, by looking at forthcoming food or their
shortcomings; at the shortages in minerals in
power, and so on. The squeeze comes actually
from the skill it takes to produce the services
you need for a high quality population. I see
no escape. We can't have these high-quality
services that are required for a high-quality population except by the humans producing them.

Knox: What do you have in mind: medical services,
educational services?

Schultz: Yes, and the list is long. It includes environ-
    ment; it includes the disease and health factors
    for they come together again. To take simple
    facts, it is so different in this country (compared
    to India) where we are getting 80 percent of in-
    puts and if we recalculate entrepreneurial effort
    and put it in here, over 80 percent of inputs
    represent human services. The difference really
    between the economies here and in India is
    that here we have high skills that others do not
    have. That is your limiting factor.

Zuckerman: I couldn't agree more, and I would just
    add this rider: it takes longer to get those skills
    and to get them applied than most people suppose.
    I'll give an illustration that applies to your future
    curriculum. When I was Chairman of the British
    Natural Resources Committee (the same time as
    the Paley Commission was sitting), we knew from
    the work of one of our research associations, and
    I am going back to this recycling problem, that
    copper and nickel were wasted in the electroplat-
    ing industry in Birmingham. We also knew that
    the waste and pollution could be stopped by very
    simple technology, and it could be shown to the
    most stupid that it was economic to do so. To
    this day, unnecessary copper and nickel are going
    into the sewers of Birmingham, adding to the cost
    of cleaning the water there—if that waste water
    can be cleaned.

Ehrlich: Should a government in these circumstances
    grab graduate students and put back this support
    of basic research? I am alluding to the fact that

at a time when we have the desperate need for this sort of thing ---

Zuckerman: That is a different point of view. We have just published a report in England which suggests that we ought to redeploy our skilled manpower and not put the emphasis on basic research.

Slobodkin: May I push this further? Someway there has to be a way of breaking out of this bind. It isn't simply a matter of, "It would be nice if there were a way." There must be a way. Does anyone have an idea?

Zuckerman: We are dealing with human beings, political institutions, vested interests, and everything else. When I leave this meeting, I am going to Rome as a follow-up of the TORREY CANYON, in which I became, unfortunately, more deeply involved than I wished. I knew nothing about oil and tankers.

Ritchie-Calder: But you knew about birds.

Zuckerman: A little bit about birds, yes. The details of the TORREY CANYON incident are well known. There has been a great deal of international interest in it. There has been a great deal of concern lest there be another tragedy of the same kind, a tragedy which is only part of the sort of tragedy which was referred to when we were talking about the concentration of agriculture, where suddenly, instead of having hundreds

of thousands of small producers, you have one
or two big ones and vast crop failures.

In spite of the understanding of the dangers
as exemplified by that particular incident, at the
present there is no international agreement about
the control of large tankers. It is conceivable that
agreement may come through the international
organizations that are dealing with the problem
now. There will be resistances, as the companies
concerned do not want to add to their costs.
Dealing with the whole problem of pollution is a
matter of social choice: How much are we prepared to spend to deal with the deleterious consequences of economic progress? Backed by
very favourable economic arguments masses and
masses of oil must be transported; vast container
ships that are going to bring iron ore to the United
Kingdom from Australia, and all the rest of it.
It is extraordinarily difficult to get another lot
of people to argue that these developments entail
social risks and before you engage in these
presumably profitable enterprises, you should
take steps to obviate the risks.

Ritchie-Calder: Tell me, Solly, what would happen
if the TORREY CANYON had a nuclear reactor?

Zuckerman: Probably nothing. I hope no one is
building nuclear reactors of a kind that would
cause the sort of disaster a lot of people think of.
In fact, the safety precautions for reactors for
the operation of the reactors (I am not talking
about the disposal of waste products), were
dealt with from the first moment that these things

were designed. It was recognized that here was
the likelihood of real danger.

Michaelis: What you are saying here in many different
ways is that the material resources, primary
material resources, don't seem to be an impediment to population growth. The associated effects
of using them in the quantity required to sustain
population growth may well become and may already be serious problems. They may not be so
recognized and, indeed, the economic balance
sheet does not often show them because in the
case of the nuclear fission product disposal from
a power station, presently one can comfortably
hide those problems under government costs;
therefore, it looks pretty good. If they had to
pay for all that, it wouldn't look so great, so you
can punch the balance sheet in favor of technical
opportunism. Nuclear power is one and the
supersonic transport, for example, is another.

We pursue certain technical ends because we
are able to, because they are exciting, because
quite often they do not run counter to vested
interests who would cry out if they were pursued.
We'd go ahead recklessly in a sense without real
regard to the economic and social costs, which
are very often hidden or forgotten until someone
has reached the boiling point of anger. You
should teach your curriculum students, I think,
to take a look at the effects I have just described
and to contrast them with the behavior of institutions of which Sir Solly speaks, because the rate
of change in the behavior of institutions is slow.
It takes much longer than R & D, than application

of technology, than the population growth or the
rate of behavior of institutions as they are now
vested.

Slobodkin: Can we go a bit further? What you
   describe is the right way to train citizens. We
   are not talking of specialists in this area. We
   are talking about the citizen who should be aware
   of this. We all have our own specialties; we all
   have our own way of making a buck; and there is
   money in poverty and pollution with all sorts of
   ways of living on these.
        Now, I am asking a slightly different question:
   what if we deliberately tried to turn out people
   aimed at solving this family of problems as
   specialists?

Michaelis: Let me answer quickly. I do not think it
   is a matter of citizens, except in the long run.
   I think it is a matter of educating decision-makers
   at high levels, people who will have the responsibility for the decisions that are being made in
   Western Europe now on oil versus gas versus
   nuclear power, and so on. These are men with
   responsibility, with training. The training they
   have had, if I can paraphrase what I have said,
   perhaps does not fit them exactly to the task at
   hand. The institutions they represent are not
   fully responsive to those tasks. But as to the
   citizenry-at-large, I do not believe you can hope
   to train them in all these intricacies--all of these
   problems with their complexity, except to
   understand that they are complex.

Davis: May I ask a series of short questions? First,
would you agree that to increase the supply of
metals, water, and so forth, for human use as
desired around the world will require a multiple
increase? For instance, to bring people up even
to the present level of the United States throughout the world would take an enormous increase in
the utilization of resources. Will this be easier
or will it be harder if the present rate of growth
of population continues?

Fisher: I suppose one way to look at it is the rate of
increase in production as against consumption.
People are both on the producing and consuming
side. If a lot of them aren't producing but consuming, then it would be more difficult. If it is
the other way around, at least from this way of
looking at it, it would be easier.

Davis: Bearing in mind what Ted Schultz said, which
I think most of us agree with, that the difference
between a developed nation and an underdeveloped
one is primarily the skill of the population applied
to the productive process, and looking at the
realities of the educational process in a country
such as Honduras, which faces a 4. 5 percent
population increase before very long, and multi-
plying out what this would mean in terms of
classrooms, teachers, and so forth, is it not
fantastic to think that Honduras is going to develop
a fine nuclear industry and all the resources it
needs. Just to get going in the task of education
and resource utilization seems extremely difficult
in such a country.

So the simple question seems: Is it easier to apply modern technology for the satisfaction of human needs with or without a rapid population growth? It seems to me the answer is clear. It is easier to apply it without the rapid population growth because that gives you a chance to educate your people and to get going.

If that is true, then the question should not be: Are we going to run out of materials? We are already out of them. The world does not have enough water, enough resources at the present time. It is a question of trying to get somewhere where we are not now, and if it is easier without population growth, we have an argument on the side of resources and food for controlling population. We need to put that question clearly and drive it home as part of the intellectual argument for controlling population.

Fisher: You drew me through several "if" conditions and I was having reservations at each stage.

Davis: I don't think these are too iffy. The first one is not iffy: that to get the world up even to the level of the United States now, much less the level of the United States twenty years from now (if it keeps making what is called technological progress), an enormous effort is going to be required. Personally I don't think it will be accomplished.

Michaelis: Let me make one small amendment, and that is the time scale. It isn't population growth but rate of population growth. Surely the United States would not have achieved its own technological capability had it remained at 5 million people.

Davis: We now have a much more rapid rate of
population growth in underdeveloped countries
than we had in the United States. Furthermore,
the world doesn't have the sort of untapped resources, even with present techniques, that the
United States had in its earlier history.

Schultz: Let me come to Kingsley Davis' side. I
think it is a mistake to assume that every country
has to become large in population and wealth from
our earlier 5 million or 20 million to our present
population in order to have the fruits of knowledge.
They are here but it isn't the small, poor countries that are going to pay the bill for most of
the advances in knowledge in the next ten to twenty
years. What makes it harder is that numbers
are increasing anywhere and everywhere. I think
the answer on his terms (also my terms) is that
the component of skills has to be increased.

If Kingsley presses this, we can arbitrarily
say zero rate of growth or just half a percent in
the next twenty years and then, of course, we
are on different ground, but staying with the
limited proposition as you put it, I think it cuts
very sharply and it strikes me that it is going
to be hard to shape the implications of the proposition. Am I fair to you in the way I put it?

Davis: Oh, yes. You see, I am afraid of this kind of
presentation of what could be a rosy picture if
numerous problems were solved by advanced
technology. It distracts peoples' attention from
the real role of population increase in preventing
the very things that would be necessary to get to
that very high degree of technological adaptation.

Knox: It seems to me all that Professor Schultz and Dr. Fisher have been saying is that there are in the gross sense enough resources--food, water, energy, minerals, air, space—and we don't use them now to the optimal advantage. There are pockets of hunger. There are people who are overcrowded. There are shortages of minerals. We don't do the best we can now, but these gross things are not to be considered as the primary reasons for taking population control measures.

Davis: I didn't say anything about their being primary. I said that the inability to utilize resources because of the effects of rapid population increase is one important reason for limiting that increase.

Knox: It seems that you are saying that there are other reasons why we should be more concerned about population growth than gross resources.

Davis: I am not concerned about resources in the ground, but about the means or capacity to utilize them. Presumably what is relevant is what is being used for human beings. My point is that if you do not have the skills to utilize resources, then it is humanly irrelevant whether the resources are there or not. For a very large percentage of the world, there are not now enough skills to use almost any resource effectively; and acquiring such skills is extraordinarily difficult with present day population growth.

Tax: May I ask a question to which I don't know the answer? We, sitting around this table,

represent a geographic area which is a small
part of the world and small part of the population,
important as we think it is, which is nevertheless
a small minority. We assume we are speaking
for the whole world. We are speaking about the
resources of the whole world, not just about our
own. We are assuming that somehow or other
as these people develop in our terms, we have
got to supply all the answers to the problems.
We are forgetting that there are the intellectual
resources of different major cultures that have
throughout history been more important than ours,
but have temporarily fallen behind because we
have gotten a certain kind of technology. We are
a bunch of "drunken drivers" at the moment and
we are saying: somehow or other we have to
figure out what to do about drunken drivers. It
may very well be that some of the people who
come from different cultural conditions will have
some answers in the course of time. I don't
want to say that you should therefore be optimistic and do nothing, but there ought to be this cor-
rective in the record.

Taylor: Following that, could I suggest that we should
challenge the proposition that we want to raise
the world's standard of living to the United States
present level, or indeed raise the United States
level very much higher. This is a level at which
boys of 12 have $250 cameras which they use to
take pictures of the Empire State Building; where
kitchens have eight pushbutton mixers; where
people have boats and yachts they go on over week-
ends and sit, never taking them out because they
are status symbols.

I am trying to say that we have pushed the
standard of living in the direction of goods and
away from other values such as more leisure, a
greater craft element in work, and so on. The
assumption that we have to put the kind of development we have used in the past, which calls for the
consumption of more materials, simply further
in the direction of supplying more and more goods
seems to be a radically false assumption. Perhaps this brings us to the question of quality of
life and perhaps I am out of turn in raising it
here, but there has been a rather built-in assumption that we are going to go on this kind of track,
and I think many of the countries that Professor
Tax referred to would even now challenge quite
radically this kind of conception of the good life,
life—oriented to goods.

Obviously, when people are starving or are
deprived of medical care, we must correct these
first, but once we have done this, the range of
choices widens.

Ehrlich: There is an interesting phenomenon, which
I find rather horrifying, and maybe Professor
Tax can tell us more about it; that is, whenever
I traveled around the world, I found that other
peoples have a tremendous predilection for wanting to pick up those things that many of us find
undesirable in our own culture. In other words,
I wonder if any change can go fast enough to stop
them from grabbing the parts of culture that they
seem to like without proper appreciation of
their own culture.

Tax:　It appears that way.　They want to take the
　　　things that they want and don't have, but often
　　　they resist taking them when they realize that
　　　these are tied to changes that they do not want.
　　　　　The Neolithic Age was the last time some
　　　fundamental great change in the world happened.
　　　Agriculture started in the Middle East and over
　　　the course of years it spread all over; people
　　　settled down in villages and then built civilizations.
　　　It must have seemed then that the world was be-
　　　coming homogenized, that everybody wanted the
　　　same things; but when the dust settled, so to
　　　speak, East was East and West was West.　Every-
　　　body had taken agriculture and the things that
　　　followed it necessarily, but as to those many criti-
　　　cal things that didn't follow necessarily, they
　　　retained their own individuality and their own
　　　culture.

Ehrlich:　That is the most curious thing I have heard
　　　all day.　You mean a cargo culture is a passing
　　　fad?

Zuckerman:　I often think about that Neolithic Period.
　　　I wish the situation were as simple today as it
　　　was then.　I have asked many people who have
　　　been responsible for major innovations if they
　　　can give me one illustration of an innovation or a
　　　technological development that has been rejected
　　　and refused?　I am waiting for the answer.
　　　　　Another thing that worries me is that while
　　　you might find the same economic pressures
　　　building up in countries, when we talk about "they",
　　　the "they" turn out to be very different among

themselves. In India, you discover such a disparity in social circumstances that it seems to
cover the whole economic spectrum. At a time
when we have half a million people sleeping on
the pavements in Calcutta and people dying of
want, you also have Trombay, which is as good
a technological outfit as you will find anywhere.
If you go to the Bangalore complex of institutions
or to the new electronics industries, you discover
the people who are generating the pressure for
the most advanced goods.

    In the time of the Raj, there may have been
a major disparity in standards of living in India,
with the British military and British civil servants living like kings and princes; but even today you still have much the same thing. The
well-educated people are building their own culture which is very unlike the culture of the social
matrix within which they live. And the same thing
is happening in China, in so far as I can appreciate what is happening in China.

    These are the two countries with the largest
populations, the populations which we believe
pose the greatest potential political trouble through
their growth and development. We were told that
the agrarian revolution in India is already causing
major problems in the Deccan, and that is super-
imposed upon the changes caused by local industrialization. I don't know of any case since the
Industrial Revolution where people have turned
their backs on technological advances because of
their possible deleterious social consequences.

Tax: That is right, but it is the pure technological

thing that they want. For example, every
American Indian that I know of will take an automobile. The automobile is to him, however,
like a horse—it is not the automobile as it is to
us. It is not a status symbol. It is something
that he always has wanted to move from one place
to another, long distances. It is a quite different
instrument, in fact.

Freedman: Isn't it true that when he takes that automobile, he takes everything else with it?

Tax: No, he doesn't. That is the whole point. He
doesn't take everything with it. Of course, he
has a problem. There is a general historical
phenomenon at work. Recall the long period after
the Norman Conquest when it appeared that
England was becoming French, and it wasn't.
The Chinese history is an even more telling case.
The Chinese took what they wanted from abroad
and reinterpreted it, but certainly the borrowing
was much more limited than one would have
supposed when it was all coming.

Japan has always been an exceedingly interesting case. If you go there now, you find that
the technology is like ours, better in many
respects. People want to learn English and doing
things in Western style is a great fad. But everything that happens every minute of the day, no
matter what the technology is, or the clothing
worn, or the language spoken, is Japanese and
not American. Our recent International Congress
there was patterned after those held in the West,
but it was strikingly different from our congresses
and, in many ways, better.

Slobodkin: Is it fair to ask if there is a theory of cultural-loading? If an American Indian is given a
subscription to the New York Times, this is a
culture-loaded thing, unless he uses it only to
start fires. And then down at the other end you
have bicycles or sunglasses, which can be
accepted in a very innocent way. They are sunglasses and you can see somewhat more clearly
and there is no cultural-loading at all.

Tax: The American Indians love tape recorders and
they use them much more than we do. As soon
as you are there, they want to get some Indian
songs or something recorded. The tapes are
passed around but not for recreation, as they
see it. There are many items like this.

Slobodkin: Dr. Davis, I am curious, does there exist
any theory which would tell you anything about
cultural loading? The only possible relevance
the answer to such a question might have is that
we are talking about how to move organizations
and institutions in ways that no one has ever
moved them. This may relate somehow to that.

Tax: Cultural loading? Define that "loading" again.

Slobodkin: Objects move from culture to culture,
assuming we can define culture and assuming we
know what "to move" means, and so on. Certain objects carry with them a set of values of
the culture from which they came. Others
carry almost none and you say that cultures have
a way of sort of snipping off a certain amount of
this load.

Tax: If they don't want it.

Slobodkin: What I am curious about is whether different objects intrinsically carry different
amounts of cultural load, and whether there exists
any theory which would tell you which objects
they are. In a sense what we are talking about
with technology is how do you move a new technology into an existing culture. It is as if it
came from the moon; it was invented by someone
and it is coming from some place. It is going to
have an impact.
        Now these other objects, like automobiles or
tape recorders or guns require some sort of response. It is conceivable that whatever theoretical
argument anthropologists develop about these objects
would give us some insight as to how we respond or
ought to respond to other kinds of innovations.

Fremont-Smith: Would food and baby care be two examples of cultural loading that are not easily lost ? I
would say food is an example of it, because food habits
are caught by the child at the mother's knee more-or-
less in the home and these, therefore, are much more
deeply imbedded. I think there is some evidence that
this is true, but I give this as an example.

Tax: There was a good study on American Indians
who are an exceedingly good case because they
have been here for a long time, consisting of
many little groups, each with its own culture.
They were here before we were, and the interesting thing is that they simply won't accept our
culture. They are conscious of its existence and

have rejected it.   That is why they are still left.
Those who wanted to accept our culture did.
They moved out and into our society and culture.
The Indians that we recognize and talk about are
those who have remained, and they grow in
numbers.

Ehrlich: But they took the automobile and the things
that all the resources are tied up in.

Tax: They took the horse once, also.   They won't
take cattle, usually, because that has a tie-in
sale.   It says you have to start doing chores and
make hay while the sun shines.   They won't take
chickens; the things they don't want, they reject.

But let me try to get at this question of food
or child-rearing.   Edward Bruner made a study
of all of the Indians in a North Dakota Indian
Reservation that were white-oriented (middle-
class oriented, if we can use that term) and he
found that in every single case, whatever the
particular case accidental or otherwise, one of
his parents, natural or foster, was white.   His
consequent white orientation wasn't genetic, of
course, but the result of early childhood experience.   Trace back a white-oriented Indian
and you find a white person in his infancy.

Similarly, psychologists at the State University of Iowa made studies of a small group of the
only Indians in Iowa to compare Indian children
with Iowa middle-class children.   They were
astounded that in the Indian children there was
no hostility at all.   They didn't hate their siblings
or their parents.   The tests that were made

marked off Indians from their neighbors un-
mistakably.

In the same way, a geographer looked at out
aerial photograph and saw at once the boundaries
of the Indian settlement, since Indian land use is
so different from that of other Iowans. These
Indians have been surrounded by Iowans for 125
years. They bought their 3300 acres of land and
they stick to it without cows or chickens or
potatoes or pigs or all the rest of these things
that you are supposed to have if you are in the
middle of Iowa. They suffer less now that trans-
portation is easier and they can go and get jobs
in towns nearby.

The automobile gives the Indians a wider
hunting territory, such as they once had; they
maintain themselves as Indians in this manner
and they accept what they can accept from us that
they want, that doesn't violate their conception
of what they have to do to be good Indians.

Segal: I want to come back to the exchange between Davis and Fisher, which I thought brought
us to the key issue with respect to the earlier
presentations. That is the question of where we
really stand on the significance, the importance,
the emphasis that must be placed on the resource
issue in the question of population policy?

I thought that Dr. Davis had put Joe against
the wall in making it quite clear that the conclusion is inescapable that, given the difficulties of
raising the rest of the world to their expectation
at least, if not to American standards, a great
demand will be made on the existing resources in

the categories that you have indicated. I think
you agreed to that.

I think you also agreed to his principle that
it would be easier—and I emphasize that, because I am going to turn to you in a moment,
Dr. Davis—if this were attempted under conditions of a lower population-growth rate.

Fisher: I am inclined to think that is right, but I am
not sure. It might be easier to raise the material
level of living in less-developed countries, or for
them to do it, if the population didn't increase so
fast, but I am not certain that natural resources
are linked to that. The social stresses, organization problems, and problems of discipline are
much more involved.

Ritchie-Calder: But if these countries are going to
develop their resources, they are going to be
developed themselves, and they cannot develop
themselves if, in fact, the education is spread so
thinly that it cannot be effective.

Fisher: Then the point of attack is on education or
training or management or extension, or something.

Segal: You are saying we cannot make the critical
argument that we have come to the point of
needing to make a decision as to the optimum
number of people, considering the need to bring
them up to this level that they expect, because
of the resource limitation?

Fisher: Keep in mind what I have said all along: I
     see nothing in the sheer resources side of the
     picture to prevent a growing population from
     making use of the base of its resources to im-
     prove itself. But, it won't happen unless we
     keep up full steam under science, technology,
     management, planning, economic advancement,
     and organization. I believe we have the capacity
     to improve our policies, institutions, organiza-
     tions, and management; this is the path we should
     be following.

Schultz: I would like to restate this, because I think
     this ought to be clear. The abundance that is
     possible with a modern economy, looking at the
     poor world, is not limited in the foreseeable
     future of two or three decades, by land and other
     natural resources. In fact the limiting factor is
     acquiring the quality in the human being, the
     agent, and here any increase in population is
     really a constraint that is serious.

Shelesnyak: You are saying that the critical factor
     is the quality of the human resources and if the
     quality must be improved, it is easier to im-
     prove a small amount than an ever-expanding
     amount?

Schultz: You start from zero to 1 percent, 2 percent,
     and it gets harder, harder, harder.

Harkavy: Let's take a break. Neil Chamberlain
     wanted to make a point, and then we'll get to
     Kingsley Davis' cities.

Chamberlain: When Ted was emphasizing the importance of human resources, it still leaves other
   aspects that lead to other conclusions.

   I was thinking of the earlier exchange between
   Professor Slobodkin and Sir Solly, in which Professor Slobodkin posed the question: Why can't
   we use the experts we have to achieve certain
   kinds of solutions that are obviously necessary?
   But, it is not simply the availability of trained
   people in other countries that we would have to
   look to for solutions; it is how well those people
   could be used.

   Having looked at it in that sense, you raise
   questions with respect to the institutions that prevent the use of people, and then one can say: If,
   in fact, institutions can be changed appropriately,
   why is it essential that the nationals of these
   countries have the trained skills? We have an
   international market in skills, so that if there are
   certain types of skills that are in short supply in
   India or Pakistan or other regions that are in the
   process of development, providing there are institutional accommodations, it may be possible for
   them to use people from the U.K., the U.S., or
   USSR or elsewhere in some of these bottleneck
   areas.

   Obviously, changing institutions may be the
   most difficult part of the problem, and yet if the
   human skills are scarce, perhaps this is the front
   where we might move or explore. Here one can
   think of the rise of the international business firms,
   that has been getting a lot of attention in recent
   years, quite appropriately. These are beginning
   to make organizational skills available on a

worldwide basis. I think we are beginning to see ways that host countries can accommodate these visitors from abroad without giving away their national sovereignty. The host countries might require that the foreign participation be a minority participation or a joint venture arrangement but still make it attractive for the foreign expert.

So, I am not sure that it is limitation of home talent, as it were, that is the critical matter in developing these resources. We can mobilize human resources on a worldwide basis, but then again we must come back to the problems that are generated by the tremendous growth in population.

So, when we talk about human resources, I don't think we have to rely necessarily on home-grown talent to unlock these natural resources.

Ritchie-Calder: I feel I ought to be involved here. I spend most of my time encouraging the sharing of knowledge and skills, and I would point out that you can, in fact, introduce the skills and you can introduce them in large numbers, but if you don't have the population with you, you are not making any headway. If you are doing it <u>for</u> them, you are not doing anything. It is not just neocolonialism, using the glib term, or anything like that. If you are doing it <u>for</u> them, you are not doing it <u>with</u> them. But that doesn't discourage the thing that we want, which is the dissemination and intro- duction of new knowledge and new skills. But if you are introducing that knowledge and skill at levels where they are not yet qualified to operate, you are, in many cases, doing a great disservice. Therefore, we are making them dependent. I am not talking about neocolonialism.

Chamberlain: I am not trying to minimize the difficulties of doing this; I am not even trying to suggest
it is a good thing, necessarily, but I would really
think that, on balance, it probably is. I am
simply saying that this is one way in which the
problem of scarce human resources might be
overcome.

   With respect to the dependency kind of
situation, I think even this is being tackled in some
degree by Mexico, which requires that facilities
in certain industries be turned over to local
management within some period of time.

Ritchie-Calder: The whole experience of the UN
development with technical assistance, and the
story of American aid, is that you can introduce
the inspirational factors (and better still if you
introduce the resources behind the inspirational
factors), but there comes the point where you are
entirely dependent on your counterpart. You cannot
do the job properly unless you are training your
counterpart at the same time.

Schultz: There is a distinction here. I don't want
to minimize at all the contribution that might be
made by skilled people, which can be very large
nor the body of knowledge that can move through
the corporations. But this is not enough, even
though we think that in agriculture this is more
nearly so than in other fields. India today is
reaching for new crop-varieties and rather
limited use of fertilizers; it has skills in its
population to move this far and maybe it is moving fairly rapidly; but if India wants to continue

to modernize and also to handle the whole pesticide complex and then fertilizer in a much more
selective sense, and then to move further in
modernization in terms of the use of tractor
power, and go on from there, then at present
Indians simply do not have the skill for doing all of
this.

The point is, you have to have mass additions
to the quality and in this case I am not reaching
for secondary schooling. I am reaching for five
years, six years of schooling to get into the
second stage of modernization, which they are
getting close to now but they don't yet have the
skills in the rural populations.

Chamberlain: I don't want to take additional time to
push this point, but I do have a feeling that sometimes we impose our standards on them. I am
thinking of a situation that I encountered in
Pakistan. There is a small clinic, staffed wholly
by Western experts with a few Western-trained
Pakistani. The leprosy problem is a significant
one in Pakistan, especially in the small villages.
It is impossible to service it from this small
clinic in Karachi, and they were then taking young
men from the villages (not educated but bright),
teaching them ways of identifying the leprous
individual. These would establish relationship
with a hospital close by and with the leper so he
could get in touch with the resident doctor in this
area. These people would then serve as follow-up
agents. This was not a case where they had
secondary school education at all; they were
trained in doing specific things to a particular
kind of operation.

Probably there are various kinds of technological advances that can perhaps be broken down into small bits of that sort and pushed ahead if there is some kind of a coordinating agent, a supervising institution, or something of that kind.

I am trying to say that I think we would be making a mistake if we thought that skilled individuals with secondary school education or advanced degrees are essential for the whole job of unlocking these resources. I think by mobilizing skilled talent from around the world, supplementing that with locally trained individuals, you could go a long way toward making these resources available and facilitating this expansion and growth which Kingsley Davis is so much afraid of.

In the process, I think you are going to raise questions about institutional arrangements, ownership rights, and a variety of other issues, but purely in terms of the technical skill barrier. I am not sure that is really quite as much a barrier as your earlier comment would suggest.

Harkavy: Mr. Michaelis, and then Professor Tax, and then Kingsley Davis. We are talking about the general theory of technical assistance, where we should not dwell too long in this conference. It has been the subject of much study.

Michaelis: I have been speaking about institutional obstacles to innovation, but institutions are by no means inanimate. These are people-problems when you get down to it. As a technologist, I might think that institutions other than the

technical ones—by this, I mean finance, business,
government, and so on—are less innovative than
my own, but I wonder. They may well be. I
don't know. I am not trying to say they are less
qualified.

I am discerning, however, a certain dis-
crepancy between the degree of questioning, the
degree of speculation that goes on in such institutions as contrasted with the technical, scientific
ones which are well represented here. One sees
less of it, one hears less of it, and I think it is
those questionings that I would like to see much
more of because it is those institutions and those
people who will have to undergo considerable
change if they are going to use all the skills that
are available in the world, if they will permit
these skills to be used. Is it neocolonialism that
prevents us from sending people to operate a
nuclear power station in another country? It may
well be but this, too, is an institutional problem
that has arisen out of the past, a political science
problem. Whether or not it is a shortage of international financial assistance that prevents us
from using commodities in an appropriate manner,
I don't know. It may be, in part, but it is hard
to affect these institutions in their thinking, and
I believe that is a real problem. An institution is
not a disembodied object; it is made up of individuals who have different views.

Tax: I just wanted to caution that we might be losing
a great deal if we don't remember that we are
defining the knowledge needed to change institutions to bring in new things. As long as it is our

definition of what is required, then it will be our
definition of what training is required; we may
find that we are not taking advantage of the natural
skills that come out of a nation's own cultures.
In the U. S. we are suddenly discovering all of
the latent skills that were hidden.
of colonialism, so to speak, with our black
population; we are suddenly discovering that there
is a lot there that was hidden beneath the surface.

Think of how much must be hidden throughout
Asia and the other countries as soon as we free
it from our own particular definition of what is
necessary. This is not to say that technical
knowledge isn't tied to the techniques, but it is
to say that when we are talking about institutions,
and in some degree about technology as well, the
native resources are much greater than they
would appear to be to us who are looking at them
as stupid, illiterate people with different ways
of thought.

Harkavy: We now turn to the question: What are the
major consequences of current and expected
population growth for the cities? Dr. Davis!

Davis: I shall try to be brief and relevant as I
can. In a meeting of this sort, we should state
the problem first. I think we have been trying to
do that, but we have not done it very directly
because we assumed that we were starting off
merely by stating facts. I shall state a few facts
about cities, keeping in mind questions that are
relevant to population policy.

For some years in our office we have been

accumulating data on urbanization and cities throughout the world. We are analyzing the data at the present time, and I am giving you some of the preliminary results of the analysis as far it has developed.

It appears that about 38 percent of the world's population today is living in what are defined as urban places. This figure is an up-to-date estimate: it relates to this year.

Knox: Are these standard metropolitan areas?

Davis: No, these are just urban. The data are of two sorts. We generally took whatever the country defined as urban, because the definition must change according to conditions. A town of 5,000 in India may be quite rural (it may be a rural village), but it is not likely to be rural in the United States; so you must pay attention to the definitions of the country. We altered a country's definition only when we felt that it was completely out of line, introducing elements of genuine noncomparability. In order to have another index of urbanization, we included data on the number of cities of 100,000 and over and the proportion of the nation's population living in them. There is 22.5 percent of the earth's inhabitants in cities of 100,000 or more.

It is clear, then, that the world is still predominantly a rural world, mainly agricultural. At the same time, however, it must be realized that even the 38 percent urban, or the 22.5 percent figure in cities, is very recent. The figure for the world today stands approximately

where the United States stood in 1900.   Actually,
of course, the rate of change is quite great.   In
recent years the world's population has been
growing about 1.9 percent annually but the rate
for the urban population has been 3.7 percent.
The city population in places of 1,000,000 or more
has been growing at a rate of 4.1 percent.

If you consider the process from the point of
view of growth and what is going to happen, 10 percent of the earth's people already live in cities of
a million or more. (When we talk about cities, we
are using the urbanized area whenever the data are
available. In nearly half of all of our cities (there
were 941 in 1950 and 1,309 in 1960) nearly half
were defined as the urbanized area rather than the
political city or the city proper.)

The number of people in the million-plus cities
is practically identical with the number who in 1950
were living in places of 100,000 or more. In other
words, the bottom size of the class that embraces
10 percent of the earth's population is now ten
times larger than it was in 1950. That is another
way of saying that the million-plus class is growing more rapidly than the other class.

Bernstein: How many million-plus cities were there
    in 1950? How many get pushed into that 100,000-
    or-over category?

Davis: In 1968, the estimate is that we have 375
    million people in the million-plus cities. The
    number of cities in this class is approximately
    200.

Stein: You don't have 1950 figures to show where the
          shift was?

Davis: Yes, 161 million people in cities of a million-
          plus in 1950, and 69 such cities. We estimate
          375 in 1968. I have projected them up to '68 just
          for purposes of showing where we are.
              Let's assume that if the urban-growth rate
          were to continue as it has done since 1950, the
          time required for the human race to become
          predominantly urban would be short. It would
          take only sixteen years from today for the pro-
          portion of urban to reach 50 percent of the world
          as a whole, and only fifty-five years for it to
          reach 100 percent.
              When we turn to the percent in cities of
          100,000-or-more, we find that if its rate of
          change were to continue, the proportion would
          reach 50 percent in thirty-seven years and 100
          percent in sixty-eight years. Even more thought-
          provoking is the calculation that in fifty-two years
          we will have half of the population living in cities
          of a million-plus. If these trends since '50
          continue, then all of the human species would be
          living in such places within seventy-six years.
              I am trying to illustrate the implications of
          the present trend. To me, it shows the impossi-
          bility of the continuance of the trends we have at
          the present time. The trend is what you see.
          The whole species would be in cities of a million-
          plus before another century. At that time, the
          population of the world would be about 15 billion,
          assuming a continuation of the present trend.
          You might ask what would be the largest city in

size under those circumstances. It would be a little hard to estimate but if it were Willkie's One World, with one economy, presumably the system of cities would conform to the rank size rule and the biggest city would be around 1.3 billion.

You must pay attention to what is happening to the rural population, too. It is a very interesting phenomenon. The rural population would drop between 1985 and the year 2000, not only as a proportion of the world's population but in absolute numbers as well. It would fall from 2.34 to 2.13 billion in fifteen years. At the other end of the scale, of course, the biggest gainer would be the classes of the biggest cities.

You might ask how serious are these projections. These are just statements taking the present trend on into the future. Since the rate of urbanization (that is, the change in the proportion urban) conforms to a logistic type curve, a point is reached when the rate begins to decline. So you would expect that the world as a whole, as it becomes more highly urbanized and hence more developed, would slow down in the process somewhat. Therefore, to be more realistic, one can take a developed country as a model in terms of which the world trend can be projected.

I have already said that in about 1900 the United States showed about the same situation that the world as a whole shows now. In 1898, the United States had the same proportion of urban, 38 percent, that the world as a whole has today. In 1912 it had the same percentage in

cities of 100,000-or-over. It appears, then, that
the world as a whole is 60 to 70 years behind the
United States in the process of urbanization.
Since countries industrializing later than we did
went through the process faster, the United States
offers a conservative model.

You might ask whether some other things are
similar as between the United States of America
around 1900 and the world today. I discovered an
amazing similarity between the present world
situation and that of the United States around the
turn of the century with respect to urbanization.
Not only was the proportion of urban to rural
virtually the same, but the growth in these pro-
portions per year was almost identical.

When the United States is used as a model
for the future growth of world urbanization, it
gives, over the short run, virtually the same
results as simply extrapolating recent world
trends. If one is talking about the next twenty
years, for example, the U.S. model will bring
one to just about the same results as an extrapolation of the present world trends. By way
of illustration, the proportion of the world's
population living in urban places will be over 60
percent by the end of this century.

In absolute numbers, the projections based
on the American model, even though it is a slow
model, are striking. For instance, the number
of people living in cities of 100,000-or-more at
the end of the century may exceed the total population that the world had in 1950. The population
living in million-plus cities may exceed the
entire urban population of today.

The fundamental difference between an extrapolation of recent world trends and a projection on the basis of the United States model lies in the total population growth. It has to be remembered that the United States manifested a declining rate of population growth after 1900. Recent world trends lead to no such projected decline. Low modern mortality is extending much more rapidly to the world as a whole than came about in the United States. The difference in population growth accounts for a good deal of the difference in the estimates of future urban populations, especially over a long period. The difference in projected urban population is more than a billion people by the two models, mainly as a result of the difference in overall rate of population growth assumed.

In other words, the United States changed not only its process of urbanization but also its rate of population growth. By doing so, it was able to reduce its rural population and thus help in the modernization of agriculture without forcing an astronomically large population into the cities. If the world as a whole tries to maintain its recent trends, including rapid overall population growth, it will experience a fantastic increase in the population of cities. In fact, in the next thirty-two years we may see five times as many people living in million-plus cities as live there now.

Tax: Now we know what the optimum pattern is.

Davis: I don't want to take too much time with this

factual account, but with reference to the sources
of growth of city populations, people still think of
the growth of cities as being primarily a function
of rural-urban migration. They are thinking in
terms of the past development of the now-
developed countries. That was the way it was,
but the truth of the matter is—and we have examined this in country after country in the underdeveloped world—it is not the way it is now. The
overwhelming contribution to the present growth
of the urban population in the underdeveloped
areas is by natural increase in the cities—the
excess of births over deaths.

Segal: Has that been true in the '50s to '60s proposition that you have been making?

Davis: We do not know the contribution of rural-urban
migration for the world as a whole because we
cannot get the data, but we can make good estimates for a number of individual countries in the
'50s and '60s.

Schultz: You are making an important point. You
are saying that our own history and our own thinking are conditioned by observing the growth of
many cities, so largely due to the exodus from
the country to the city. When you look at the
world, you would not expect this. You would
expect a large part of the city's increase to come
from sheer increase in numbers. Is that what
you are saying?

Davis: Yes.

Ross: Or the developing nations, really?

Schultz: Yes, the world.

Davis: You see, in the highly developed ones, we have reached the point where there are no longer any farmers to come to the city. In terms of the farm population, there are big out-migrations still. In terms of the cities, there is not much because the cities outweigh the farm population.

Schultz: To support you, there is the study by Ed Denison on rates of growth in the European complex, and to the American economist's surprise, a very large fraction, a large part of the increase of the labor force in the non-agricultural part of Europe still came from the country since World War II, notably in Italy and France.

Davis: At the present time there is a very high rate of natural increase in the cities of the underdeveloped countries. One reason for this is that these cities have very low death rates. It used to be, for instance, early nineteenth-century Britain, Sweden and France, that the cities were death traps. People came there in abundance, and, if they were lucky, they survived. Although they came often at the best age for survival, young adulthood, the death rates were very high.

Urban fertility, compared to the rural, was much lower, so that many cities in the early development of present industrialized countries were not replacing themselves. They were depending entirely on rural urban migration for growth, growing rapidly with the hordes of people from the country. Thus they created a demand for agricultural products. This made it relatively easy to modernize agriculture, because excess manpower was being drawn off the farms.

Under present circumstances, it is much harder to make the case that even with rapid urban growth, the countryside is encouraged demographically to modernize rapidly. It looks as if, even though hundreds of thousands (or even millions) leave the rural areas, no great dent will be made in the high natural increase in those areas. The trouble is that the cities are providing their own new labor in an extreme degree. They are growing rapidly, but the source of that growth is different from what it was historically.

Or, to put it another way, rural to urban migrants, coming to the city in India, are competing with newborn people or the youth already in the city, for whatever jobs the city can provide. The problem is overall rapid population growth. The whole population is divided into rural and urban; if it grows rapidly, the increase must manifest itself in one or the other sector, or both. As a matter of fact, the rapid increase of population is showing itself in both sectors in the underdeveloped countries. The rural population is growing more rapidly than it normally would at this stage of development, historically speaking, and the city population is growing rapidly too.

In my opinion, it is a fundamentally new

situation. The present city growth is another
complicating factor, making it extremely difficult to get the kind of institutional structure (a
rather rarefied type) necessary for real technological advance. The problem is perhaps more
acute in the countryside than it is the city because agricultural people are not getting the
opportunity that they need. Since the underdeveloped countries are still predominantly
agrarian, the situation of a double population—
in the city and in the country—is economically
and politically hazardous.

Soon I hope we will have more information
on what is happening demographically in the rural
areas in relation to the land supply, but it does
not appear, on the basis of present information,
to be good. The cities in particular are
politically unstable.

Zuckerman: Why?

Davis: People can starve to death or suffer various
kinds of inadequacies in the country without
getting together to mount a political protest.
With rapid population growth and not much
economic opportunity, it is easy for the city
people to band together and resort to whatever
is necessary for extracting concessions from the
powers that be. The concessions are not necessarily economically productive.

It will be very difficult to solve these urban
problems. Even though the developed countries
are more urbanized than the underdeveloped
ones—about three to four times as urbanized—

there are so many more people in underdeveloped countries that about half of the
urban population in 1960 (48 percent) was in
underdeveloped countries; also nearly half of the
city population and nearly half of the cities themselves (46 percent of all the cities of 100,000-or-
over) were in underdeveloped countries. So there
are urban problems on a massive scale in the
underdeveloped countries, just as there are urban
problems on a massive scale in the highly developed
ones.

Most urban problems, or problems in the
city, are traceable to the rapid growth of cities.
Recently a group of American city planners returned from Europe and, as Americans nearly
always do when they return from a foreign area,
reported that city planning abroad is much better
than in the United States. The difference, however, is not due simply to European superiority.
If one wants a pleasant city, easy to plan and easy
to live in, one should go to one that is not growing.
It should not be San Francisco or Los Angeles.
These cities have real problems because changes
occur overnight.

The authorities are constantly trying to solve
a problem that they created by solving another
problem. Under such circumstances, it certainly
is hard to plan. What would you plan for? Would
you plan for the population of 1980? Or would
you go ahead and plan for 1995, when the
population will be doubled. The plans for 1980
would certainly be unsuitable for 1995. Where
would you stop? The continued population growth
creates insoluble dilemmas for city planners.

For example, the problems created by suburbani-
zation and the decay of central city are created in
large part by rapid growth. Why would people
leave the central city if this were not the ever-
more-conjested hub of an ever-larger-human
agglomeration?

Knox: Would you say New York has been growing
      rapidly lately?

Davis: The New York metropolitan area grows just
      about as fast as the population of the United States.
      Over many decades it has remained about 8 per-
      cent of the total population of the United States.

Knox: And what do you call an urban area?

Davis: An urban complex, the actual area of urban settle-
      ment. It expands in area as well as in population.

Zuckerman: When you ask rhetorically if you plan for
      1980 or 1995, are you asking us to suggest an
      answer or are you going to provide it?

Davis: My point is that you can't provide for the
      future with the rate of population growth.

Zuckerman: I don't know which countries were visited
      by your city planners but we have in the United
      Kingdom with a population of about 53 million,
      major governmental projects for regional develop-
      ment. From the postwar development of towns,
      lessons have been learned and I believe I am right
      in saying the official view now is that you ought

to plan for the biggest city, and that you ought to take a complex of several small ones within a related area and build them up into what might be called here a mini-megalopolis. Can you indicate from your studies which is the right course—big or small cities? Planning has to take place.

Davis: It seems to me that any arbitrary limit on town size is going to result in a multiplication of towns. If there is no more distance than there is between some places just outside the London metropolitan area now, it is practically one complex anyway. My point is that I see no solution to urban problems with the continued population growth. Any plan is going to become inappropriate eventually, and thus be a problem itself rather than a solution. In short, you cannot plan cities without planning population.

Schultz: Kingsley, may I turn this around for just a moment? About seven or eight years ago I drew lines of a map of the United States, starting roughly with the 100 Meridian, coming down to the Dakotas, and so on, going west until you hit the Cascades and Sierra Nevadas. Leaving out Southwest Texas, you have about half the area of the United States. The population in this area has been declining relative to the rest of the country; it was then about 7 percent of the population. I have always been puzzled why the drift has been to the two coasts, if you please, leaving empty this extraordinarily large part.

I go back to Joe Fisher and the preference we

are supposed to have for wilderness to get out
of the urban complex and crowding.   Let me
jump to the problem the Canadians are facing in
part of their middle north and our Alaska.   More
people come back than go north.   There is a
30-40 percent income differential in favor of
holding even those who are there.   The Alaskan
population would take a real dip if you pulled out
the Armed Forces that are stationed there.   The
population is only a handful.

Now I return to the United States where
people don't stay in half of the country, piling up
in what you call ultimate metropolitan areas.
Does this really say that we don't value space,
that we don't value wilderness, that we don't
really want it even if we can earn 30-40 percent
more in a beautiful part of Alaska, parts of
Canada, and that large half of the United States?

Ehrlich: I think you are absolutely right.   One of the
things that I learned from becoming a propagandist was: I started out with the impression that
people want to save Yosemite Valley; that people
jammed into Los Angeles were unhappy about
living in the little ticky-tacky houses in the smog.
I quickly learned that was wrong.   They had never
"had it so good" as sitting in front of their TV
sets in their little ticky-tacky houses.   This is
a very real problem.

Davis: But that is not the question we are considering.

Schultz: I know, but I think there is something about
preferences.   We talk about preferences as if

people really want to live and have space and want
wilderness. Do they really?

Davis: They want both.

Schultz: Do they want space?

Davis: One of the fastest expanding types of vehicular
commodity today is the trailer or the cabin
cruiser. It enables people to travel and to have
the convenience of home while they are travelling.
A very lively aspect of real estate today is the
selling of parcels of rural land to urbanites who
want to get out and play.

Schultz: That is up in Michigan, but when you get
into northern Canada, up to the area I was talking about, nobody is there. In the Black Hills,
you can buy yourself 40-50 acres "for a song."
Go to Alaska and they will pay you to stay there.
There is something strange about our preferences
for this crowding.

Ehrlich: They don't want to stay there permanently.
I have been going to the western slope of Colorado
for many summers. It was empty eight or nine
years ago in the summer, but now the house
trailers have moved in, and they all park at the
same campground. They have moved themselves
out of Los Angeles, next to a trout stream, but
with exactly the same spatial distance to the
next trailer.

Davis: It is utterly ironic. The place that has nobody

in it is "unspoiled" as yet. Being "unspoiled"
means that few people are there. Later, they
tell you, "Well, I don't go there any more because,
you know, it has been spoiled," which means
there are a lot of people there who, of course,
came because it was "unspoiled." Although
people may come to cities for certain purposes,
they like to get away from them, too. They like
to get away from the crowding.

Taylor: We are talking about the United States as if
        if were typical of all such situations. The United
        States still has a lot of space.

Schultz: But we don't use it. We don't seem to want
        it.

Taylor: This doesn't tell you very much about the
        Peking area.

Davis: One answer is the cities themselves. In
        industrial countries they have been deconcen-
        trating for decades; people are moving out to the
        suburbs to get away from high-density city living.
        It has been a continuous process, and again it is
        one that, with continued growth, becomes more
        difficult. You move out to the countryside, and
        pretty soon the erstwhile countryside is crowded
        with others who have done the same. Then you
        move out a little farther to the next suburb. In
        the process, the engineers are paid to build a big
        freeway so that you can still, even though you
        are that far out, drive back to the city. The
        activity of building and servicing the highways

and of commuting bumper-to-bumper on them all
counts as part of our allegedly high level of living.

Bernstein: People don't go much past the sewer lines,
you will often find, and such facilities take quite
a concentration of people. Dwellers don't settle
in when it is really wilderness and farm. They
settle in when it can be crowded.

Zuckerman: I wonder whether some of the paradoxes
you have been enunciating could be pulled together so that one could see where we are going.
First of all, I understand from you that there is
a trend toward growth of cities as population
increases, and that process is accelerating very,
very fast. If it continues we will have a situation
in which 100 percent of the world population will
be in cities or urban areas. You say this as
though this were something of which you disap-
proved.

Davis: Oh, I don't care. I won't be around, anyway,
at that time.

Zuckerman: The implication of your remarks is that
this is something which should be averted if at
all possible. But you say next that people want to
be urbanized. At the same time, they want to go
someplace else, and then you imply that there
is no planning of cities, and no planning possible.
Is that really the case? Can anybody who wants to
extend the area of urbanization on the eastern
seaboard where we are meeting? Can he fill in
the gaps?

Davis: Not if there is an effective effort to maintain
agricultural activity in the region. That is why
many planners express a preference for multi-
family housing.

Schultz: You mean legally; can't you go where you
please?

Zuckerman: In England you cannot, but yet mistakes
are made and we have learned from the mistakes.
Let me give an illustration, some of it my own
opinion. One of the biggest exercises in urban
renewal was Birmingham, which is a city, if you
take in contiguous populations, of let us say
nearly 5 million now. It extends all the way to
Coventry to the east and north to Wolverhampton.
There was a major program of renewal of the
center, the bulk of which has been completed,
but if you go there you will find that much of the
center is unoccupied. The shops aren't full and
the restaurants are unoccupied. Some now argue
that a mistake was made. The mistake wasn't
in spending the millions that went to the renewal
of the center. The mistake was in permitting
people to spread outside the limits of what was
the public investment in renewal.

Schultz: Why was that a mistake?

Zuckerman: Because now you have got patchy development outside and an unoccupied or partially unoccupied center. Whereas the center, which is
well designed, would have accommodated a great
many more. It was a mistake from the point of
view of the resources used.

Schultz: We have a lot of literature which says that
    the British planning that you are describing has
    made mistakes and looks just as bad in terms of
    what it has cost society as the helter-skelter
    process that prevailed before. The Russians
    are having this experience. They have tried to
    ration the big cities and here, again, the same
    thing is emerging.

Zuckerman: I am going to be the last to deny the
    mistakes. I gave you earlier an illustration—at-
    tempting to limit the size of a town to 100,000
    and having unduly costly overheads. I have
    pointed to another mistake, where it was within
    the power of the people who were putting up the
    money to prevent what was a poor return on
    capital, at the same time as they used up land
    unnecessarily and spoiled certain open spaces.
        The new lesson, as I understand it, is to try
    to combine a number of adjacent small towns
    covering an area, let us say, of 20 square miles,
    and deliberately turn these into the focal points
    of a major city; to try to attract industry in such
    a way that you build a city around the several
    focal points so that it becomes one vast complex.
    At the present we are in danger for lack of
    planning. Southeast London is attracting popula-
    tion against the wishes of the central government.

Davis: Why?

Zuckerman: It could be very costly. We are going
    to have a channel tunnel which is going to open
    south of London. The channel tunnel might mean

a redesign of the transport system, and by transport system I mean much more than roads.   But
that isn't taking place yet.   The channel tunnel
is a real project.   Let's say it will be finished by
1980, by which time the natural rate of growth
for France, England, Germany, and all the others
who will be 'tunneling' to and fro, will be well
above the planning figures of yesterday.
        We all seem to see the difficulties of plan-
ners, but what I got out of Kingsley Davis' remarks is that we oughtn't to plan because it isn't
worthwhile.

Davis: I want to ask you a question.   Why are the
    people moving to the southeastern section of the
    London metropolitan area?

Zuckerman: I don't know.   The reason, I suppose, is
    that southern London is quite close to the coast.
    It always had a big population.   It is easier to
    establish small industry there.

Ritchie-Calder: One of the things that always im-
    presses me in these discussions is that we al-
    ways talk about trends and start to plan for them
    instead of saying, "This is not a prediction;
    this is a prognosis."   It would be much wiser if
    we started planning away from it.   It so happened
    that we did a survey of southeast England and
    started to plan for the development of southeast
    England when in point of fact any wise social
    decision would have been to plan away from
    southeast England.   The reason why you had the
    enormous development is, first of all, we have

not only our banking center, our port of London,
but we have our government. Half of London is
concerned with looking after civil servants.

But the result is that the first development of
London was along the great West Road, the public
utility road, and it was much cheaper to pay high
rates, high costs on that road in order to get
short hauls into London. You see, this brings
up the whole question of the development of your
transport system. Why not subsidize people to
transport goods so that it is just as cheap to bring
it to London from the north of Scotland.

The "social cost" of London has been fantastic.
The government did step in and say no more building in the center of London. But, already, everything had congregated inside. All of the services
had to follow. The transport system is cracking
because 10, 000 people are pouring out of one
building—it is the story of Manhattan all over
again—but it was lack of foresight, in my opinion,
to accept a trend, which had no great option in it,
because light industry was aggregating around it.

Davis: If you have such intense problems in England
with a relatively small growth of cities, just think
what the underdeveloped world is having, or will
have, with its extremely rapid urban population
growth.

Zuckerman: But you haven't answered my question.
Are we because of this natural growth of cities
to which you have referred not to do what
Ritchie-Calder said, to say, "That is what is
likely to happen if we don't plan against it
happening"?

Davis: Let me finish my story. As long as you do
    not do anything about the population growth as
    such, the planning doesn't make sense. This is
    too important a factor to omit. I am weary of city
    planners who say to me, "Now, can you as a
    demographer tell me what the population trend
    is going to be so we will know what we have to
    plan for?"

    The population should be part of the plan.
    The population growth should be subject to con-
    trol. As long as you leave that uncontrolled,
    especially in the underdeveloped countries where
    an extremely high population growth seems prob-
    able, the planning is futile. Unless the control
    of population is incorporated into city plans,
    these plans will really be nonplans.

Harkavy: What do you mean by that?

Davis: Many population control measures could be
    discussed. For instance, build houses that are
    too small for a family, and limit even those.
    Put the Family Planning Service in the very
    center—really build it in. People don't take this
    seriously. We are so much in the habit of
    thinking we will do city planning for whatever
    population is coming along.

Segal: I think that was the answer. I was going to
    ask him to say that.

Michaelis: It surely should not surprise us, as it
    did a few minutes ago in the discussion, that the
    trend into the city and away from open space is

almost an irreversible one. Surely the whole
system of distribution of material goods, of the
provisioning of services of all kinds, is based
on certain mass markets which are, in economic
terms only attainable within certain concentrations.

If a man goes to the wilderness in his trailer,
he only goes generally as far as the range of the
nearest television station, because his kids are
still going to want to see their pet programs. He
stays near a supermarket where he can buy food
at a price he can afford. A farmer would probably
sell it to him twice as expensively. It is part of
his nature, isn't it? He is living at a certain
standard of life and he isn't made, as a man, for
wilderness any more. He would like to get to a
tennis court and there wouldn't be tennis courts
where there are only one hundred people. There
wouldn't be the economic incentive to have a
tennis court and maintain it for one hundred
people.

Ehrlich: It is very curious to me, just as a general
comment, that technologists seem to be terribly
drawn into facing fantastic problems of sewage
disposal, of urban planning or converting citizens
to responsible use of resources and to supporting
immensely expensive projects to try to treat the
symptoms of overpopulation. But technologists
are not very willing to promote the only thing that
will give us a chance of curing the disease. They
won't push for population control.

If this tremendous effort and money will go
in one direction, happily we will build the

freeways, find the money for the sewage disposal somewhere, for cleaning up the air, for using the resources properly, for planning the cities more and more and more.

Shelesnyak: Then the question is, how can this be done? We all agree that the situation is critical; more must be done—urgently. Everything we have gone through, so far, indicates that the reality of the problem is pretty well accepted. But how are we going to get this thing airborne?

SUNDAY MORNING SESSION
September 29, 1968

The conference reconvened at nine-ten o'clock,
Dr. Harkavy presiding.

Harkavy: Ladies and gentlemen, I think the program
for today will be slightly different. I suggest
that we change the order to controlling population
growth. I am doing this primarily because of
Paul Ehrlich's remarks: "Well, all the rest of
this stuff is too hard to do. Let's control population growth." Also Ron Freedman and Shelly
Segal are deserting us at the end of the day. We
will be able to confront family planning as we know
it, in contrast with something we have labeled
here "social control of fertility" and also biological control of fertility. The other Shelly, Dr.
Shelesnyak, will follow Shelly Segal, presenting
the biological control picture.
    Let us start with Professor Ronald Freedman
on the questions: How good is family planning?
What are the prospects for large-scale family
planning programs? I might say that if there is
any individual in the world who has been more
creatively involved in the evaluation of family
planning programs than Ron Freedman, I don't
know of him.

Taylor: I would like to say that I am deeply disappointed that you are leaving out sections which would have interested me most, and which I think will make the discussion entirely unrealistic if you leave them out.

Harkavy: We are not leaving them out. We are postponing them largely because Freedman and Segal are leaving. I believe that these issues could easily take the whole day, and we would be without the benefit of these other presentations.

Taylor: You will get to them this afternoon?

Harkavy: I expect that we will get to them this afternoon and tomorrow morning. From time to time, I think Kingsley Davis and others have asked, "Are we talking about controlling population growth or aren't we?" Much discussion seemed to be going off in directions that aren't exactly relevant. I think we can achieve more relevance if we first attack issues of how to control population growth.

Ehrlich: Well, we are accepting a point of view that it is absolutely desperate that we get on with controlling population growth right now, because that is the context in which this other section has to be discussed. Otherwise, we can go on idenfinitely with the same kinds of programs.

Freedman: I get these fulsome introductions from people like Bud Harkavy, and it is very easy for him to say such nice things because in the competition I qualify as one of the three best with the two other people who are doing what I am doing.

How good is family planning? Everybody agrees it is good—but good for what? To start with a summary, looking back to my position about six years ago when I first really became involved with evaluating the action program, things have gone much better and much faster than I expected. I think it is all so new that we still don't know how well it will go. My considered guess is that it is clearly not enough in itself, but that it can do a great deal, and more, than some of the critics of the programs have indicated.

In answering this question, how good is family planning, or in introducing the discussion, there are some criteria that we have to keep in mind: What are we expecting? And I would like to refer back to a statement of Dr. Ehrlich yesterday, because if it has to meet his standard, it obviously isn't good enough—that is, for example, when he says that the course of events in Japan was catastrophic. I would say that if these various programs could result in a series of demographic events like those of Japan in the postwar period, it would be very good indeed. If that is not good enough, then we are in desperate trouble.

The fact is that the net reproduction rate in Japan is and has been below one percent. There was a very dramatic drop in birth rate there after the war, not as the result of an organized effort but as the result of the

legalization of abortion, and their growth rate
now is still above one, largely as a result of the
heritage of the past high birth rates, and we are
not going to overcome that sort of thing overnight.

When we ask how good is family planning, I
take it to mean, how good are the programs that
have been organized essentially in the last two to
seven years. How good are they? They vary.
What are they accomplishing? We have to say
that they are very new and there has not been time
to test in any definitive way either their success
or their failure, or what they can do.

I have already indicated that I think there are
some optimistic signs, but such large-scale
deliberate organized efforts to interfere in human
reproductive institutions are a very new thing in
human history. The nature and conditions under
which they will have various effects, we don't
know much about. The world is very different
now than it was when birth rates declined in the
West; the new conditions and programs are still
under test and they need to be studied.

I wanted to take a minute (and I put this Rube
Goldberg diagram on the board) to talk a bit about
the complexity of the study. We don't have to
postpone action forever, but I want to point out to
some of the people who are not familiar with the
field some of the complexities involved. We are
interested in fertility; what is happening to the
birth rate so far as the Family Planning Program
is concerned. The "intermediate variables" are
between fertility and everything else. This is a
term which Kingsley Davis and his wife, Judith

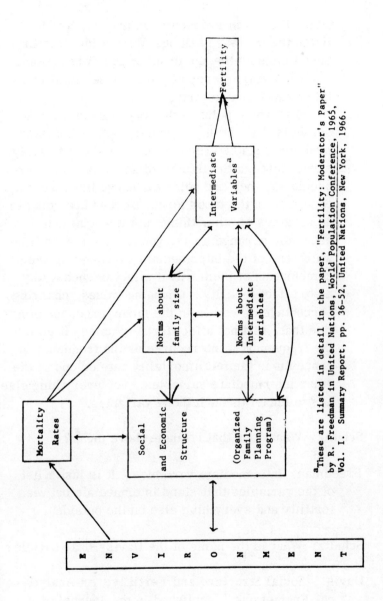

[a]These are listed in detail in the paper, "Fertility: Moderator's Paper" by R. Freedman in United Nations, World Population Conference, 1965, Vol. I. Summary Report, pp. 36-52, United Nations, New York, 1966.

Blake Davis, introduced in an article, which
listed the number of things which affect fertility,
such things as the age of marriage, when people
marry, the frequency of intercourse, fetal mortality rates and so forth.

The whole point of the way this diagram is
set up is that nothing over here <u>before</u> the intermediate variables (indicating) can affect fertility
except <u>through</u> the intermediate variables. When
people say they are going to change the percentage
of women in the labor force, or they are going to
do all kinds of other things in the social and
economic arrangements, you must ask each time
which one of the intermediate variables or which
combination of them will it affect in such a way
as to affect fertility. Changing values, changing
percentage of women in the labor force, anything
like that, will not affect fertility unless it affects
the frequency of intercourse or the frequency of
conception, the fetal mortality rate or one of the
other intermediate variables. So, everything else
has to funnel through those variables.

Schultz: What does that triangle there mean?

Freedman: Intermediate variables. It is just a list
of the variables that stand intermediate between
fertility and everything else on the outside.

Schultz: What is the name of the Davis-Blake article?

Davis: "Social Structure and Fertility: An Analytical Framework," published in the <u>Journal of</u>

Economic Development and Cultural Change
about 1955.

Freedman: I have put into separate boxes here the
values (norms) about family size and the values
(norms) about these intermediate variables which
are sometimes independent of the values of family
size, sometimes dependent on them. There are
all kinds of feedback and interacting variables.
Mortality enters the picture. Social organization
that affects all these values may also have an
effect on the intermediate variables without
reference to the values. For example, the nature of the religious organization or the economic
organization may have an effect on fetal mortality
independently of any of these values. This should
be a much smaller box, but what we have now,
this little insert in the social organization box
is the organized Family Planning Programs that
we are talking about. This new, artificial,
planned innovation has been introduced into this
complex social-biological complex. The question
now is, what difference this innovation makes.
How does it affect the functioning of this whole
system? That is really the problem and it is not
simple to answer. We have to act in the meantime, but we also need knowledge of what the results are in the long run.

    By short-run criteria, I would say that the
programs appear to be most successful in places
where other conditions appear to be favorable by
our preconceived ideas of what favorable conditions are. This is in places like Taiwan, Korea,

Hong Kong, Singapore, Malaysia. But I hasten to point out that I don't know of anybody who would have predicted in 1961 that even in these "favorable places" the birth rates were going to fall as sharply in the next five or six years as happened. Furthermore, as I will try to indicate, they are falling with a rapidity and in a pattern that makes it plausible to assume that the programs are making a contribution to the decline, at least, in the short run.

It is very hard to argue, obviously, what is going to happen in the long run and whether this would have happened anyway. When you get into the social field, the question of what would have happened in history if you hadn't had so-and-so is a very, very difficult subject. But, of course, if no decline had occurred, there would be nothing to argue about. Something has happened.

In such critical large populations as those of India and Pakistan, for example, we do not yet know how much Family Planning Programs can accomplish, for several reasons. First of all, the "significant" efforts are only a few years old. You might ask, "significant by whose standards?" I admit that anybody who looks at the Indian programs, although they are old in time, would say that until three or four years ago there was not much input. There was a program but there was not much input. You can argue since there isn't an input, that is an indication of failure in itself. Even now in India, although there has been some improvement, I would say that it is impossible to know whether the programs could

have a significant effect in some parts of the population—at least, if they were carried out. They
are not being carried out according to plan.
There are all kinds of plans, and there has been
some new progress but, basically, the programs
are not being executed.

We can argue whether the plans are right
or wrong, but we don't know if the plans would
make any difference unless they are executed.
I think it is significant that about three years
ago, both in India and Pakistan, there was, for
various reasons, better organization and more
input, sometimes grossly inadequate, but it re-
sulted in a greater apparent result. Since we
don't know what the birth rate is in these places,
we don't know if the program had an effect on the
birth rate. I think it may have been effective in
some parts of India, but probably not significantly so.

We do know that during the most recent
short period of time they are having (maybe) 1
to 2 million sterilizations a year and 1 million
or so IUD's inserted, despite the fact that most
of the program is really not working.

Returning to my diagram, I think that most
of the demographic-social-scientific community
would agree that the reproductive levels of the
society involve a set of culturally defined sequen-
tial sets of behaviors in families which have this
kind of complex interrelationship. Other people
would organize this diagram differently; we have
lots of quarrels about relationships. For example the social and economic institutions of

the country are important, but we know pathetically little of the specific character of their relationship to fertility variables, even in specific countries. We need to study those relationships, doing everything we can with the knowledge we have in the meantime to get the best possible results. But it is imperative to increase the knowledge base by systematic studies, which we are perfectly capable of making, so that we will have more to go on three or five years from now. This is not to say that we shouldn't do everything possible at the present time.

I was in India a year ago, involved in consultation with people there. I was with some people who were making assessments about the program there, and they wanted inputs of certain kinds. They were using inputs from other countries for these calculations that they were making, and I commented that these are probably very inappropriate, because conditions are different in these other places. They replied that was all they had.

I was bothered very much when I asked the question, "What are you doing now so that you will have the inputs three or four years from now?" The answer essentially was, "Nothing." I think that is a tragedy.

Taylor: The area was Taiwan, Korea, and ---

Freedman: I was in India and I had data. Since I had been working in Taiwan, Korea, Hong Kong, Malaysia, Singapore, I had data from those countries. The set of data from Taiwan was relevant and might have applied in some aspects. Whether it applies or not, we don't know until we get more data from India, but the thing that bothered me was that some people had to put those data into calculations without viable plans for collecting their own data in their own situation.

I learned that without certain kinds of social and economic changes (over in that box to the left), changes in reproductive institutions are unlikely or impossible. That is a broad statement, but in a general way, most social demographers would agree that this is true. For example, how the family context fits into other institutions, and to what extent the whole society is organized on kinship lines and what rewards come from the family—these are crucial. I think almost everybody working in the field agrees with that. However, when it comes to a guide for action in specific cases, we don't know how much change is needed in what social and economic institutions as a pre-condition. We also don't know in many countries how much change has already occurred in some of these factors. Recently Ansley Coale and some of his co-workers have been studying the situation with respect to the fertility decline in Western Europe and are concluding on the basis of what happened there, that we are extrapolating.

Schultz: Europe?

Freedman: This is all of Europe, really. They have data mainly for Western, Central, and Southern Europe and are beginning to get some data from Eastern Europe. In general, I think they have evidence that the situation was not as simple as the social theory would have us believe as to what was necessary for fertility decline.

Zuckerman: Could you amplify? What was expected?

Freedman: For example, my colleague, Paul Demeny, has recently found some historical data for Hungarian villages and provinces in which the birth rate was very low in areas which were largely agricultural, largely illiterate, and with none of the characteristics that are supposed to be the pre-conditions for fertility decline. This historical research has just started, but it is beginning to raise some questions as to how fundamental the social and economic factors are and the particulars of this classical general framework. I still haven't abandoned the framework, but it leads to some questions.

Davis: Does he have an explanation?

Freedman: No. He has some ideas but they are not very convincing. It is negative evidence.

Tax: A monograph is coming out shortly on an Hungarian village in which the men do not stay in the same house with the women—a recent change. They are horse people, and they stay in the stables.

Whether they stay in the stables with the horses
because they want a lower birth rate, or vice
versa, I don't know.

Taylor: You said "historical," but what historical
    period is referred to?

Tax: It is memory culture of the people who are
    living now, the way they were twenty years ago.
    I was only suggesting that Europe isn't as homo-
    geneous as some people think.

Freedman: That is precisely the point. They have
    divided all of the European countries into a large
    number of local areas and, using parish registers
    and other things of this sort, they are recon-
    structing the demographic history and trying to
    relate it to other variables for as many local
    areas as possible. The idea is precisely that
    Europe was not and is not a homogeneous whole
    and that the demographic history in different
    parts is different. This new work is opening up
    some doubts that I think are reinforced, in part,
    by what we are seeing in the Far East.
        This boils down to the need for tests of what
    all-out Family Planning Programs will do under
    various conditions. We have some tests now,
    I won't say these are all-out programs, but tests
    of what pretty good programs can do where the
    conditions are favorable. The criticism is made
    that it would have happened anyway. Maybe so
    and maybe not. I think, when such programs are
    mounted in places where the conditions are

different, we have to wait and see. We are capable of doing this scientifically. The scientific community of the world can do this.

There are a number of places in which efforts have been made where I would have expected nothing to happen and where I, for one, was surprised. For example, a colleague of mine worked in Thailand some years ago in a rural area where there was a lot of illiteracy and where you could reach much of the population only by boat. It seemed a most unpromising project to me, for the pre-survey indicated that most of the people knew nothing about contraception and biology. But they started a program, serving quite successfully a significant number of people who wanted contraception when available.

I am saying that we cannot assert categorically that these programs are not going to work. We have not, in my judgment, tried them. I would be the first to admit that we also cannot assert categorically that it is going to work in new places that are less developed. I think there is a fairly high probability that they will not work in the same way in India or Pakistan, but they may have a considerable effect.

Schultz: Ron, may I interrupt? While there is great value in your being so comprehensive and careful, it seems to me it may be too careful in the sense that the parents wishing children may be responding from the standpoint of the satisfaction of having children and what they have to do to get these children and the satisfaction they get from it may be much more universal than the extraordinary homogeneity that we impose. I have spent fifteen years arguing with colleagues in economics and the argument that I have confronted is that farmers all over the world are so culture-bound that, in some real sense, even if they had opportunity, they wouldn't respond. I think evidence is piling up that there are many of these peasant communities with great differences in culture that when they have the opportunity, do respond and the response is similar, in a sense, to what one is seeing elsewhere.

It may be true that we are dealing with a kind of rationality on the part of parents that is universal. The satisfaction of having children is a value that is positive.

You come with a new technology, a new birth control technique. The response may be as universal as it is to what I called yesterday the modernization in agriculture. It shouldn't be ruled out as when you introduce a new type of crop or planting.

Freedman: Let me add something to that. Where I have made some observations, which covers a good deal of Asia, most good surveys in which parents are asked what kinds of families they want, almost universally they say that they want to have children and they want several children at least. However, a very large minority of the parents in all of the places where I have knowledge of these studies say that they want to have fewer children than they are having—particularly if mortality has been falling.

In all of the places in which there has been a serious Family Planning Program carried out, there has been a very significant response from the parents, taking this opportunity. I would also say in almost every case these were places in which the social scientists and political leaders would have said that nothing was likely to happen. The people are too backward.

My experience, Sol, is that American social scientists are much more ecumenical in their view than the leadership of the countries with which we are dealing.

Schultz: What does that mean?

Freedman: It means they are broad; they are ready to accept anything. We don't say the people are backward. My observation has been the indigenous leaders are the ones who say that their people are backward. They say, "The only way we have to solve the problem is to forcibly sterilize all our peasants. They are too uneducated," and so forth. From what I have seen the peasants are intelligent people within the limits of their education. In terms of their own problems, they respond within a reasonably rational framework.

The new programs are not all-out. They don't solve the whole problem, but given the short-time horizon, I think they are a very significant development.

Ehrlich: I wish you would show me that the program

is going to lead to the control of the population—
not something that will be reversible if the
people's attitudes change in response to a local
labor shortage and so forth. In other words, I
want to see if these programs will lead in a
clearly defined manner to some sort of population stability and then reduction. I am not saying you have to get it instantly, and I am not
saying these programs aren't valuable.

Freedman: I have never said and I don't know any
responsible person who has ever said that these
programs will do that. I am all for other things
that will reduce population growth but, if that is
your goal, these programs are a very important
contribution toward it. Whether the other things
you suggest will work is hypothetical. I don't
contend these are going to solve the problem or
how much they will do. I don't know anybody
else who does. We don't know yet. All you
know is that these programs have worked where
they've been tried effectively—worked at a certain rate.

Ehrlich: That is sort of a tautological conclusion.

Davis: How many places has the program been put in
effectively? Let's have that first.
　　　If you confine your cases sufficiently, and
leave out all the others because by definition
they are not effective as programs, there is the
danger that you are biasing the results.

Freedman: I have already indicated the big areas where they haven't worked.

Taking the general point of view about the necessity for other kinds of broad social changes, with which I agree, we still don't know if the necessary conditions are already there. We don't know to what extent these other conditions can be changed, and now we don't know enough about what the Family Planning Programs can contribute to them.

I come now to the places where something has been done and where you have what I consider to be relatively good programs--and I remind you again that all this is about five or six years old, or less. The Taiwan program is one which I consider to be the oldest good program. It goes back effectively to 1961-1963. In what sense has this effort been a success? It has been successful in a number of places in the sense that many people have accepted contraception and have practiced it. In the three places I know where studies have been done, we have evidence that after a period of three or four years (although many people have given up the contraceptives that they were given initially), the great majority are doing something about family planning. They have, during the intervening period, many fewer births than they would have had if their previous fertility had prevailed.

The places that I have in mind admittedly comprise a small list. My point is that there ought to be a longer list. Frank Notestein may be able to add to this, but I would say that the places where we have some evidence of this kind are Korea, Taiwan, Hong Kong, Singapore, and some evidence from Malaysia.

Notestein: Probably a little in Pakistan. It is awfully hard to prove.

Freedman: I wouldn't rate Pakistan as a success yet. Too early.

Notestein: No, no; it is just the beginning of a little effect.

Freedman: I am rating these places as a success in the sense that large numbers of people have accepted change within a relatively short period of time and the birth rate is falling quite rapidly in these places. The question is would it have fallen anyway? I think it would have fallen any- way. How much would it have fallen anyway? I think the changes in fertility seem to be re- lated to the programs in this field.

Let me present the kind of evidence that we have. It is admittedly partial, indirect, and not all in. In Hong Kong, the birth rate fell rapidly between 1961 and 1965. An analysis of that in- dicated that it was mainly an artifact; it was mainly due to changes in age composition and partly to changes in the marriage pattern, and very little to changes in the fertility of married people. However, between 1965 and 1966, the birth rate fell 10 percent in one year, which was a rather large decline. It has fallen another 7 percent between 1966 and 1967.

The Hong Kong Family Planning Association had a intrauterine device program started in late 1964. You can look at the data as to how many women got the IUD and their age distribution, and it fits with the change in fertility. In 1965 and 1966 the birth rate fell. Previously it had fallen in the older age groups. In 1965 and 1966, the 10-percent decline was due to a decline in the younger age groups, in particular in those age groups that had been using the IUD, and also in lower status groups than had previously been practicing contraception.

You can write that off on the ground that, given a little time, this would have happened anyway. Maybe so, but given a problem of this sort, I think we have to accept this sort of evidence. There is no reason to believe that you would have suddenly had a 10-percent decline in marital fertility rates in these particular age groups, in these social strata, without this particular program. The women were ready; I do not deny it, and there were favorable conditions, I do not deny that. I don't think anybody knows how long it would have taken without that intervention.

Davis: May I ask you a question or two before you go on about Hong Kong? What is the abortion situation?

Freedman: There have not been any systematic studies. I have been there four or five times and it appears that, for reasons I don't understand, there is not a lot of abortion. I think one

reason that there may not be is simply that birth
control is advancing very rapidly. Quite apart
from what the Hong Kong Family Planning
Association did, there are a lot of people who
are getting contraception through the drug stores
and through private doctors. A survey done in
1967 indicated that about 60 percent of the people
practicing contraception (and there were a lot of
people practicing contraception) begun through the
Family Planning Association.

Segal: When Ron talks about the activities of the
Family Planning Association, you should not have
an image of the typical Planned Parenthood clinic
as we know it here in the United States. The
Family Planning Association in Hong Kong runs
family planning services in every maternity
hospital that delivers a large number of women,
which means that a large proportion of the women
who are delivered—because they do have a high
proportion of the births occurring in hospitals
in Hong Kong—are provided with family planning
service at the time of their delivery.

Davis: A second question: What is the comparison
between your picking off the latest decline, I
take it to be fertility in Hong Kong—how would
that compare with the rate of decline in fertility
in Tokyo in, let's say, late '40s the early '50s?

Freedman: I haven't looked at it specifically but my
guess would be that it would certainly be no
faster and probably not as fast.

Davis: Which, that Tokyo would not be as fast as Hong Kong?

Freedman: No, I would say Tokyo probably went faster.

Davis: Which was mainly with abortion at that time?

Freedman: That's right.

Davis: So, an alternative possibility would have been to open up more abortion centers?

Freedman: Sure. There were many alternatives. I should supplement what Shelly Segal said by saying that there are also many clinics outside of maternity hospitals and this is, of course, an ideal situation. It is a restricted population and easy to reach. They have, I think, about seventy clinics scattered throughout the island.

Davis: What is the current gross reproduction rate in Hong Kong?

Freedman: Offhand I don't know. I would guess that it is probably in the neighborhood of 20 this year.

Harkavy: Please define gross reproduction rate.

Freedman: It is an estimate of the number of female babies a woman will bear during her reproductive years under current fertility rates.

Zuckerman: You are dealing with a pretty

heterogeneous population in Hong Kong, and the proper comparison for me would not be Tokyo but Singapore, and the Chinese population there. Do you have those statistics?

Freedman: I am coming to Singapore in a moment. Let me say that the decline in Singapore has been very rapid. There has been a decline in fertility that greatly accelerated during the last two years, I believe as the result of a highly organized program. The birth rate now in Singapore, when you standardize age, is lower than it is in Hong Kong, but they have the same sort of thing. They had a private Family Planning Association which was fairly active, but in the last two years there was a large acceleration in the decline, which I think can be traced to this program.

Zuckerman: Did this apply to both the Malayan population and the Chinese?

Freedman: The decline has occurred in all sectors of the population. Of course, Singapore is predominantly Chinese, but the Malayan population has also been a part of the decline. They start from a higher level.

Hoagland: Did you obtain any information as to what may be going on in Mainland China with regard to fertility control?

Freedman: I would rather postpone that; I am not an expert on it. I have some ideas and I could say something about it, but I think it takes us off the main topic.

I began working in Taiwan in 1962 when the
birth rate was close to 40. It is below 28 this
year. It had been declining. There is no question
that all the conditions for decline have been
favorable there. In my opinion, however, there
has been a change that was not expected. There
are two pieces of evidence that I want in the record. First, all the studies before the program was introduced indicated that contraception, sterilization, and abortion (which is common
in Taiwan) were predominantly practiced by the
upper strata, that is, the better educated, the
better off, and the urban. A program was introduced. The birth rate decline accelerated, and
the overwhelming majority of the new users
were drawn from the lower strata that these
programs are attempting to reach.

Frankly, we thought that we weren't going
to have much success with the farmers, the
illiterates, and so forth. They responded more
than the other groups—and that is understandable,
the other groups had alternatives—but they did
respond and a very large part of this decline is
due to that. This probably would have happened
in the long run anyway, is my guess, but I think
it is very implausible that in a short period of
time you would get that kind of switchover without the organized program.

We have another kind of evidence that I
would like to see more available. Taiwan is an
ideal place to do these things because the statistics are very good. The island is divided into
362 local administrative units and because the
Japanese set up an excellent population register

which the Chinese have continued, we had each
year age-specific birth rates and marriage rates
for each of these 362 areas. These data are much
better, by the way, than any I know of for any
European country or any Western country.

For each of these areas we have measures
of percentage in agriculture, educational level
of men and women, density of population, distance to the nearest big city, and a variety of
things that would go into the social organization
component.

We also have for each of those 362 areas
data on the program: how many woman-months
of effort each quarter have gone into field work
in the organized program; how many doctors are
available. (Those are our two principal measures
of program input.) We have for each area the
number of acceptances, that is, how many women
got an IUD inserted, and now that they have
started a Pill Program, how many women have
started on the Pill. In addition, we have mortality rates.

When you put all of that into a multivariant
analysis, what the data show, as expected, is
that you have higher acceptance rates and lower
birth rates where you have lower mortality and
where you have higher education. All of these
things are true, but after you have taken into
account as best possible all of these effects, one
important fact emerges, namely, that effort
makes a difference. The acceptance rate is
related, after all these other things are taken
into account, to the effort in the program.
Furthermore, the decline in the birth rate is

related to these efforts and to the acceptances after taking into account, not only all of these outside factors, but the preceding decline in the birth rate.

You will recognize that this is a very complicated type of analysis, for all kinds of qualifications have to be made, but I doubt very much that the basic conclusions are going to be changed.

In by judgment, we need that kind of evidence to answer the questions that we are asking. We can look at these data and find what combinations of percentage in agriculture, density, effort, and so forth, have made a difference. We are just beginning to do this. Those of you who are impatient, may I remind you that in the natural sciences it takes time to do these things, too. In the social demographic field, for example, you must wait at least nine months to start, and then you select some data and process it, and so forth. Those are the kinds of data that I am talking about.

There has been a very interesting development in Singapore. That is the one place I know of where there has been a program that has been based on the Pill. It is an unusual situation in that they have, I believe, the largest maternity hospital in the world and about 85 percent of the babies in Singapore are born in this one hospital. Every mother is visited when she comes to have her baby, and a very large proportion of the women are given appointment to come to a clinic afterwards. About half of them come, and the birth rate has dropped sharply during the last two years, much more sharply than before.

Zuckerman: And you have also taken the political changes into account?

Freedman: No; I don't know what that would mean.

Zuckerman: Well, possible lack of employment of the Chinese, and so on, as a result of the United Kingdom's reducing its naval base there.

Freedman: That would be in anticipation, you know, because, after all, much of that had not happened before the time I am talking about. Many of those changes had not occurred and the level of unemployment had not yet gone up, and as I understand it, it is still an anticipated level of unemployment. That may affect the situation, I don't know.

Davis: You mentioned age-standardized birth rate. What is it in Singapore now?

Freedman: It depends on what you standardize it on.

Davis: All right, the gross reproduction rate.

Freedman: Standardizing it on the 1961 Hong Kong population, which we did for various reasons, I think it is now down to about 24.

Ehrlich: What is the death rate?

Freedman: I don't know, but my quess is 7 or 8.

Davis: That is a pretty high birth rate for a city of about a million and a half people.

Freedman: Korea has close to 40 million people and they began a program about 1963 or 1964, several years after Taiwan.

Unfortunately, they have poor demographic data in Korea. Piecing together what we can with estimates, it seems fairly certain that the birth rate has been falling. It would be difficult to imagine that it had not been falling because during this fairly short period, I think close to 30 percent of the women in their child-bearing years have received services through the program. The major thing has been the insertion of an IUD; secondarily, vasectomies, and they have the beginning of a Pill Program. The data that are available indicate the same kind of shift I discussed earlier with respect to Taiwan. There is a lot of abortion there, and I think there is good evidence that the abortion rate has increased as a result of the program, although that can't be demonstrated. It is illegal but there is a lot of it.

There was the same sort of shift from practice in the higher strata, in the urban strata, and so forth, to predominant use by illiterate women, rural women, and so on. Actually, Korea is behind Taiwan in development levels and the rate of development, the rate of literacy, things like electricity, and so forth. But in the last couple of years, the rate of economic development has picked up considerably.

I will stop with this, repeating what I said

initially. Even though these are selected populations, I don't think anybody expected this kind
of rapid change in the short period of time. I
doubt very much that anything like this would
happen in India and Pakistan. However, I guess
that considerably more would happen than many
people think, and I will reassert that there
hasn't been a significant effort in these countries
with all resources mobilized.

It may be that it is the nature of those countries that they can't organize themselves to con-
duct such an all-out effort. That is a dismal
hypothesis. I won't accept that, under existing
circumstances and given the nature of the problem,
until a more substantial effort has been made
than I think has been made to test things out.
I will conclude by saying that I believe very
strongly that these programs play a very significant role in getting toward a goal of low rates of
population growth. I also believe that they are
not all that can be done, and they pose no obstruction to these alternate schemes.

Schultz: If one really begins to look at the evidence
and draw inferences, that gives us something to
build on. I don't think you would quarrel with
the view that compulsory school attendance of
five to eight years, the beginning years, is
another strong program effort which would have
influence in reducing the birth rate.

Freedman: Education, particularly of women, is
one of the most powerful facilitating variables
in all of these cases where there is any evidence.

Schultz: Has anyone looked, or is it possible to look around the world for behavior where there has been imposed a strong program for public school attendance, really effectively in force, where one could follow it through for a while and see what that evidence would show?

Freedman: Kingsley's mention of Japan is a very good case in point, but it is very complicated. I don't think there is any question about the fact that the Japanese birth rate fell as fast as it did and many other things happened after the war as the result of the remarkable level of educational sophistication and literacy that were there. My own interpretation is that the birth rate should have and would have fallen before the war if there had not been organized barriers to prevent it from falling, and after the war, given all of the facilitating conditions and the educational literacy, and so forth, the birth rate fell very sharply, but it is complicated by all these other things.

Zuckerman: One could use, for example, the recent example of immigration to England of Pakistanis and Indians into cities like Birmingham with enormous populations, where the children are subjected immediately to the same educational processes as the English children. There would be an opportunity to study this problem.

Schultz: But, there the social environment might make a difference. There are many other things that change, too. I am asking for the data to

work toward evidence, for I believe what you
say is correct.

Freedman: There are a lot of data that show that
fertility is related to education. I don't think
there is any doubt about that.

Schultz: There have been countries that have imposed
compulsory schooling, quite well carried out,
and I would like to see just how much complementary effect it has had. You are saying it runs
alongside, and it is reinforcing, and I am quite
sure this is true. I would like to see the same
thing done for this factor because it is another
extraordinarily viable policy that countries can
have. If we could demonstrate that this has a
strong effect, and if they want to get their birth
rates down, this would be very important evidence.

Freedman: It seems we could make a very strong
case for that. Isn't the problem an economic
problem?

Ritchie-Calder: Isn't it a self-contradictory one?
You have a large growing population and you don't
have the education facilities.

Segal: A question was tabled a moment ago which I
would like to come back to, and that was the
question of the selectivity of these examples from
the list of countries that have announced for a
national Family Planning Program. Freedman
has emphasized this but I think it needs

reiteration. Those of you who read one of the background papers written by Berelson, "Where We Stand," will recall that there are perhaps thirty countries around the world that have announced for a national Family Planning Program as a policy, within the framework of the Ministry of Health or the comparable governmental body.

I know of no such case in which you could say that the program has been attempted, implemented, and been a failure. I think the ones that Ron has selected are those where a fair chance has been given to see what you could do under proper organizational structure. If you take, for example, a country like Turkey, which announced for a national Family Planning Program three or four years ago, and search the country for the number of people hired by the government and working full-time in Family Planning, you might find three. Are you going to say that this is a national Family Planning Program that has failed? It is obviously a program that was never organized and put into effect.

In Kenya, there is one man in the entire country who works full time on Family Planning and he is an American. There is a Kenyan who spends about a third of his time on Family Planning.

Shelesnyak: Shelly, did you say there is no country that has made a population policy that has been successful, that it has failed to achieve its goals?

Segal: That is right.

Shelesnyak: What you are really saying is that
announcement of a population policy doesn't
count.

Segal: What doesn't count?

Shelesnyak: You can't put "success" in a score sheet
except to say fifteen countries have made a
pronouncement.

Segal: Let's not use semantics about the proper term
in my introduction. I am trying to make the
point that I think all of us who are interested in
Family Planning do a great disservice to the
potential of this kind of an operation by misin-
terpreting the level of activity that has occured
in the span of time. This is something that Ron
has pointed out. There has not been enough time
for evaluation even in those intermediate places,
like India and Pakistan where a sizable effort
has been undertaken. There has not been time
to spread through the entire country, nor for
statistics to be available for proper evaluation.

Shelesnyak: There is more than lack of time in what
you say. It is a lack of implementation of policy.

Davis: Yes, India is the prime example.

Freedman: In India that is true and I think that
Shelesnyak's and Kingsley's points are well
taken. I think India and Pakistan announced their
programs long enough ago that there could have
been a test if the programs had been carried out

and we would have to say that they haven't carried
through on original plans. There should be an
analysis of why they haven't. The kinds of cultures they have accounts for one position. Before they can have an all-out program, perhaps
some other things have to be changed.

Segal: India has a smallpox immunization program
supported by the WHO and every international
organization you can imagine for over twenty
years and now only 30 percent of the eligible
population over the time period have had primary innoculations. Fewer than 5.1 percent
have had booster innoculations.

Zuckerman: Have you evidence for different parts
of India? India is a vast country and the various
programs are run locally. I was talking to the
Minister of Health for Baroda a few weeks ago
and he told me that his parish contained 30
million people. We were discussing the Family
Planning Program, which he is responsible for,
and he vigorously believes that they are achieving
considerable success with it.

Freedman: There are pockets of India in which there
has been some success. My last personal view
of the data and field situation was a year ago
March. At the time I think it could have been
said that there was no state in India where you
could say that the program had been a success.
Some states appear to have a declining birth rate,
but I don't think you can attribute it to the program.

Davis: Could I come back to what seems to me to be
a logical question? Let's ask what we are doing
at the present. We are attempting to say whether
or not a certain type of policy has had an effect.
Obviously, there is some correlation between
fertility decline and the use of contraception,
but the question now is whether or not a policy
of large-scale introduction by government, or
at least the government-tolerated group in the
country, has had an effect.

Freedman: Are you distinguishing policy from program?

Davis: No, let's call it program. I am willing to use
a broad term here.
    It would be a sad situation if the major pro-
gram carried out efficiently had no effect, and
I am afraid that this twenty-year job would be in
danger. But what is the real comparison? How
does it compare with another program or another
policy? But, there is no other.
    Let me come back to Ted's example. Has
education been tried? Has the education of women
been tried anywhere to limit the population? No,
so you can't compare the effect of that with a
Family Planning Program.

Freedman: May I comment on that, Kingsley? In
Taiwan and in these areas that we have looked
at, it is true that if you hold the other things
constant in these local areas, the more women
that have higher levels of education, the lower
the fertility.

Davis: Yes, of course. Use of contraception—if women use contraception, this lowers the birth rate.

Freedman: That is not what I am saying. The program got them to use contraception.

Davis: Suppose we had a program that gave more education to women over and above what is likely anyway. That is the comparison. That is the question.

Notestein: No, no.

Davis: Let me ask you another question. Is there a policy of promoting female employment for comparison, that is, a policy deliberately instituted for the purpose of limiting fertility? The answer probably is "no." Where is there a policy of paying for the education of men and women as long as they remain unmarried? Has that policy been followed?

Segal: Incidentally, the answer isn't "no" on the first one. For years, Iran has had a policy of freeing women from the home and putting them into educational employment opportunities.

Davis: I think that I would use your words, Shelly Segal, in this case and that is an inadequate program, which you couldn't use for evaluation. There is probably no more evidence there than in Pakistan.

Notestein: One of the troubles, Kingsley, with education is that we talk about a practical program.
All of these countries desperately want education and they will support it for its merits more
quickly than they will as an aid for birth control.
It is so much valued for itself.

Schultz: If I were to think about the choices of policy
that a government may consider and make its
selection with the assumption it wants to reduce
the birth rate, it seems that Family Planning
pays off. I am not saying that it is all that can
be done.
      Now, what other kinds of policy choices are
there that a government could act upon even
though they don't know what the effects will be?
One is the education of the children. You argue
for education for women, but I would say start
with children, and include the women.

Freedman: I think there is enough evidence that makes
it very clear from everything we have seen that
if you raise educational standards, particularly
for women, contraception will be practiced more.

Schultz: Is this what the evidence will show? I have
tried to get the evidence and it is very hard to
get anything substantial. I am not worried that
the evidence will argue against the proposition
that you just pointed to, but it is hard to get.
      The other policy choice is jobs for women.
I am also convinced that jobs for women is a
viable policy choice, but I haven't seen the

evidence. We have it in the United States in the Glenn Cain study and some others, but I have not seen it for a developing country.

To bring in the biologists, the evidence may show that bringing down the death rate may be a powerful influence in reducing the birth rate. We have sort of boxed in the medical people saying that reducing death rates has just messed everything up. It may turn out, if we allow a period a little longer than a decade, programs that reduce the death rate may be one of the forces reducing the net reproduction rates. If true, we ought to find out.

Ehrlich: All you can do, though, is wait for that.

Schultz: No one has looked at it in terms of what is implicit in what I am saying as an hypothesis.

Taylor: Is there a danger of a time lag here?

Schultz: I have seen some data on this that implies that a decline in the death rate is a factor bringing down the net reproduction rate.

Taylor: What is the lead time?

Schultz: One generation.

Ehrlich: Where has this occurred that it hasn't been combined with industrialization or something else?

Schultz: No, no, it is just the death rates coming
    down.   The rest of the economy is split into
    specific sectors.

Davis: It almost looks the opposite in Latin America.

Schultz: I know, but the important thing is, unraveling
    all the factors here and accounting for the inter-
    dependences, to be sure you are not looking at
    the wrong things in terms of cause and effect.
    It is not that resources spent on Family Planning
    do not pay off, but there are also other things
    that may.

Ehrlich: I wouldn't like to pose that question quite
    yet.

Slobodkin: This all sounds like agricultural research
    before the invention of R. A. Fisher. That is,
    something has been done and it cannot be done
    as a controlled experiment by the nature of the
    project. That is, you take a place; you have only
    one Taiwan to work with; you have one Hong Kong
    to work with.

Freedman: You can separate the parts of it, though,
    and I think that makes the difference. You can't
    make it as clean as you have in the laboratory,
    but then you from the natural sciences generally
    jump to the opposite conclusion, that is, that we
    can work without data and that our opinions and
    passions should govern.

Slobodkin: I was thinking that we have a phenomenon,

presumably at least in part due to some treatment in this case, and we have a variety of alternative treatments being brought up by other people. Has anyone played with the idea of a quasi-controlled experiment with a series of areas chosen—three at a minimum, six would be better so that you get some kind of an error term—in which you have one treatment applied, two treatments applied together, and then the second treatment applied alone? First of all, in principle it could be done; it is an internally controlled system. There is no area in which you say, "We are doing nothing and that constitutes a control"; but it ought to be the case that in the area where both treatment A and treatment B are applied, you get a stronger effect than with treatment A or treatment B alone.

This may turn out not to be feasible because a government tends to be simple-minded; the general intellectual level of government seems to be somewhat lower than the participants in government, in a curious way. You can visualize, for instance, two treatments being applied and finding themselves in a situation of competing for the attention of the same government, both being of a weaker form than if they were applied along.

Segal: I think it is a very good point and well made.

Schultz: Puerto Rico has run the experiment on all three.

Slobodkin: May I suggest that instead of doing it with

government support, it would be better if it
could be done on external support so that it
would be possible to use either intrauterine devices or bed-reading lamps (which I heard
Margaret Mead mention as an effective contraceptive device) and support the two treatments
with equal strength. Does this make sense?

Freedman: In my judgment, it would be very difficult to do it without consulting the government.

Slobodkin: Consult, yes, but have your resources ---

Freedman: On a small scale, I agree with you perfectly, that there ought to be more of this.

Slobodkin: Is there any of it?

Freedman: There is some of it in various ways. Let
me give you an example. This is a nuts-and-
bolts kind of example. It can be elaborated.
In Taiwan, one of the questions, where they have
been charging for these things, what happens if
you give contraceptive materials away? So, they
have given the IUD insertion away, rotating areas
for free insertions. There has been some experimental design put into it and they have tried
to find out if this does any good. I think there
is good experimental evidence to show that
doing this for a period of time makes a significant effect.
    That was done with variations of other things.
There is no reason, in my judgment, why this
could not be done with more important variables

in these places, and I think you would get government cooperation in most cases. A lot of it can be observed naturally. There is an element of selection there to begin with, but I wouldn't rule that evidence out. If it doesn't turn out favorably with the selection, then you know that you are in trouble.

Slobodkin: I will define the Golden Bough fallacy (I have never seen it defined in print), because I think it relates here. Frazer posed the question whether a sacred king was killed in the grove of NENNI every seven years. He wrote twelve fascinating volumes about analogs, similarities, and related phenomena, and at the end of those twelve volumes you don't really know whether a sacred king was killed at the grove of NENNI. We have the same kind of thing seeming to crop up here occasionally. The treatment has been applied, something has occurred, and we have a whole series of plausibility arguments that then arise to which one can select counter-plausibility arguments. This is a very poor business when you are talking about a serious problem.

Zuckerman: I recognize the difficulties, and it may very well be that we will end up with a kind of Frazer analysis—analogies, historical post-mortems, and all the rest of it. But your general question about experimental situations in which you will get governments to cooperate in a way that will favor one group of people as opposed to another strikes me as not being realistic, not because governments are stupid but because governments could not survive if they did that kind of thing.

Let me give you an illustration. A short time ago a big commercial undertaking in England wished to introduce cervical smearing for the diagnosis of cervical cancer for all of its female employees. It was stopped by our Ministry of Health, for the simple reason that the knowledge of what it was going to do had spread, and there was a clamor for general service. The Ministry could not respond, and they had to ask these people to hold off until such time as the diagnostic procedure could be applied more generally.

Davis: Why were they not able to do this?

Zuckerman: Money, trained people, manpower, technicians.

Davis: Couldn't they just put an extra tax on tobacco?

Slobodkin: I am not saying that governments are in fact stupid, because governments work within the sort of constraints that Sir Solly is pointing out and we cannot expect them to work differently.

Segal: I think Larry's proposition should be analyzed in some depth. If you mean, Larry, an experimental design to test the merits of particular aspects of what would be defined as a Family Planning Program in terms of a program to motivate people and supply them with services

for contraception, there are experiments in which
variables have been established. Experimental
areas have been set up to see whether, using
Ron's experiment, for example, attempts to
motivate the male as well as the female are as
useful or as economical, effective, as attempting to motivate the female along. Other areas
have been set up where the effort has been made
to evaluate the use of the intrauterine device
under circumstances in which it is the only
variable as compared to not using it; or using
the oral contraceptive, and so on.

But if your question is more general and
gets to the point that Kingsley has been raising:
Is it possible to set up experiments in which
Family Planning, defined in this manner, is the
programmatic input in one place and some element of social change is the variable in another
place ---

Slobodkin: And a third one where both are being
used.

Segal: If you have that sort of proposition in mind,
of course, you ask if anyone has played around
with the idea. Lots of people have, but the
practical aspects of this sort of experimentation
are very difficult. They are probably not impossible.

Let me give you an example. An ideal place
probably for such an experiment would be a
rather small area where government cooperation really means the cooperation of one or two
people, and such a proposition was made for the

Barbados in the Caribbean. At the time, we were trying to develop a program for an outright Family Planning Program for Barbados. Incidentally, this was under the guise of a cervical smear cytology program for cancer detection— for various reasons. We wanted to learn something. It wasn't simply a disguise; we wanted to know if the propagandistic value of saying, "We are going to try to help you, to prevent you from getting cancer," would have some advantage in attracting people to Family Planning service. About the time that was being developed, a very intelligent plan by a couple of your countrymen, including David Glass, was proposed. This plan involved a system of social change, including legislative changes that would be antinatalistic, incentives of other economic sorts, and so on, that would tend to affect fertility.

I visited Barbados. Perhaps I was an ineffectual representative of this concept but the reception with which it was received, as far as having any practical implications, was terribly discouraging.

It may be that there are ways of doing this and if there are, I don't think that anyone who is a so-called Family Planner would shy away. No one who speaks seriously of Family Planning has ever thought of Family Planning instead of economic development and the kinds of things that lead to reduction in fertility, but one has to deal with the practicalities of the situation.

Ehrlich: Let me say that I really have nothing to

disagree with Ron Freedman about. Everything
he said is reasonable because, under certain
circumstances, a Family Planning Program will
bring down the birth rate. I think there is no
evidence that a determined program in India,
properly initiated, would necessarily fail. It
might very well succeed and it might fail. We
are in an area of doubt about what will happen in
South America, India, and so on.

I am not sure that other programs, if
Family Planners had started pushing different
programs twenty years ago, might not have got
further advanced today than we have. But that
is fruitless to discuss because we didn't start
anything else twenty years ago. But I am not
ready to say that Family Planning has not im-
peded other efforts. I think at a very super-
ficial level you can say that it has been used as
an excuse for pushing down abortion, and there
is some evidence that abortion can be very
effective. I believe the U.N.'s standard line
for putting in Family Planning Programs is that
they will be a weapon against abortion. Whether
or not it has been an effective weapon against
abortion, I don't know. I suspect it has in many
places.

Freedman: I might just interject that both in Taiwan
and Korea, there is no question about the fact
that illegal abortion has been an important
aspect of the program, because a large number
of people have given up contraception. When we
interview them and get a detailed fertility history,
it turns out that they are sufficiently motivated

that about 65-70 percent of the pregnancies that
they have, after once beginning in the program,
are aborted. So abortion probably has increased.

Ehrlich: That is cheering. I think, however, that the
major problem here is that it would be wrong to
look at Family Planning as sort of a winner in a
competition of various kinds of methods that have
been tried, whether or not they have been equally
pushed. Actually, Family Planning is not one
scientifically put-forward method, as you all
know; it is really an idea that has been pushed by
a social movement that started out under dramatically difficult circumstances. I am reminded of
the attitude of some people in family planning in
Planned Parenthood world population groups that
characterizes the first generation of people who
got evolution thoroughly accepted into schools.
They started at a time when this was a very
unacceptable idea. They fought tremendously
hard battles; they got a tremendous amount of
abuse; and they finally got evolution accepted.
It has become, fortunately I think, a "true"
dogma, but it has become one of the most dog-
matic areas of biology, and these same people
who brought this in have been responsible for
forming a very tight group and pushing this idea
very hard.
    The face of population control to a politician
or somebody in public life is represented by
Family Planning. Family planners have pushed
their idea very hard. I think this historical
development has limited our choices, whether
we like it or not.

When a country recognizes it has a population problem, it usually announces a Family Planning Program. It will then put a few teams in the field and that's that. It is my feeling, that whether or not the other methods have been tested, we ought to broaden the approach and start making a lot more noise about other possible methods.

Hoagland: What methods?

Ehrlich: I think there is a very big area of uncertainty. Let me say, however, that I am disappointed at the amount of reticence in trying other programs because we don't know what is going to happen, or because other programs are uncertain, or because they may have certain unfortunate social consequences or create certain difficulties in societies that are not ready for them, and so on. I don't understand this reticence when we are talking about programs, for instance, of establishing vast monocultures over most of India, where we already know the kinds of catastrophic results you can have from that.

In other words, this reticence is not in our general tinkering with the environment. In fact, we are very happy to go on with all kinds of programs with almost no long-range consideration of the consequences. I am not saying we should do automatically the same thing in these other areas, but I feel very strongly, that we can't afford to continue to put our major emphasis with the politicians in the form of Family Planning, particularly with the uncertainty that you bring up in the desperate areas of Latin America, much of

Africa, India, and so on. This does not mean that I am against Family Planning, because I think if there were no evidence of bringing down birth rates, I would think Family Planning is still valuable. If a woman is going to have fifteen children, it is better that she be able to have them in her own time, with her own timing and by her own choice. In other words, it is not a question of my being for or against Family Planning. It is a question of the posture that people interested in population control present to the world.

I feel that whatever direction population control goes in the world, we should be the leaders in it, for the reasons that (a) it is a place where those of us in this room can have some influence and contribution and (b) because we have got the resources. Also I feel very strongly that it does not behoove us to push for population control anywhere until we have faced our own serious problems at all levels. At one level contraceptives are not available readily to all citizens of the United States. At another level we don't have any governmental policies about our population size.

So, I feel the first and most dramatic order of business is for Americans to institute political action to get our government firmly in a position where it can say, when it tries to influence, in whatever way, the rest of the world, "We are doing it at home. We are not trying to outbreed you. We have recognized the seriousness of this problem. We have taken the following dramatic steps to handle our own population problem. Now we would like to ask you to do other things."

Now, what should be done in the rest of the world is a fantastically complex problem and I think all of us would agree that the solution will have to be different for each country. I notice that Dr. Berelson supports the idea of attempting communications, a greater effort at establishing a TV type of communication system to at least give us a channel of information for whatever kinds of information we want to feed into these populations. Attempting to raise the educational level is, of course, dramatically difficult when you have a rapidly rising population.

What else can be instituted, I think, may come out in discussion. Personnaly, I am disgusted by the possibility of having to consider some kind of "coercion", such as (when Chandrasekar) proposed compulsorily sterilizing Indians with more than three children; the possibility that we might have moved in with paramedical personnel, with helicopters, to help with the tremendous logistics problem which was immediately raised. I must say, however, presented with the possibility for disaster, I am not sure that a little bit of friendly coercion in this kind of area would not be better to letting events simply run their course. I would point out that the United States Government has not been at all reticent in applying coercion when it felt that its short-range political interests, rightly or wrongly, were at stake.

Bernstein: With brilliant success!

Ehrlich: You beat me to it. I think the issue that is
immediately raised, and one which ought to be
investigated, is whether or not that kind of support
would have worked. In other words, was there
some way in which we could have influenced the
Indian Government, for instance, to back
Chandrasekar. After all, it was an indigenous
idea; it was not something raised by somebody
outside the country. A politician in that country
put his neck on the line and got his head cut off,
obviously. But, it is conceivable to me (and I
may be naive) that the influence of a country,
which at the time was putting a very large amount
of effort into feeding that country, might have
helped Chandrasekar further down that road.

     I think that ends my speech, except I do want
some information from Dr. Freedman before I
leave. We heard earlier that it was impossible,
essentially, by incentives to keep the birth rate
up or down, and you said they had managed it
artificially in Japan before the war. How did they
manage it ?

Freedman: I didn't say they managed to keep it up or
down. What I was saying was that it was my interpretation, shared by some Japanese historians
and demographers, that the birth rate did not fall
before the war, when it should have, but that it was
held back.

Ehrlich: How was it held back, or how do you think it
was held back ?

Freedman: They had essentially a military government

and I think there was very strict legislation
against contraception, abortion, and so forth.
You couldn't import any information; Margaret
Sanger was kept out; and a whole series of things
like that, apart from all of the ideology which
went against it. There was actually specific
legislation against family planning. I think there
were other cultural factors.

Ehrlich: To argue against my own proposition, there
is, of course, the point that Japan's success with
abortion after the war is probably connected with
the fact that they were used to marching in lock
step when the orders came down, when the government influenced the ---

Freedman: You have it all wrong. The abortion program in Japan was adopted by the Diet as a result
of popular demand, as a result of the great up-
swing of illegal abortion.

Ehrlich: You think the government was not interfering?

Freedman: This was not a government program. It
was legalized. I would say this was the voice of
the people speaking under the new liberal regime.

Ehrlich: I gather that industry has pulled its support
out now in large part because they are afraid of
the cheap labor competition from Hong Kong, and
so on.

Freedman: Who has pulled out?

Ehrlich: The industrial support present at first has
    now been gradually withdrawn from the abortion
    program because there is concern ---

Freedman: My understanding is that abortion is still
    a "Blue Cross" benefit in Japan.

Ehrlich: I am speaking just of the support of the
    industrial companies that put money into the pro-
    gram.

Segal: There is no money in the program.

Davis: I wanted to make a suggestion in the handling
    of the discussion to keep two considerations
    separate: one is the possible effective policies
    with reference to population control and the other
    is the acceptability of such policies. If you get
    the two mixed up, I think each consideration
    interferes with the other. Somebody comes up
    with a suggestion of a policy that would be effec-
    tive if it were adopted. We then say straight off,
    that it is unacceptable. The question of acceptabil-
    ity in advance of trying something is extremely
    difficult to answer. Because the acceptability
    question is hard to answer, and may be wrong,
    it should not interfere with consideration of what
    policies would be effective if they were adopted.
    That is an independent intellectual consideration.
        A further reason, to me, for keeping those
    separate is that the argument and evidence about
    potentially effective policies is a part of what I
    consider an important aspect of this whole game,
    which is the intellectual aspect. I am dubious about

and I am uncomfortable by too much American effort abroad with reference to reproduction, or with reference to anything else, so far as that goes. I would rather see us make a convincing case about both the necessity for population control and about the potentially effective measures any official in a foreign country has ready at hand. There they are. He can then ask for technical assistance if he wants to, and the intellectual underpinnings are already there.

In the case of Latin America, for example, programs have been started when, in fact, the officials have not been thoroughly convinced of their case and they tend to run scared when opposition arises. We want them to be able to make a convincing case so that separating the question of acceptability from the question of effectiveness, if adopted, seems desireable for clarity in our discussion.

Michaelis: Let's come back to some basic things. Procreation is the individual's choice, regardless of his level of affluence—the one choice, I guess, the world over that any individual can make. If the national will in any country or region desires that birth rates shall be lowered drastically or quickly, intervention can generally occur only through incentives or penalties. Therefore, I am ruling out education because it may take too long.

Harkavy: As chairman, let me respond both to Kingsley and Mr. Michaelis points in the terms of the structure of the meeting. The topic of our agenda, "Can the social and political environment be manipulated?", refers to the range from positive incentives to lower fertility to negative sanctions. I hope this will be discussed from the point of view of feasibility, morality, and acceptability.

Hoagland: I want to comment on one point. About ten years ago Mr. Chagla, Ambassador from India, was very outspoken about the need for fertility control in India, saying on radio and television that India needs a safe, cheap, reliable oral contraceptive. He was very interested in the development of the so-called Pill, and when Pincus was in India, he interviewed Mr. Nehru and others in the government and they agreed that it was of great importance to see if the Pill would be useful in controlling population there. The manufacturer, the Searle Company, agreed to furnish enough pills to treat two million women indefinitely. This pleased everybody, but nothing happened.

Freedman: Did they really say indefinitely?

Hoagland: Pincus said so, but it may not have been indefinitely; it was a very long period of time. Nothing happened; various reasons were given that didn't seem adequate—but they didn't use the Pill.
     Only six months ago I talked with a person who had been in the Indian Department of Health at that time, who claimed the inside knowledge. He said that the reason the Pill hadn't been used was that if they had accepted them and treated

2 million people, the demand for a much larger
number of women to be treated would be so great
the government couldn't have afforded it.

Zuckerman: Until they were ready, they couldn't
handle the problem but now, of course, it is
national policy.

Segal: I just want to say that you are quoting a source
and there is no distortion of the facts as you know
them, Hudson, but I suggest that the interpretation of that particular incident is different from
other sources. I followed it closely, living in
India part of that time, and I was involved in some
of the discussion. I don't think it was because
they feared it would be a success. I think (quite
the contrary) there were grave doubts as to whether
it would be successful. They doubted if they had
the basis to go ahead in a system that was quite
different from the United States. If you remember,
for example, in the United States at the time, FDA
regulations stipulated a two-year limitation on the
span of use of an oral contraceptive. It was
several years later that that limitation was taken
off.
        The question of whether it should be used in
India under medical conditions were quite different.
Did they have enough information essentially to
use this method quite differently from the way it
is being used in the United States? In the United
States, even today, the oral contraceptive is a
prescription item with a package insert including
medical restrictions that are not feasible; so
India's dilemma in the early years with regard to
the oral contraceptive was understandable.

I might just also add that there were some
very sticky economic and political issues involved.
For example, Searle's offer was tied in with sending a man who turned out to be a swindler, who
brought with him a large supply of pills for study
and proceeded to sequester all of them under his
own personal control and doled them out on a
kickback basis. This became known to the Indian
Government, and had a terribly detrimental effect.
As a matter of fact, when the history of this is
written, I think the unfortunate, although well-
intended, efforts of the Searle Comapny in the
early years probably did a great deal to set back
the true evaluation of oral contraception in India.

Hoagland: I am very glad to hear this version and I
believe you are right. My informant was a person I met very casually and he said he had been
associated with the Department at the time and
this was his understanding.

Ehrlich: Was he responsible for the anti-IUD rumors
which apparently had some influence on the un-
acceptability of the other method ?

Segal: That was another episode that I am afraid
involved the same company.

Shelesnyak: It is important, however, so far as
political attitudes are concerned. I attended the
International Planned Parenthood Conference in
New Delhi in 1959. There was great fanfare.
Nehru opened the session. The main point that he
made as he welcomed all of us who were interested

in not having too many babies, was, "Don't you
come here and tell us about having too many
brown babies." That was the headline the next
morning.

Ritchie-Calder: I wanted to ask Paul Ehrlich what
alternative methods he has in mind.

Ehrlich: I think this is something that would vary from
place to place. One of them, of course, is making the attempt. I think we have learned a lot
about ways of handling media and educating people. This doesn't mean a five- or six-year education. It means opening new communication
channels to the people of the "other world". This
could have many simultaneous effects. It could
teach better methods of agriculture. It could lead
to general modernization and awareness of the
world situation. That is one of the things which
could accomplish a great deal, and accomplish it
at a cost of peanuts compared to other programs.

Ritchie-Calder: Are you proposing an alternative to
Family Planning?

Ehrlich: What I have written as a propagandist about
Family Planning has not been hedged the way I
would hedge statements made to a professional
group like this. Family Planning, as a movement, has not worked in the field of population
control and I see no reason to feel that it will.
This does not mean that it has not lowered birth
rates in some places. I think there is a sharp
distinction between lowering birth rates and

population control. In part, the difference involves
the time period. If I felt we had a hundred years,
we could go on with thirty more years of family
planning and if at that time birth rates and death
rates were roughly the same and we saw the trends
continuing, we could say fine, let's leave it at
that.

Ritchie-Calder: May I ask you, on the communications
side, what would happen if, in fact, you do not
promote the idea of family planning in India and
cannot move the people with the present methods?
You are creating a demand that nobody is going
to fulfill. You can raise the issues of population
control, but I haven't found any place in the world
where they are concerned about the global population problem, except in the highly sophisticated
countries.

Ehrlich: They are not even concerned enough in the
highly sophisticated countries. I watched carefully the year-end news round-up programs last
year, now nine months ago, in which all the
problems of the world were summarized by TV
reporters brought back to home base for round-
table discussions. I did not hear one mention of
population as a problem, and it really has not
been dealt with as any kind of issue at all in our
political campaigns.

In other words, I think we have a very serious
educational job in the developed world where we
already have the communications systems, where
we already have educated people, where in most
of the United States our overpopulation problems

are thrown back in the people's faces day after
day in terms of symptoms. We have not even been
able to get people to face, as Dr. Davis pointed
out, the necessity for including the desired size
of population in our planning.

Ritchie-Calder: I would like to come back to Kingsley
Davis' point and split these two things off and see
what we think is a population policy. I want to be
pro something. I don't want to be against the big
population, I want to be for a small population,
and then we have to make up our minds what, in
fact, the population policy is, not just that we are
"agin it," "agin" a large population.
    On the matter of acceptability I feel that,
basically, just as the matter of the schooling
problem and education that Professor Schultz was
talking about, it is making certain that there is
great understanding of the problem. It is a very
intimate problem. It is not something that goes
out on the Voice of America where you deplore or
encourage. In UNESCO at the next General Conference we are considering the question of a communications satellite and one of the purposes is to
promote understanding of Family Planning.

Ehrlich: One of the things that has not really been
tried is honest-to-God big economic incentives.
I would like to see some analyses of the cost of
increased population and of giving really big
economic incentives. I don't think the analyses
have even been considered.

Tax: Around this table we can obviously agree that we

want quick reduction of population growth. This is easy. And we could certainly agree, at the start at least, that we feel no government should encroach on the freedom of its own people to organize for the purpose of birth control by any methods. Beyond that, it is likely to be complex and instead of having these methods compete with one another, we can surely begin as we go over the biological and other things to be additive and to set up a mechanism by which you can discover which are the best in which places, or which are likely to be most effective.

From that point of view, I believe you could then get away from the ethical arguments, and so on, because that would be locally determined to some degree. You couldn't get anything done except if people want to do it and we don't have to worry about that. We would simply try to discover all the different ways that one might work in various places if one had the freedom in those places. You would try to get a great many ideas, biological and otherwise, and encourage working it out.

Harkavy: May we turn to the issues of birth control technology, its status today, and its prospects for the future. I have asked Shelly Segal to start. As Director of the Population Council's Bio-Medical Division, he has been in the forefront of these developments. The Council's Bio-Medical Division is now just about the only nonprofit institution in the world devoted to biological research for fertility control technology. I also salute the work of the Worcester Foundation in pioneering the Pill.

Segal: I am at somewhat a loss, because as the dis-
        cussion developed earlier I started to jot down an
        outline of how we might attack the subject of the
        biological aspects of fertility control, but the tenor
        of the discussion is so different from that of today,
        I find this outline a bit obsolete. I had listed such
        esoteric things as the evolutionary basis of fer-
        tility control, and so forth.

        Instead of doing that, I would like to be a
        little more pragmatic and give you essentially a
        progress report on where we stand in terms of
        available contraceptives, what the prospects are
        for the short range of new developments, and
        a two-bit crystal-ball look into the future.

        It might be useful to tell you what I think is
        the importance of this whole area of contraception
        from the biological, biomedical science point of
        view—where it really fits into the total scheme of
        population consideration. Let me take that last
        block that Ron Freedman had called fertility and
        redefine it: consider this block as the total num-
        ber of women in the world in the reproductive age
        group or the goal population for our purposes, and
        I think it would be fair to say that at the present
        time a rather small segment is using some means
        of fertility control, by will, to regulate the size
        and spacing of the family. So one simplistic way,
        perhaps, of defining our objective is to get this
        front moved so that all of the hundreds of millions
        of women in the reproductive age group are re-
        producing in a controlled fashion.

        There are various ways to get from here to
        there, but I think it is important to say that no
        matter what the indirect method, the method that

affects the intermediate variable group, eventually
the women must do it by either abstinence, contraception, abortion or sterilization. I don't
think there is any other way. Of course, abstinence has various sub-definitions, but there is
no other way, in my opinion, that this can be done
acceptably. I am excepting infanticide, homosex-
uality, sodomy, and that sort of thing.

Bernstein: Is there no possibility of actually changing the
size of the group? You define it as the group in the
child-bearing period. I have been led to understand
that there has been a very significant change, rather
short-run, in the onset of the menstrual cycle. Is
there no possibility of delaying the onset of the period
during which child-bearing is possible?

Segal: I would be able to subdivide one of my other
categories that way if you are going to use a
biological means to do it, but to save time I will
concede that that may be possible, although I don't
really see a practical method imminent.
        If I use this definition, if this seems to make
sense, I suggest that we can help move this front
forward by more effective utilization of the
available methods, by better organization to make
them available, by better motivational efforts to
make people want to use them, and so on. Even
if we do all that, we are going to be far short of
our objective.

Chamberlain: Shelly Segal, I am not quite clear what
your objective is. You speak about that front and
you are trying to move it to the other side. As I

listened to you, I thought you were saying that this is self-controlled by this population you are speaking of here which doesn't get really to the point that I think Kingsley Davis was making, and Paul Ehrlich was making, about social controls.

Segal: I will come to that in a moment.

Chamberlain: Is your goal, what you are trying for, self-control, self-limitation?

Segal: Yes. I think that if we stay still in this framework of voluntary adoption of the method to regulate birth, it would also be conceded that as we view the limitations of the existing methods to do this, we could carry this front still further by making available more readily adopted methods. That is to say, there are enough limitations with the existing methods to be a barrier to total achievement of the objective. This is the idea that I want to present, that I think it is a mistake for people to think simplistically about the panacea of a new method, that the new method is going to be the Pill or the IUD or the innoculation, that it is going to make all the other problems go away. I think this is ridiculous; we should not misinterpret the enthusiastic efforts to develop new contraceptive methods as being a program of greater priority than or more important than, or in place of all the other things that have emerged from this discussion. We are talking about a potential contribution to a segment of the total job. I felt that was important lest I be misinterpreted as trying to sell contraceptive development as the answer.

First, with regard to the existing methods, beginning with Gregory Pincus contraception was modernized by the attention paid to the endocrine aspects of the reproductive cycle. That doesn't mean there wasn't a great deal of research on reproduction endocrinology going on before that, but this was really the modernization of contraception in terms of applying modern scientific knowledge. Prior to the oral contraceptive, with the possible exception of the suggestion of the use of rhythm some twenty or thirty years before, all methods were based on the rather antique scientific fact that to prevent fertility or prevent pregnancy, you had to prevent sperm from meeting the egg. In the process of applying this principle, cultures all over the world and throughout history have tried to devise ways of preventing this, and the sperm has been confronted with an ingenious series of man-designed methods to prevent this—vulcanized roadblocks, lethal pools, and many things.

I think it was Margaret Mead who made the interesting anthropologic finding that even among Australian aboriginal societies, a method was designed to achieve this purpose, essentially, by means of a ritualistic operation which involved creating a fistula at the base of the penis to allow the semen to escape at the time of ejaculation. At micturition, the aperture was artificially closed as a flautist might do the same thing.

The oral contraceptives have now changed this. We no longer depend solely on preventing the sperm from making their ascent to the arena of fertilization. With the development of the oral

contraceptives, the combination of progestin and
estrogen, the attack is made at a critical point
in the reproductive chain of events necessary for
reproductive normalcy. Ovulation is suppressed.
At least that is the primary basis of the action of
hormonal contraception as now being used, although there are probably secondary effects as
well.

This method, first introduced in the late
1950s, has been very widely adopted, particularly
in the upper strata of societies all over the world.
I don't know the present estimate of oral contraceptive users but I guess it is somewhere between 12 and 15 million women.

It is also, I think, noteworthy that the impact
of the oral contraceptive in the less developed
countries and in the lower strata even in the United
States, has not been very great for whatever
reason, whether it be economic or poor decision-
making on the part of government. The intrauterine device came a few years later and, has been
used widely in developing countries and has cut
across the socio-economic scale. The estimated
use of intrauterine devices around the world is
somewhere between 5 and 7 million. There is a
great range here because figures for the United
States are hard to get.

These are the two modern methods that have
been applied to any large extent. There are
several others that I will come to in a moment
that are in some stage of experimentation, but
these are the two methods that have been widely
adopted in the context of recent national Family
Planning Programs and also on a private basis
in the higher segments of the economic society.

The fact is that there still are some serious questions about each of these methods and we cannot be complacent, thinking that these methods are now firmly entrenched. They will always be available, and anything that we do will be in addition to these. I think if Goodie Pincus were still with us, he would be the first to acknowledge that there are several difficult, unanswered questions about oral contraception. The burden of proof on those who view with alarm some potential hazards is a terrible burden. You cannot establish that proof exists; you can only point to the fact that there is evidence, which causes concern.

Let me cite a few things that people are continuously studying. The effect of continuous steriod administration on liver function has never really been established, particularly in cultures with a low nutritional level or with a high incidence of parasitic infestation as compared to the United States where these are not important factors. There is theoretical evidence to suggest that we must be concerned about it.

There are several studies indicating that there is a significant influence of hormonal contraception on what would be defined as the pre-diabetic or the creation of a pre-diabetic. There is a change in glucose tolerance and a change in circulating insulin levels and, incidentally, not in occasional cases. We are talking about 38 percent of the women showing changes in glucose tolerances that are reminiscent of the pre-pregnancy changes in a similar percentage of women in pregnancy.

The issue of cervical cytology and the development of pre-cancerous lesions of the

cervix has been with us since the onset because
of the large amount of experimental evidence in
monkeys (Sir Solly took part in this work) and in
mice (Lipschutz' work). There is early evidence
that there is something to be concerned about
here, and until now there have not been any meaningful studies on what is happening with long-term
use, although there is now some interest in this
subject.

So, we have some questions, and if one takes
a pessimistic view, one has to acknowledge the
fact that even oral contraception, as we now know
it, a very valuable tool, may not be available in
the unlimited distribution category for the long-
range future. To look at it another way, we can
say it is even not available by that definition today because, after all, in most countries where
it is widely used, like the United Kingdom and
the United States, it is a prescription item that
involves a great deal of medical surveillance if
it is to be used in the approved way.

Unless we are willing to say to other countries, "You can do with this method what we
would not do in our own country," then we have
got to accept the limitation of what this implies
for countries that do not have the medical system
to distribute the method the way we say it should
be used. There are countries, (apart from India
which was mentioned and where the story is very
complicated) that to this day, for reasons which
they consider to be medical reasons, have not
authorized the use of oral contraceptives.

The intrauterine device, like the oral
contraceptives, gives some degree of medical

anxiety. Again, as with oral contraception, the
possible long-term effect on the cervix cannot be
predicted. No one can state with impunity that
it will not cause histologic changes in the cervix
or the uterine wall, for that matter. This remains
to be seen. Here, the theoretical basics of experimental evidence is not quite as broad as in
the case of the use of estrogens, but until such
time as long-term followup studies are possible,
one cannot discount this possibility.

There is evidence that where there is a pre-
existing high incidence of pelvic inflammatory
disease, this may be exacerbated by the process
of inserting and using an intrauterine device.
This appears to be a very minor issue in terms of
actual risk percentage, but still it cannot be
discounted.

This is a rather pessimistic picture for you,
not because I am predicting that these things will
happen, that we will lose these methods, and not
because I am trying to build up a good case for
more funds for support on other methods, but
because I think you have to keep some of these
issues in mind in trying to understand why there
have been hesitancies in one quarter or another.
It hasn't been a simple matter of: here is a
method, let's use it. There are other considerations that are accounted for in trying to make this
decision.

As for other methods that appear to be
imminent, I think you can only put into that
classification things that are actually in some
state of clinical investigation at the present. It

seems unrealistic to assume that an idea, which
will involve a physiologic alteration that is
developed even today, will be available in two or
three years. I think there is an automatic lag
period of up to five years before the idea of today
or tomorrow will take form in a finalized product that can be distributed for mass use. There
is the question of toxicity studies, both in animals and in human subjects; the establishment of
biological effectiveness (although these two types
of study can go on concurrently), and the engineering problems of actual product development. This
can only be done when you know exactly what
dosage and what form of administration, and so
on. It is a time-consuming process.

There are several new developments now in
the stage of clinical investigation. In the field
of hormonal contraception, there is a completely
new concept in hormonal contraception now being
widely investigated. This is a hormonal contraceptive that eliminates the added estrogen
present in the conventional oral contraceptive and
reduces the progestin component (the other hormone in the mixture) to a small fraction of the
levels now being used. It is a new concept. It is
a new concept because it no longer requires
ovulation suppression as the basis for its activity.
It is an attempt to develop a hormonal contraceptive that works at some level peripheral to ovulation itself. Those of you who are not biologists,
this, essentially, is the simplified diagram. (At
blackboard) If that is the pituitary gland and this
is the ovary, here is the fallopian tube and uterus,
and the pituitary sits up here and is the target

for present hormonal contraception. The idea is to prevent the production of the protein hormone produced by the pituitary which is required in order for the ovary to develop an egg and to release it. It is an excellent spot to attack but it of course, also suppresses completely the cyclic activity of the ovary, so that this is obliterated and in its place is substituted an artificial cycle based on the cyclic nature of taking the Pill— twenty-one days on and a few days off, and so forth.

What is now involved is an attempt to do something much more focused, to allow the pituitary and the ovary to go through the normal monthly cycle but to prevent the series of events after ovulation and before implantation. Experiments reported recently (the first report was in 1965 by Rudell and his collaborators in Mexico City), have established that it is indeed possible to interfere with fertility in some undefined manner, but after ovulation, by the continuous administration of a very low dose of the progestin alone, a dose that will not inhibit the pituitary, that will not prevent ovulation, but which will prevent in most cases the normal subsequent events leading to implantation. This is called a continuous microdose progestin therapy.

At the present time, one such product is actually on the market in a limited geographic region. It is being test-marketed by the Syntex Company and its subsidiaries in France and North Africa, and the results are rather encouraging. It does not have the 100 percent theoretical effectiveness that one expects of the more drastic hormonal contraceptive, the Pill, but its pregnancy protection rate is rather high. The pregnancy rate with women on continuous oral progestin therapy is calculated to be somewhere in the neighborhood of 3.8 when given orally.

Slobodkin: Pardon me, what does that mean?

Segal: It means 3.8 pregnancies for 100 women using it.

Shelesnyak: What is the unprotected value?

Segal: It depends on the population. This would be roughly 70 or 80. It is a vast difference. This is compared to the intrauterine device which is about 2.5, and again there is some variation and some range of reporting, but it is at about that range.

    This is its use by oral administration, as tablets that are taken every day. In addition to chlormadinone acetate, which as I say is being used now on a commercial basis in France and North Africa. It is being tested in a number of other places, including many countries in South America and Asia as well as the United States; five other companies have introduced their own synthetic progestin for testing as a micro-dose contraceptive on this same principle. Megestrol acetate is one. It is a close chemical relative to the initial compound. This is a compound that has a joint licensing arrangement between a British drug house and the Mead Johnson Company in the United States. Incidentally, we at the Population

Council have acquired non-exclusive rights to this compound for use in governmental non-profit programs so that we feel unrestrained in whatever studies we want with it.

Another that is being studied in the same manner is norgestrol. These are all synthetic progestins. They are steroids. They are related to the progestins that are now involved in the conventional oral contraceptives.

Thyndiol is being tested. I have forgotten the other two, but there are six.

It looks as if the development of this continuous micro-dose progestin concept is providing a new type of oral contraceptive. It retains all the disadvantages, the logistical disadvantages of a pill-method; it requires the supplying of pills and the woman to take it every day. It has the additional disadvantage over the existing oral contraceptives in that one is working at a very carefully calibrated threshold of activity so that missing a pill now and then is going to be a much more serious matter than was the case in the conventional oral contraceptive where you could get away with a few days of pill-missing and still have a high level of protection. Also, the side effect with this is the interruption with the normalcy of the menstrual pattern. About 30 percent of the women who initiate this method have some complaint about the abnormalcy of pattern—either they are spotting sometime during the month or the menses is too scant or too heavy, or something or other.

So it is no panacea and it has problems. My own view is that it does not have major implications with respect to new methodologic advance for programs.

There has been one slight modification which has helped with regard to the cycle control problem, and that is to put the hormone in an oil suspension in a gelatin capsule rather than in a dry tablet, which apparently helps regulatize the daily absorption rate so that you don't get a lot of peaks and valleys in the blood curve and, therefore, you get a better level of cycle control. That however is sort of a pharmaceutical advance rather than an ideologic advance.

There is an advance that I think is a little more than just pharmaceutical preparation and that is the development of the concept that if this micro-dose principle works and gives you an antifertility effect based on the long-term administration of this drug orally, then we could administer it in some way that would give a long-term blood level but would not require daily pill-taking. Working on the hope of finding something that would do that, an interesting possibility has developed. There is a material that is a synthetic rubber, called Silastic, that is widely used in plastic surgery. It is known that this is acceptable for implantation under the skin in the human organism. There are literally thousands of cases, for example, of youngsters with hydrocephalus who have had Silastic valves inserted under the skull with tubes that drain either into the caval vein or through the diaphragm into the peritoneal cavity, some of these lasting for a long as twelve years. Histological studies have been done on the local tissue reaction to this subdermally implanted Silastic.

Restorative plastic surgery has been going on for about twelve or fifteen years using the same material, so we know it is acceptable for subdermal implantation. It causes virtually no local tissue reaction and, as far as carcinogenesis is concerned, one can only say that there is no evidence that it is a serious problem or any problem in this regard, but it would require long-term evaluation.

It has the interesting property that in its solid form it is something that looks and feels like a synthetic rubber. There is a solubility coefficient for a number of chemical substances, including steroids, so that steroids actually dissolve in the wall. (Drawing) Let us consider Silastic, one capsule with crystalline material in the lumen. A certain amount will dissolve into the Silastic wall until saturation is reached. Once the wall of the capsule is saturated the release rate from the Silastic wall into the body fluid will be dependent on the differential solubility in the surrounding body fluid as compared to the Silastic itself. This is a two-phase system.

You have a reservoir in the capsule constantly replacing that crystalline material to maintain saturation of the wall; and release at the outside face surface. This means that one may expect to achieve a constant release rate over a long period of time. This differs, from release rate from an implanted pellet. Hormonal pellets have been available for years. Over a period of weeks or months the pellet gets progressively smaller and the release rate declines. The Silastic implant has more linear secretion for the major part of its life-span.

All of the biological work has been done to establish the necessary facts about the biological activity in animals, the release rate. All of this has been done in vitro. The release rates have been worked out, so that we have now established the geometry of the size pellet with the particular hormone that will give a daily release rate for a period of time. This could be as long as a thousand days, at a level that should give an antifertility effect in the human female based on what we know about the oral dose that has been used for a long time now in women. All of this has been done, and, in fact, the most preliminary clinical trials have been initiated by colleagues in Brazil and Chile. We have learned enough about the activity in the human to be rather optimistic. It is not fair to say that any of the serious questions about human applications have been answered. We are just at the point of having an opportunity to do studies along that line.

This, then, is another line of investigation that is being attempted.

Schultz: What would it cost, Shelly?

Segal: The actual cost has not yet been worked out. The amount of hormone involved is negligible so you can forget the cost of the hormone. We are talking about the release for megestrol acetate, for example, of 35 to 50 micrograms per day. In terms of cost, you can just forget it.

I don't know yet the cost of the Silastic. What we are using so far is experimental material that has been provided gratis. We have had some

negotiations with the Dow-Corning Company that
controls this material and my guess is that it
could not be, for an implant that will last for
three to five years, more than 50 cents, and it
could be as low as 5 cents.

Davis: The real cost is medical labor.

Segal: Yes, that is where the real cost is. As I have
pointed out for some of the other possibilities,
there are great disadvantages to this, too. As
of now, the great disadvantage is the requirement
of some kind of medical establishment or para-
medically trained people to do the insertion.

What you do after the period of use remains
unanswered. Do you just leave the capsule in
and forget about it; if a woman wants another five
years' worth she puts in another one. Or do you
have to remove it surgically? As a matter of
fact, the question of how long it would last is
open. With this particular compound, megestrol
acetate, and the particular material, Silastic,
which is dimethylpolysiloxane, the release rates
are such that a three to five-year period is about
as practical as one can get, considering the
spatial relationships.

The solubility characteristics of other poly-
mers are different, so that if it is not dimethyl,
diethyl or dipropyl might have different release
rates. Norgestrol, we know, has a different level
of activity. Norgestrol is a terribly interesting
compound because 60-70 micrograms a day taken
orally is all that is required to get this micro-
dose antifertility in the human female. We know

from our various biological studies that the continuous release over a 24-hour period through this
capsule implant procedure—sort of an infusion
method—cuts to one-tenth the requirement of oral
dosing to get the same biological effect. When I
said before that our capsule release is 35 to 50
micrograms per day, this isn't an accident. We
wanted this because we knew that in the human
female you can get an antifertility effect by oral
administration at a dose level of 350-500 micrograms. We knew from a rather extensive series
of animal studies that the dose relationship for a
comparable biological effect was 10:1—and we
used several biological parameters—by the oral
route as compared to the implant route of administration, was 10:1, so this is what led us to this
kind of a release brake requirement.

Similarly, when you think about the norgestrol
with an oral activity of 50-70 micrograms, this
means you are talking potentially about (it would
have to be studied out) 5 to 7.5 micrograms per
day being released in order to get the same kind
of biological effect. That gives you a completely
different spatial requirement. One could then
work toward an implant much smaller, or the
same size with a much larger life span, because
there is more space for storage and all of that.

Hoagland: Shelly, I didn't hear you say how large the
implant is.

Segal: The implant is 1.5 centimeters in length and
something under 2 mm. in diameter, which makes
it possible to insert it through a 12 gauge needle.

Davis: You don't think the woman could insert it her-
     self?

Segal: I don't know. I think that the mechanism of
     supply and distribution has to be looked at.

Ehrlich: Paramedical personnel could be trained to
     do this.

Shelesnyak: Is it subcutaneous or intramuscular?

Segal: Subcutaneous. There is a difference in the
     absorption rate between subcutaneous and intra-
     muscular which has to do with this phase of the
     system, the differential solubility here, but at
     present we are working on subcutaneous.

Fisher: Where is it implanted, again?

Segal: I think that doesn't make much difference. We
     have found that regardless of where you put it in,
     in the neck, back, rump, it doesn't matter; so
     you can have a certain amount of individual pref-
     erence. The early clinical trials are not de-
     signed to teach us that. The early clinical trials
     are on women from whom it will be removed after
     we have gotten the information required. In these
     women it has been placed here in the forearm so
     that the surgeon is certain that he won't have any
     difficulty in finding it after the six months' or
     nine months' period.

Zuckerman: May I ask a technical question about dose
     levels and daily absorption rate? In the case of

implants of crystals and pellets, some thirty years
back, we estimated the rate of absorption by
weighing pellets removed at various times. I
understand that you are talking about three-to-
five-year lifetime of these various capsules.

Segal: Right.

Zuckerman: Since the date here is 1967 in your paper,
how did you estimate these various rates ?

Segal: There are two ways. One is by setting up a
series of implants with radioactively labeled
steroid and then doing evaluations of the amount
released of the radioactivity in vitro into a physiological water bath in which the ambient fluid
was physiological under temperature conditions
or control. Periodically over a several-month
period, 24-hour release rates are measured to
establish the level of the curve. At the end of a
six-month period, or whatever it was, the remaining radioactivity is measured to check with
the daily release rate observed at periodic intervals.

Shelesnyak: Are all these measurements made only
in vitro ?

Segal: That is in vitro. There are other physiological
studies in the rat that have gone on over as long
as two years, with estrogen in this case, because
it was an easy end point to establish. In cas-
trated female rats it is just simply following how
long it will maintain the vaginal cornification over

a two-year period and at the end of that time removing the capsule and seeing how much hormone
was left so that one could project how much longer
it would go if the animal's life-span were to continue.

We have been getting to a progestational end
point in the rabbit. We have been able to maintain
for fifteen months now the progestational endometrium of an estrogen-primed ovariectomized
animal with nothing more than the implant at a
properly adjusted release rate. Periodically,
animals have been sacrificed and the amount of
remaining hormone was weighed so that one could
project how long it would have lasted.

That is where we stand with the implant. The
major questions remain to be answered but I have
no warning signals, as yet, that anything will go
wrong.

Others are investigating other types of contraceptive developments. You may have heard
about a long-term injectible, that is, a depot injection of a large amount of progestational agent
that is then released from the site of injection
over a rather extended period of time, which
depends on how much is injected primarily. One
of these preparations is provara, a hydroxy pro-
gesterone acetate. This compound at 150 mg, a
different level now) in micro-crystalline supension
(injected intramuscularly) will last, absorbed from
the injection site, for about a three-month period.
This is really ovulation suppression therapy. In this
case, the effort is to get enough hormone absorbed
from the depot injection site daily for a three-month
period to suppress the pituitary, prevent ovulation,

and not worry that you get amenorrhea as a result of it, which apparently is not a serious
problem for many women.

A larger dose, like 400 mg. injection, in a
1 cc. depot injection, will last for six months or
slightly longer; and again by suppressing the
pituitary for six months will give an antifertility
effect for as long as that depot site remains active.

This method has problems. It has been rather
widely tested. In many countries, studies have
been made on thousands of women. Some of the
studies have been carefully examined; most, however, have not. The main problem is the uterine
bleeding. A completely chaotic pattern of bleeding is being created. No one can predict whether
a woman will bleed more or less continuously,
will spot, or will have amenorrhea. It is a rather
chaotic pattern and I am astounded frankly that
women will put up with it to the extent that they
do, according to some reports.

This pattern is a great problem as indicated
by even the most enthusiastic proponents of this
depot injection are giving monthly supplementary
estrogen therapy to control the bleeding. So I
really am not too enthusiastic about it. Once you
do that, you lose the simplicity of the method.

Ehrlich: With all the tremendous advances that are
being made with micro-encapsulation, is anybody
looking into getting linear release, or even inter-
rupted release by the proper mix of capsules?

Segal: Yes, some sort of a micro-spansule principle.
It has been investigated and one pharmaceutical

engineering firm come up with a contract for a micro-encapsulation procedure that will give this without the need for the capsule. But, it has been hard to do, I must say. We made a several attempts in our own lab; we designed one, a pressure cooker, that will explode a mixture of cholesterol and the hormone in melted form into a huge plastic bag, and then we took the little recovered globules and tried to size them out to get a range from tiny to extremely tiny, but this was difficult.

Unless I have overlooked anything, that is about as far as I can go with studies of the physiological means actually in clinical investigation.

Taylor: You haven't mentioned male contraceptives.

Segal: Presently there is no male contraceptive under serious clinical investigation.

Michaelis: Why is that?

Segal: I am coming to various possibilities now.

Zuckerman: Before you get into other possibilities, some of the things you referred to in the background paper were about possible suppressants of the hypothalamus and pituitary, which are in the distant future. I would like to hear what you have to say on the issue of lag periods. You said about five years is the lag period for these particular things.

Segal: I should qualify it. If we are interested in a

method in America and perhaps also in the United
Kingdom, that will be developed under the necessary regulations and sanctions of the regulatory
agencies, the FDA and ---

Zuckerman: My point is quite different, because the
lag period has been over thirty years for the
development about which you are talking. As far
as general principles are concerned, both the suppression of ovulation and the transformation of the
uterine environment have been known since I was
a student. Suppression of the primate ovary was
achieved in the early thirties, and I remember
publishing a paper in the Lancet showing that it
could be done with androgens as well as progestins
(those were the days before the oral steriods) but
everyone felt they were coming—but certainly the
experiments were in the days of the pellet. I
remember indicating that here was a way of suppressing the human ovary, but warning against
its use, because of side effects—such as growing
a beard.

The problem of contraception wasn't my main
interest. I was trying to derive a general theory
about the histogenesis of tissues which are responsive to steroids. I was concerned with a
basic scientific question. My observation about
the suppression of the ovary was a practical by-
product. But the practical byproduct was there
in the same way as was the Grafenberg ring in
1930, which stimulated the same kind of interest.
At a time when interest in the Family Planning
movement wasn't as strong as it is now, these
contraceptive measures interested the upper

classes. When I first heard of the Grafenberg
ring, it was certainly in relation to its use in the
higher income brackets.

But it has taken thirty years since then, in
spite of the availability of knowledge, to get to
the present stage of development. All the refine-
ments about which you have been talking are, in
fact, not changes in fundamental scientific knowledge but improvements in the exploitation of what
we knew. What, for example, is the difference
between Whittle's first jet engine and the advanced
jet engine you find in use today? The basic
principles are the same, and yet it has taken all
this time to produce today's engines. I would like
to know, since I do not believe that one can reduce
the time lag for introducing things that have not
been devised and where even the physiological
principles are in dispute, how we can speed up the
process of application of what is known. It doesn't
seem to me worthwhile, at a meeting of this kind,
to discuss matters which are not on the table, in
the pipeline, where there is uncertainty and lack
of assurance about the basic knowledge. To me
these things do not make up an exciting story.

Segal: I think your comments lead to what I am attempting to get to now, that is, those things on which
there is general scientific agreement. There are
certain principles established as to their possible
development into a contraceptive methodologic
advance. How do we speed up that process? These
things are already being evaluated clinically.
They could be accelerated, perhaps by months,
a year or so, by a greater concentration of effort.

When we talk, as we will now, about such
things as the development of compounds that will
maintain the <u>corpus luteum</u>, or things that may
influence the receptivity of the endometrium for
nidation by hormonal means, I think we are discussing a broad period of investigation, and we
don't get from there to the possible application of
these principles.

Zuckerman: It is more than that. Many of the things
that you are speaking about are in such dispute
that, frankly, I would not accept them as being
even quasi-established.

The business of interfering with the receptivity
of the endometrium is something which is very
important and it is possible, as I think you indicate in your background paper, that your new
micro-dose therapy does disrupt the preparation
of the endometrium for nidation.

I assume that developments would occur in
that field. For example, my understanding is
that the IUD does not have its effect by accelerating the transport of the ovum down the fallopian
tube. I think that has definitely been shown not
to be the case. In the experiments that I have
gone into, and the results that I have seen, seem to
to show that IUD's affect the endometrial environment in some unknown way.

I suggest that here is a new field for experimentation: What are the factors that are respons-
sible—as you say, ovulation is not affected by
your micro-doses, so the effect must be distal
to the ovaries. The changes might be tubal; they
might be endometrial. With IUD, the clinical

change is endometrial.   Here is an area for a lot
of basic research.

(The conference recessed at twelve-forty
o'clock.)

SUNDAY AFTERNOON SESSION
September 29, 1968

The conference reconvened at two-five o'clock,
Dr. Harkavy presiding.

Harkavy: Let me propose the afternoon's business.
Shelly Segal will finish. He will be followed by
Shelly Shelesnyak. We shall then go on to questions of population policy, the guts of the meeting.
Merton Bernstein and Lyle Saunders will speak
on these.
I am wondering if we can then come back to
such "minor" matters, ecology and the quality of
life, on Monday morning. Sir Solly will then
summarize, and we will be finished.
Shelly, will you continue.

Segal: I have told you where we stand with existing
methods and outlined those procedures that are in
some stage of clinical evaluation. When we get
beyond that, we get into a broad spectrum of
possibilities, the likelihood of which depends upon
our particular scientific faith. There are some
possible items given assumptions that not everyone agrees to. This means that since these
assumptions are not generally acceptable, there
is also a great deal of work needed on basic

289

points to reach a point of general scientific acceptance as to where to go ahead. For example, there
is the question of capacitation, a term introduced
by Austin and Chang some years ago, suggesting
that before sperm can actually fertilize ova in the
female tract, they have to undergo a subtle and,
as yet, ill-defined final maturation stage in the
female tract which endows them with the ultimate
fertilizing capacity. Thus, the word "capacitation."

From a theoretical point of view, it would
seem ideal to go ahead and try to find out what
the capacitation factor is and attempt to interfere
with it. Indeed, I do think that is a worthwhile
thing for scientists to be investigating. Many
are. But at the same time, there still is disagreement as to whether capacitation is a definable
phenomenon, and there is conflicting evidence,
depending on which species is looked at. So, there,
a lot of basic work is needed.

Similarly, one possible basis for an after-
the-fact contraceptive which could be taken once
a month, or whenever a fertile cycle is expected,
is the interference with the function of the corpus
luteum. It has been established in all species
studied that the early function of the corpora
lutea is essential for the initiation of a nidation
process. Yet there is still disagreement among
biologists as to whether the uterus normally
produces a substance that interacts with the ovary
to maintain corpus luteum function. A lot of work
is necessary at this level to get some agreement.

I am not going to try to outline the great
number of potential leads along this line. I only

want to make a general comment about this.   As
I survey the activities, one thing is clear: almost
all attempts to carry research, from our present
stage of knowledge to ultimate application in terms
of contraceptive methodology, can be defined as
attempts to interrupt a known or suspected endocrine link in the reproductive chain of events.
That is to say, you can limit, almost to the
exclusion of all others, one subspecializing group
of biological scientists in whose hands has fallen
the almost complete responsibility for developing
new contraceptive methodology.   At the recent
International Congress of Endocrinology, I posed
this issue to the endocrinologists: this is a highly
responsible challenge that has been put in their
hands; that without the efforts of endocrinologists,
there is really very little else going on.   This is
a shame.   I don't think we have found a way of
involving the scientific talents and interests of
other biological scientists—as well as scientists
in other aspects of activity.   There are isolated
exceptions.

Hogan: Shelly, may I ask what is the status of reversibility of vasectomy. Is there any progress here,
because this is a remarkably efficient way to
control population if sterilization is accepted and
if it were possible to reverse it. If this could be
reversed, it seems to me it would make its
acceptability very much greater. I keep hearing
very different stories about that.

Segal: There are a handful of people who are working
toward this objective. There are three approaches.

One way is to develop a temporary tubal occlusion instead of a separation by surgery of the vas. Attempts to do this have included the use of such things as the Silastic we were talking about in the liquid form, which is a body-temperature-vulcanizing variety. If it is injected in a liquid form, it then vulcanizes into a more-or-less-pliable, but solid, plug. Several have attempted this in animals. One group has tried a few human subjects, and it doesn't look as if it is a simple, easy-to-finalize kind of project. There are all kinds of secondary problems.

The second way is to try simplifying the surgical procedure to increase the changes for reversibility. There are several projects afoot but it is hard to say what will emerge.

I think the idea that you can technically simplify this operation and make a great advance in that direction may be overstated from time to time. It is a simple operation as it is, and I cannot envisage now a procedure that would be simplified to the extent of not requiring an incision in the scrotum. In the human, the spermatic artery and the vas run side by side and even by palpation it is hard to define each separately.

The third type of experimentation along this line is being done by one or two men, only. In particular, Dr. Lee in Korea, is attempting to confirm, in humans, experiments he has done in animals on the antifertility effect of the presence of a foreign body that does not necessarily occlude the duct in the vas deferans, but it is not too much of a variation.

Ritchie-Calder: Shelly, what is the position on the
    immunological approach?

Segal: As you know, there has been a lot of talk about
    a possible inoculation of some sort to impart
    infertility, either permanently or for a long period
    of time. The problem here is to identify the
    particular antigen that will be used. There has
    been an effort to extract from either spermatozoa
    or from the testis tissue itself a specific tissue
    antigen that would not cross-react with any of the
    other tissue antigens of the body—as this, of
    course, would be unacceptable—but would in the
    male immunize against the particular protein
    involved so that spermatogenesis would be inter-
    fered with, or, in the female, cause the formation
    of antibodies that would somehow interact with the
    deposited spermatozoa on the surface and render
    them incapable to fertilize.
        There are some serious immunologic ques-
    tions in this approach. It has not been established
    that there are such tissue-specific antigens that
    can be extracted from testis or spermatozoa that
    will not cross-react with other tissues. There
    have been attempts to purify testis extracts that
    can be used for immunization, but even the most
    highly purified ones cross-react with other tissues,
    and this essentially would be the same as setting
    up an auto-immune disease process. One of the
    tissues that the most purified testis extracts
    cross-react with now is the brain. So, it is a
    problem.
        Other sources of antigen are being sought.
    In our lab we have done (lots of other people have,

too) experiments with highly purified gonadotro-
phic hormones, the hormones from the pituitary
that actually control the function of the gonads,
the testis or the ovary. But these have never
really been fully purified, so it is difficult to get
an immunologic effect that influences only gammete
production of the gonad and not hormone production, and once you do that you have the whole
balance fouled up.

There are a few other sources of antigens
that are being investigated and I think these are
in a preliminary stage of development. In this
connection, Dr. Kenneth Laurence has, I think,
made an interesting discovery in working with
specific iso-enzymes involved in steroid production. The step for the conversion of a precursor
pregnenolone, an essential hormone for the initiation and maintenance of pregnancy, requires a
particular enzyme. This enzyme is produced not
only by the ovary but also by the placenta and the
adrenal. It wouldn't do you any good to immunize
a human organism against that particular enzyme
if it would also interfere with the life-supporting
adrenal function. But it appears that even though
it is the same enzyme in terms of its function—
it is iso-enzymic—it is slightly different
chemically from the one that is produced in the
adrenal. This may be a basis for specific immunization that would interfere with specifically the
function of the ovary and not the adrenal.

Fishman in Boston and several others have
now shown that some of the omnipresent enzymes
that are produced by many tissues (also by the
early placenta) appear to be somewhat different

when they are produced by the early placenta.
Alkaline phosphatase, which is a very important
enzyme for a lot of body functions and wouldn't
ordinarily be thought of as having any specificity
in the reproductive process, now appears to be
iso-enzymic again for the early placenta, and it
might be possible to get it into this whole area of
specific iso-enzymes as a source of antigen. But,
this is in a very early stage and there is not much
that one can project about future possibilities.

Zuckerman: Earlier you were asked a question on
the duration of reproductive life in the female;
you indicated that this is a subject about which
very little is known. I am wondering whether it
is worth pursuing as a possible area of experimentation. It is known that about the time the
female ovary stops liberating oocytes, the meno-
pause ensues. The question is whether or not one
could, by some treatment, reduce the stock of
oocytes at an early age to a point that you restrict
the period of the reproductive life of the female.
One way I know of doing it in rats, is not a good
way. It is the simple process of irradiation.
That is obviously not the way to deal with human
beings. We have not followed it up from the point
of view of radiation but isn't there some radio-
mimmetic drug not as dangerous as beamed
energy that might have this effect?

We know, too, that the male ejaculate has to
have a certain chemical constitution in order to
work. I wonder whether or not one couldn't
reduce or change the activity of the seminal tubules
or accessory reproductive organs without, as it

were, completely stopping their function. You
would be reducing the period, in the case of the
female, within which conception is possible; and
in the case of the male you would reduce the
changes of conception.

Shelesnyak: I would like to introduce in my comments
some of these other possibilities, and this is one
of the types of things, and also elaborate somewhat on the immunological aspects.

Segal: If it will introduce that broader subject, I
think all would agree that until now, any experimental evidence along this line has not been
discarded because of a personal bias with respect
to acceptability or feasibility, but there have been
problems with the leads that have developed until
now. For example, the radio-emetic drugs are
terribly toxic, the ones that until now have been
developed. Radiation itself, of course, has a
lot of generalized problems.
    With respect to preventing the onset of puberty:
You can prevent this in a laboratory animal but
you do it by a way that in a large portion of the
animals it not only delays but actually prevents it.
The administration of steroids in the neonatal
period on a dosage base phenomenon can in some
animals delay and interrupt the normalcy of
ovulation. In others, however, it prevents it
completely, so that no one has ever sorted out
a way to bring this under control as you have
suggested, which is not a bad way.
    Shelesnyak will talk about the possibilities
for not worrying so much about the onset and the

termination of menstrual patterns but their length.
Why not a six-month cycle instead of a
one-month or twenty-eight-day cycle? I think he
will talk about that.

One more word about the male. In looking
for something that might be an effective contraceptive method by immunologic means in the male,
for a long time we have concentrated on spermatogenesis itself, stopping or reducing spermatogenesis. This is fine, but I think that we must
accept in this approach the need for a rather long
period of investigation before anyone could reasonably suggest clinical application, because we know
from experiments by Austin and others that
spermatozoa are not necessarily good or bad.
It is not an all-or-nothing effect, for there are
various stages, and if one starts fooling around
with the spermatogenic process, you must always
be certain that you are not interrupting the sperm
production in such a manner that some sperm are
being produced which, while having the capacity to
fertilize, are abnormal enough to cause embryonic
abnormalities as a result of the male genetic input.
This is, I think, a very serious consideration in
attempting to develop and evaluate agents that
affect spermatogenesis per se.

There are other possibilities that would not
interfere with the miotic process or the process
of sperm formation from the germ cells while
attempting to interfere with the fertilizing capacity already-produced and now-stored spermatozoa
in either the epididymis or as they are a part of
the ejaculate. There is a very complex chemistry
to the seminal fluid. We don't fully understand

what all the components are there for, but it seems
a reasonable postulate that some interference with
the normal biochemical constitution of the fluids
in which the sperm find themselves at different
stages could prevent them from ultimately obtain-
ing a fertilizing capacity. Work along this line
should be encouraged and there is some effort, but
at the moment there is no particular item that I
could single out and say that it is getting someplace.

Zuckerman: Just to rise to what you said, the French
authorities before the first World War carried out
an inquiry into infertility in sailors on battleships
due to heating of the testicles.

Harkavy: John Rock, as a matter of fact, has been
experimenting this way with what is known, of
course, as a Rock strap. Doctor Shelesnyak says
that he is "not responsible" and therefore can
range widely over a series of more "way-out"
possibilities on fertility control.

Shelesnyak: He knows and I know. Perhaps I should
elaborate. I have no programmatic responsibili-
ties in carrying out birth control processes or
supporting projects, but I think one thing should
be clear—at least it is clear to me—that there are
two distinct approaches. One is the family unit,
the individual birth control of the family planning,
and the other is fertility control as a public health
measure which involves some other approaches;
that is, the one is an effort by which we attempt
to achieve, first of all, individual selection but an

all-or-none phenomenon. We don't want any babies, not that you don't want 20 percent less; you just want a method or system whereby you have no children except when you want them.

In this area, there is no latitude for error. Ordinarily, pharmaceutical chemists and most practitioners are permitted latitude for error when designing or using therapeutic measures. Total effectiveness is not required; side effects are tolerated.

When it comes to birth control techniques, if there is a failure, the technique is in serious disrepute. The technique must be perfect with no secondary actions. The science and technology for attempting to depress fertility is, I think, an area where the scientist should be encouraged to focus his research. The sociologists and the politicians are going to have a tough time putting across this approach, that is, general depression of fertility. We are even less advanced in this than ten years ago. At all Family Planning meetings on birth control, someone would turn to us and say, "Well, Doctor, let's assume that tomorrow everybody agreed to birth control. What could you offer?" We would probably mutter and sputter, "Well, there really isn't much we could do except mechanical sperm blockers."

If we do convince the community to accept a, say 50 percent, depression of fertility, it simply means that all of us will have to try harder. Nevertheless, there will be no interference in the individual's choice beyond that of trying harder.

Yet, if we turn to the biologist, the fact is that no one, so far as I know, (and, Shelly, correct

me if I am wrong) is attempting to study or to
explore techniques or methods to depress fertility
per se.

Slobodkin: Are you referring to fluoridated water and
that kind of thing?

Shelesnyak: I am talking about any biochemical, any
pharmacologic agent, or any stress factor, anything that can be presented to the community at
large, without their participation.

Slobodkin: Or knowledge?

Ehrlich: Either way.

Shelesnyak: Without their participation. We have as
yet no substance, no approach; but it is more
serious that we have no concerted effort at exploring either methods or even fundamental physiological processes that would be most amenable
to that attack. Shelly Segal has been talking about
a focused attention on a very limited and specific
site, or two sites, in the whole range of reproductive processes: ovulation suppressors, sperm
blockers, and perhaps some interference in
transport mechanisms; and with essentially the
same substance or class of substance, steroids.
Perhaps we could also add hormones.
    The IUCD is an historical accident. We don't
know how it works; that does not matter. But
these are the only two things. As for more
generalized approaches, the subjects are areas
in which the investigators' biologists aren't even

encouraged or stimulated. I addressed the 24th International Congress of Physiological Sciences in Washington on this problem—only because I fussed to friends when I saw the original program four years earlier, noting that they had paid no attention to reproductive biology. They had a symposium on lactation. As a result of my comments, I was invited to talk about the needs concerning reproductive biology. In this area, physiologists, collectively, are relatively un-concerned.

Engineers, psychologists, sociologists, even biologists themselves, so far as I am concerned, have not been as effective or interested in this field as they should be.

There are other areas certainly which war-rant exploration. I agree with Sir Solly that there is a time lag, whether it is five or thirty years. The fact still is that each time lag is at a zero starting point, and in some of these things we haven't reached the zero starting point yet.

Incidentally, there are other immunological approaches that can be explored on the basis of understanding immunological factors of progesta-tion. At any rate, it seems to me and my Rehovoth group that implantation involves an immunological mechanism; the existence of any immunological mechanism offers a possibility for an immunological blocking mechanism.

May I invite your attention to the fact that, as fundamental and interesting a phenomenon as it is, the sex drive hasn't been given enough serious study and attention. It may be an approach to fertility control if we can modify it.

Ehrlich: Air pollution may help that.

Shelesnyak: Larry asked me about something like fluoridated water. The problem of putting something in the water supply is of great magnitude, even if you have it, for you must remind yourself that even in the United States only about 40 percent of the water supply is piped. In other words, you must have centralized sources of distribution.

As far as food is concerned, you have the same problem, and then someone suggests, "Why don't you put it in salt?" That's fine if you have a substance that has a range of effectiveness from nannograms to micrograms and everyone gets a common source of supply. There are people who use just a little bit of salt and some people who use a tremendous amount. There is a distribution problem.

Ehrlich: You have children in both sexes and farm animals to watch out for.

Shelesnyak: That is right. In considering its suppression, one must recognize that fertility is a product of both male and female. Methods should act on either sex or on both sexes.

One other point. We know that stresses interfere even with menstrual patterns, certainly with ovulation, and with activities in the male. It is quite possible, judging from experiments, with animals that sound and various odoriferous substances influence both implantation and ovulation— in rats, at any rate. We should make some effort at exploring the possibility of using these.

If we can generate enough interest and stimulate enough activity in the investigation of possible fertility control methods, we ,will get out of our endocrinology rut. Better, perhaps, than getting out of the endocrinology rut would be broadening the base. This would be a real contribution. In this respect, I think we have not used enough of the technology or spinoff from aerospace studies and from electronics.

Let me take an example: a pre-ovulation sensor. There is an interesting aberration in some primates, including man, with respect to sexual patterns. In most mammals, the female is receptive to the male only at specific, limited times—a time that is associated with ovulation and high potential fertility. It is interesting that both the female and the male, somehow, get the message prior to actual ovulation. They are aware of this before ovulation takes place. In some instances, they are triggered. This means that something is going on in the female that is transmitted to the male in most mammals.

I think there is a possibility that an evolutionary vestige exists in man. As a matter of fact, certain things do take place, whether we can detect them or not. With the proper instrumentation, then a warning, 24 hours or "x" number of hours before ovulation, will solve the Catholic Church problem.

Slobodkin: You can imagine a perfume that changes odor.

Shelesnyak: I don't want to try to solve the problem here; I just want to raise the question. Perfumes

obviously are used on the positive side of this.
There are undoubtedly mechanisms on the negative
side, not necessarily repressive—just suppressing.
I mean something which turns you to reading
rather than writhing. On that note, I think I
should stop.

Harkavy: I have taken a chairman's prerogative to go
up and draw something on the blackboard which I
think will be a connecting link between this interesting biological interlude and the questions of
population policy. This presentation was originally
proposed by Barney Berelson.

If we put the number of acceptors of a given
method of fertility control on the horizontal axis
and their degree of motivation on the vertical
axis, we draw a curve that illustrates the obvious
proposition: if people are highly motivated, there
will be many acceptors. But we can shift this
demand curve, to use the economist's expression,
by offering a better contraceptive. We should
have more acceptors with a given level of motivation.

This demand-schedule concept is, to my way
of thinking, an answer to the argument that motivation is the key. Highly motivated people will
even use poor contraceptives. But less highly
motivated people—the condition of most in the
developing world—will be more likely to use contraceptives if they are effective and easy to use.

While we encourage work on all aspects of
improving family planning and shall explore the
area "beyond family planning," we believe that the
most important contribution our Foundation can

make is to encourage the development of new contraceptive methods. This is a field that is very
poorly supported. We have calculated that,
including research by drug firms, there might be
$25 or $30 million a year going into all aspects of
contraceptive development.

Zuckerman: This is worldwide?

Harkavy: Yes, worldwide. This is a very generous
     estimate, because we are including in this total
     basic research and training of people who are
     engaged in aspects of reproductive biology that
     may be relevant to fertility control. It is a very
     rough estimate. Compare this with resources
     going into cancer research. The National Cancer
     Institute had a budget of $175 million in 1967; the
     American Cancer Society added $19 million in
     that year in support of research; several other
     foundations added more. In other words, one may
     contrast $25 or $30 million in reproductive biology
     research worldwide with about $200 million for the
     cancer research in the United States alone.

Ehrlich: The government put $50 million into rat con-
     trol last year.

Harkavy: That is right. Furthermore, this is an
     area where there is a weak institutional structure
     to support contraceptive work. The pharmaceuti-
     cal houses themselves, of course, are primarily
     concerned with a return on their investment. We
     really can't count on pharmaceutical houses, pur-
     suing their stockholders' interests, to devote major

resources to development of products that are cheap and don't require repeated use. It costs a drug firm some $5 or $10 million to develop and test a product that will obtain Federal Drug Administration approval. Perhaps it may be possible to offer a subsidy to a drug house so that it will have the incentive to work on contraceptives appropriate for mass use in developing countries. Such an idea may have a lot of bugs in it.

Reynolds: May I ask you a question? There is one thing that triggered me. You said that the question of subsidizing the pharmaceutical or drug house has a lot of bugs in it. When you call it subsidizing, it does, but what is the matter with supported research and development for such a product?

Harkavy: I think, in fact, that that is what you do.

Reynolds: That is the way most technological progress is made, as a matter of fact, in every other field except medicine.

Harkavy: There is much accumulated experience in the Space Agency and the Defense Department with just this kind of subsidized research. We must see what lessons for contraceptive development can be learned from this experience. Our natural clientele—both a foundation's and NIH's—is the academic institution. The mission of the academic institution is not to develop a product, but to develop knowledge and to advance the disciplines.

Schultz: Not so.

Harkavy: You don't agree?

Schultz: No. The distinction between product and
knowledge is misleading because these two concepts overlap. Suppose that there is any advance
in knowledge from research, the new knowledge
consists of either of two classes of entities (or of
both): (1) entities that are transformed into new
skills and when they are acquired by human agents,
they represent new forms of human capital; and
(2) entities that are transformed into new materials and when this is achieved, they represent
new forms of non-human capital. Firms for
profit will undertake only research and development from which they can capture the benefits
from research. If all of the benefits accrue to
those who pay the cost of the research, profit-
oriented firms (persons) under competition will
arrive at a general economic optimum (private
and social) by equating marginal cost and returns.
If, however, not all of the benefits accrue to
these firms, they would equate marginal cost only
to the point where marginal returns that they can
capture are equalized. Since there is a large class
of research which has the attribute that some or
even all of the benefits are widely diffused ending
up ultimately as a consumer surplus, it is necessary to "socialize" this part of research in order
to arrive at a general economic optimum. The
latter is to be viewed as non-profit research
activity. There has emerged a lot of mythology in
Washington in the post-war period, justifying
federal funds for all manner of research regardless of the class of entities it produces and

regardless of whether the benefits from them can
be captured by firms for profit. The non-profit
class of research is not restricted to universities
for there are many other non-profit research
organizations.

Knox: I just want to say that there has been some
more mythology contributed to this subject here.

Reynolds: The whole aviation industry was built on
the basis of R&D (Research and Development)
contracting. Admittedly, the R&D contracts
came principally from military agencies but nonetheless commercial aviation's capability grew out
of this.

Knox: In many fields of the physical sciences—I can't
say that this would be true in the social sciences
area or in the humanistic disciplines—there is a
gray area between what is suitable for privately
financed applied research and what goes on in
many universities. There are quite a few men
who spend a substantial part of their time, while
actually members of the faculty doing the kind
of applied research that leads to commercial
products.

Schultz: You are using the applied and basic research
distinction, assuming that it is not an arbitrary
classification. Clearly some applied research
produces results, all of which. cannot be captured
by a profit-oriented firm although it were to pay
the cost of such research. Similarly, there is
some basic research from which the fruits can

all be captured by the researcher and therefore
it can be optimized under competition by firms for
profit. Research, the products of which cannot
all be captured by the researcher, must be organized under nonprofit arrangements and the entities
that are produced should enter the public domain.

Knox: Let me just take the example of pollution control. It would be very difficult in many industries
to see a profit-making potential in pollution control research accept a long-term view that unless
something is done here, even the industry itself
may have its difficulties. But it certainly cannot
be justified on any basis of return to the stock-
holders or new-product development, or anything
that would normally be considered to be the
research function of a profit-oriented enterprise.

Slobodkin: I think you are wrong. At the moment, you
are right but, in principle, it needn't be that way.

Knox: But it does happen; that's all I am saying.

Slobodkin: It does happen but paths can be established
without too much fantastic social reorganization.

Notestein: But nothing you said is in opposition to
what Schultz said.

Knox: I thought he was drawing a much sharper distinction.

Schultz: I was redefining. The results are really a
definition of the research entities.

Reynolds: I was talking about a product here, a product that happens not to be the most immediately economically rewarding one, so that the company doesn't put out the R&D cost in development. I think that is entirely different from what you are saying.

Schultz: It is the public domain.

Segal: It depends, I think, on the level at which the R&D company is expected to get into the act. I don't know what it has been in space science or in aviation science, but we have not overlooked this possibility. Everyone interested in this, has talked to all the development firms, Arthur D. Little and the whole lot, and in this particular area they are at the point of asking what we want them to do, and they will do it.

That is not very helpful, because we are looking for what should be done as well. That is the whole ball game at the present time. There are lots of ideas that can go on at the level of the university and we don't need to farm them out, so to speak. There are plenty of good, talented people at universities working at this level; but beyond that, we have not been able to get help.

As far as the oriented industry is concerned, in this case the pharmaceutical industry, an example might establish Bud's point. Their response to the rediscoveries or the publications regarding the Silastic is very interesting. This work has been going on in our laboratory and some at the University of Illinois. There have been publications. It is well known to everyone

that Silastic has this property of releasing steroids over a constant period of time.

The pharmaceutical industry's response to
that is, I think, fascinating. At least two of them
have now undertaken projects to develop a product
that will make use of this principle at the same
time getting a nice commercial product. What
they are doing is not the implant, which would be
50 cents for five years, but they are devising a
little Silastic ring (something like the rim of a
diaphragm or the rim of a cervical cap) that
contains a certain amount of the hormone. A
woman can insert it intravaginally and get the
local release and absorption in the vagina or on
the wall of the cervix. They are developing it
to last about three months.

If you are developing it at all, you could make
it last for one hundred years. I can assure you
of that. I am not speaking off the top of my head
because we probably have worked more with this
than anyone in the world. You could make it last
for one hundred years and you could, if you
fiddled around a little bit with the amount of
hormone you put in and the release rate, make it
last for three months. They are making it last
for three months.

Ehrlich: It could have been just two weeks, or some-
    thing.

Slobodkin: Is there a way of breaking through this in
    the veterinary medicine area so that the same
    compound might be of use in connection with steer
    production or meat production?

Segal: Oh, it is being used.

Slobodkin: You could get the R&D that way.

Segal: One of the major ways that it will be used in the veterinary field is for synchronizing estrus in sheep so that one can have lambings spaced over the year rather than seasonally.

Slobodkin: Would you get any help from the R&D here?

Segal: Some, but the important work to refine these principles for human application is not being done in industry or by anyone else.

Knox: Shelly, don't you think that if they came out with a three-month duration ring, and another firm decided to put one on the market that would last six months, that the one for six months would run the three-month's one out of business?

Zuckerman: It depends on the advertising.

Segal: The point I'm trying to make is that it hasn't happened. The facts are there and the way it is going now is interesting in terms of the comparison between our objectives, say, the way we are going at it, and the commercial product.

Zuckerman: May I make a general observation about the point, because I have had a certain amount of responsibility for spending public money in the R&D field, and I have had considerable experience as a researcher. I haven't the slightest doubt that the pharmaceutical firms would be operating as effectively in the field of birth control agents as they have in the field of stilbesterol or antibiotics, if they had a real lead. What we haven't got at the present moment are any leads beyond those applications in the pipeline, which Shelly has told us about.

If we could get down to the point of formulat-ing issues in an absolutely clear way; if we knew that those issues had been agreed upon, turned into problems, leading to solutions and if these things had practical value from the point of view of contraception, I haven't the slightest doubt we would find the pharmaceutical firms there.

Segal: That is true.

Zuckerman: That is the difficulty. Not so very long ago, a party from the National Academy came over and met the officers and some members of the Council of the Royal Society for a weekend meeting. The Royal Society in London has got, or did have, a Standing Committee on Population, and the Chairman of that committee was invited to come along and give a résumé of their deliber-ations and the conclusions they had reached. The discussions ended in one brief sentence. Some-body on the American side, turning to the Chair-man, said, "Well, have you people got any new insights?" There was a dead silence. We then moved on to the next subject.

This is the problem. There are certain things that have been clearly established about which Shelly has spoken this morning. For example, we do know how to suppress ovulation. The new work that he is describing will, I hope, also prove sound; that is to say, we need not suppress ovulation but we can impair the fertilizing capacity of the sperm.

At this moment in time, the established pieces of knowledge about which Shelly spoke are the only things on which we can work with absolute conviction. I feel that rather than speculate further about unknown physiological problems, it would be wise if we turned to those indirect, faster methods of influencing family behavior of the kind that you indicated you would like to see the group discuss.

Bernstein: May I break in to ask a question: I got the impression that among the biologists most concerned with this area, there is tremendous impatience that if something won't pay off in one, two, three, or four years, it didn't seem worth looking at. Am I correct?

Segal: I think you might have that conclusion because of my poorly planned presentation. There is a whole broad area that I didn't include that is sort of lost in the preliminary document that describes the tentative leads which need a lot of work at the basic level, and certainly there is a great deal of attention given to that—as well as support.

Shelesnyak: I personally see no contradiction in what Sir Solly says about promoting what we know; I wish to stress that we should do more to get an

understanding for developing a general fertility
depressant.

Harkavy: Let us now turn to the next step. We have
this listed under "Social Control of Fertility,"
for want of a more felicitous term. We ask: Can
the social and political environment be manipulated? Professor Bernstein was invited to talk
on the general topic of "Consequences of Population Growth on Political and Social Organizations:
Individual Liberty." Professor Bernstein has
been involved over the years in the field of social
legislation. Population policy is an area in which
up to now practically no legal scholars have been
involved. Therefore, I was very pleased that
Professor Bernstein agreed to come to this meeting to initiate our discussion on population policy.

Bernstein: My presence here indicates the tough shape
that you are in, and in the few weeks between the
time that I knew of this and today I have had to
supplement what general interest I had with some
quick tooling up, because apparently no individual
scholar has—let alone any group—made it his
business to deal with institutional and legal
aspects of population control, which doesn't mean,
of course, that nothing has been done. What, in
fact, has happened is that the demographers and
other groups have become involved, including the
biologists and sociologists, who addressed themselves to the questions. They are specialists in
related areas, but are not specialists in the
means of possibly effecting institution change.
Hence efforts to produce plans for change have

been a by-product of the efforts of social and physical scientists who generally do not concern themselves with legal and public policy proposals.

I get the impression that there is a paucity of information and effort in trying to ascertain the effects of population upon institutions and political organizations, which would be the predicate for going forward to try to find out what you might do.

The title of this meeting is, "Growth of Population: Consequences and Cures." I think the cure, means whatever curbs growth. But, you seem to agree that for quite some time the cure is not going to be "complete" and, if the growth continues, what, indeed, will be done about the consequences of growth?

In order to deal with that, you must know what are the consequences of population growth. From what I have learned, I deduced that most of the views on the consequences of population growth are primarily speculative, once they get past the verifiable proposition that when there are many children in the family, the amount available for the nurture of the family is divided and, therefore, there is less for each. As an observable consequence, a very large number of those who are poverty-stricken or in dire circumstances occurs in large families.

Slobodkin: May I interject at this point that the precise sociological and organizational consequences may, in fact, be speculative, but the cosmic consequences in the sense of ecological consequences, effects on total air quality and so forth, are not speculative.

Notestein: Rather more speculative, I would say.

Slobodkin: We can inject that now.

Bernstein: The total consequences of a growing population have not, so far as I can see, been more
than speculatively dealt with, and yet some of the
speculation here I found to be somewhat deficient.
For example, in the opening remarks of Professor
Notestein, the projections of population were
given. In his and other presentations, projections
of food supply and supporting social and economic
organizations were made which apparently would
be adequate to sustain the larger expected population without catastrophe. It was noted that
some qualifications were required. But I found
a consideration absent of what, as an independent
variable, is the impact of population growth on
all these other factors. If the family is made
more inefficient by larger numbers, isn't society
made more inefficient in some measurable way?
Or does everything go on a straight line?
        I, too, have speculated. One can posit—at
least on a very unscientific basis it seems to be
so—that larger populations require both private
and public organizational bureaucratization. That
might seem to be all bad, because bureaucracy
is supposed to be inflexible and impersonal. Yet
one might suggest that there are countervailing
factors: when there is a sufficiently large population, which I will leave undefined, it is possible to multiply variations in need so that they
can be served, whereas in a smaller population
it wouldn't be economical to take account of
variations because they were too few.

That is somewhat abstract, but let's say in a
client population, 98 percent of the group to be
served have a fairly uniform requirement and 2
percent have variation. In a small population,
say 100, it may not be worthwhile to try to serve
that 2 percent, whereas in a group of a million,
serving the 2 percent may be not only possible
but absolutely necessary. Given the technology
we have today, which may in part be attainable
because of a large population, it may be possible
to serve individuals more effectively than in the
past. I think this has been a major factor in
modern society, resulting in superior quality of
goods and services in our society today as compared to an earlier handicraft period.

But there is a notable resistance to centralization of authority and bureaucratization. The trend
toward centralization in the United States has been
off-set by great interest, agitation, and pressure
for greater local control of governmental activity,
some of the governmental activity involves private
organizations, notably in the antipoverty field.
Neil Chamberlain suggests that this is rear-guard
action—or may be.

Chamberlain: A concomitant action, almost necessarily going along with the centralization. You
have to have some decentralization in order to
permit centralization to go on in other respects.

Bernstein: That is what I was thinking. I got the
impression from your paper that you thought
perhaps that greater local control is doomed.

Chamberlain: No, no.

Bernstein: I agree that you need it as an offset to
greater centralization to accommodate the local
needs and wishes, and the desires of
local groups for participation.

These developments create a need for a
great deal of creativity in the area of government.
We haven't solved our basic problems of federal-
ism. Yet we have piled on top of these unresolved
problems the need to devise entirely new governmental mechanisms of greater centralization
dealing with larger units, such as the metropolitan
authorities. Yet, at the same time, we build
entirely new levels of government, not merely
for the school system but, affecting housing control, recreation, and many other areas where
demands for local power may develop. The
racial situation merely exacerbates these needs.
I don't think it is the only factor operating for
decentralization. A large part of the problem has
been the ossification of bureaucracies. I think
a good example is the New York Board of Education.

The problem of adjusting to population pressures is complicated by the fact that we don't
know a great deal about how accommodations do,
in fact, take place. There has been an observable
tendency in urban situations for family units to
become smaller. That can be for a number of
reasons. I don't think that the actual factors
operating have been completely studied or isolated
and weighed. I judge that to be the case, and if
it is so, it seems that there is a basic lack of

information which to build schemes for manipulating institutions to affect population growth and family size.

We have examples of attempts to deal with certain manifestations in the field of public welfare. There has been a considerable amount of concern (putting it mildly) about illegitimacy among public welfare recipients, and we have on the books a statute providing for aid to families of dependent children. That statute provides that federal funds, accounting for roughly 85 percent of the funds expended and delivered into the hands of recipients, will be unavailable as benefits to mothers and children where the proportion of illegitimate children to the entire child population of a state exceeds what that proportion was in January of 1968.

So far, it has not been in operation, although the effective date was July 1, and nobody knows how to put it into effect. There has been a tremendous amount of resistance on the part of local authorities. You might be interested to know that the welfare authorities in the state of Georgia are contesting, or seeking to contest, the constitutionality of this provision, so there is some question.

Harkavy: Mr. Bernstein, doesn't Title V of the Social Security Act refer to dependent children under the definition of Aid to Dependent Children legislation rather than illegitimate children? Is this a point of fact or am I wrong?

Bernstein: No, no, it is addressed in fact to illegitimacy although you are correct that the group to be measured is that which qualifies because of the absence of a father.

Segal: But it is addressed to illegitimacy within the aid to dependent children program, which is a very small part of the total federal welfare support.

Bernstein: Oh, I agree.

Harkavy: The point is right, but I don't think they are actually taking a census of bastards.

Bernstein: Oh, no, that is true. But here you have an example of an attempt at institutional control by providing incentives and penalties of a dubious sort. Nonetheless, the program, I think, ought to draw attention to that and it ought to be studied to see how this kind of mechanism works. Does it have any effect upon the production of children? (I have strayed from the effect of population pressures into a related field.)

There are suppositions (that may turn out to be correct) that crowding has an adverse effect on population; that it results in more aggressive activity; that it increases the possibility of war; that it may have a deleterious effect upon the efficiency of population. Yet, as was commented here, we have noticed a good deal of propensity toward crowding and concentration. As Kingsley Davis pointed out, larger and larger groups concentrate in comparatively small areas,

despite the fact that there are large areas physi-
cally available, certainly in this country, that
could sustain population.

We have developed in this country a doctrine
of a constitutional right to travel a little hard to
explain, because its constitutional underpinnings
(I must say) are a little obscure. This grew out
of attempts to limit passports to keep travelers
and newsmen from going to politically questionable
places, like Mainland China and Cuba.

Ehrlich: And doesn't it go back to the California case
where they attempted to limit immigration into
California, internal immigration?

Bernstein: The Edwards case didn't generalize to the
point of a general right to travel but turned more
on equal protection grounds. What happened was
that California tried to exclude immigrants who
came to participate in the higher benefits of the
California welfare laws and it was made a crime
to transport people into a system in this effort.
The Supreme Court of the United States held that
this was a denial of equal protection; that this
kind of exclusion was not possible, but there
wasn't approval of a right to travel.

However, there are cases currently pending
before the Supreme Court of the United States
dealing with the residency laws, where the welfare
provisions of the Social Security Act specifically
provide that states may require residence of a
specified duration as a qualification for the re-
ceipt of welfare. In the Aid to Families of Dependent Children program up to one year

of residence can be required. Several states have had just such provisions, warranted by federal law. The constitutionality of those provisions of federal law has been attacked in several courts. Connecticut, Rhode Island, and a few others have declared them unconstitutional; in Pennsylvania, there have been two different results from two different panels of the Federal Court of Appeals. The Supreme Court will consider those challenges to the legality of the state, with federal statutory warrant, to limit movement throughout the country where the purpose is to hold down the local welfare roll.

Shelesnyak: Something is not quite clear. I am trying to tie what you are saying to the more fundamental thesis of social legislation as a potential means for population control, or the possibility of using social legislation for the regulation of population growth. Are these related in an indirect manner, by relationship simply to welfare cases?

Bernstein: This is the sequence which leads to the discussion. The subdivision was not merely growth but population pressures, and as noted here, there has been a concentration of population in urban areas. A possible means of dealing with this would be the effort to disperse population, and I am commenting upon legal devices presently in force that are designed to limit population movement, which will be decided before the impact upon larger issues of population concentration will ever be brought into focus. This has already happened in the Connecticut birth control

324 GROWTH OF POPULATION

case, in dealing with a particular problem, that is, the anti-birth control devices statute of Connecticut. Very important legal doctrines were decided that will have an impact upon the future in this area, despite the fact that those larger concerns were not really in focus.

Ehrlich: Didn't that establish the right to have as many children as you want?

Bernstein: The right to marital privacy was established. At least Mr. Justice Goldberg, joined by Chief Justice Warren and Justice Brennan, delivered their views that any attempt toward compulsory limitation of conception would also run into the same principle. It seemed a little premature to decide that issue so broadly.

Shelesnyak: In other words, apparently a small local or localized phenomenon can be, as you see it, an instrumentality for legislative processes which would have a more generalized effect. How would they compare to basic legislation directed toward fundamental problems?

Bernstein: Would you put that again?

Shelesnyak: As I understand what you have been developing, it is that legislative instrumentalities, historically, that relate to the problem of population growth and cure have been generated on the basis of problems that were rather limited and specific; for instance, contraceptive devices in Connecticut led to something much more general.

Bernstein: Yes.

Shelesnyak: Legislation, restriction of welfare funds to certain types of groups and families, interfered with migration. In other words, the general problem, however, of legislation toward interfering with or regulating population growth is an entirely different order of magnitude for a different type of problem, isn't it?

Bernstein: That may be, but I don't think so. One of the difficulties in the residency law cases is that it is difficult, perhaps impossible, to demonstrate, on the data at hand, that these residency laws had any inhibiting effect upon population movement, so that you could establish that freedom of movement had, in fact, been interfered with. Some courts have assumed that this would be the result of a residency requirement and it may not be true.

All I was trying to say at that point is that we already have one very broad constitutional decision and others pending that may have a terrific impact in this area. Those decisions will have come about without a consideration of the larger problems of population control; they may stand as an impediment to future activity.

Another set of problems arises with what is the impact of population growth upon individual rights. I take it that this is quite apart from what it is that you are going to try to do about population growth, which also involves problems of individual rights. I suggest that larger populations, plus other developments such as the increases in longevity, which I think may be expected, will lead to larger institutionalized populations.

Slobodkin: You mean in hospitals, orphanages, and so on?

Bernstein: Yes, mental hospitals and private extended-care institutions, as well.

Ehrlich: What about simple loss of rights like the right to own a gun or to fly your airplane wherever you want, or to drive your automobile at any speed you want, or to dump your sewage over the fence? It would seem to me that there is a vast area of loss of rights and we don't have to get into something as specialized as institutionalizing people. There are these prior things, the tremendous restrictions of freedom which we see around us that have been escalating for a very long time.

Bernstein: I am not quite sure at what point in time the right to dump your garbage over the fence was lost.

Ehrlich: It is not a point of time. It is a matter of population.

Slobodkin: It is illegal in some areas.

Bernstein: Well, yes, whenever there was somebody else on the other side of the fence.

Ehrlich: Precisely; that is the whole point.

Bernstein: But that is a right I really don't cherish
very deeply.

Ehrlich: It is very expensive to give up that right.   It
costs a lot of money not to be able to dump your
sewage or your garbage over the fence.

Slobodkin: Do you own a septic tank ?   It is relative,
because you actually pay cash for the loss of the
right to pour your sewage away.   You have to
buy the septic tank.

Bernstein: Maybe my sense of values just doesn't
have me focused upon those as the kinds of rights
I am concerned about.   I am perfectly willing to
have you do it, but I haven't addressed myself to
those particular instances because, frankly, they
don't strike me as inalienable rights or ones that
are serious inconveniences.   I think there are
some serious inconveniences.   I don't miss the
right to bear arms, I might add.

Ehrlich: But there are all kinds of restrictions on
your individual freedom, no matter how defined,
which we can see being applied progressively.
I agree with you that I don't cherish the right to
throw my garbage over the back fence.   Of course
there is the right, for instance, to own any size
home that you want, or the right to plant your
land as you wish, or the right to own pets.   There
is a whole long series of restrictions that may not
be expressed as rights, although I can assure you

that the people involved desperately do express
them as rights. In other words, you will find
when the time comes to stop owning dogs because
we can't afford the protein, the dog feces, the
noise, and perhaps the rabies that will become
epidemic, you will find a tremendous fight developing for the right to own dogs—perhaps one of
the most serious rights ever proposed. I think
you must consider people's attitudes toward these
privileges, if you wish, if not rights.

Taylor: You have areas in Britain where you can't
build a garage on your property without permission; you can't fell a tree more than 18 inches in
diameter without permission, and so on.

Bernstein: I can see a point when life gets very intimate and it is difficult to avoid great concentrations, then the incursions might get serious. But,
frankly, some of your illustrations don't move me.

Ehrlich: But that is because you are looking at it at
this point in time. I think if you brought the
average American of just 30 years ago to the
present he would find that things have grown much
more rigid and that his "rights" have been restricted. Now you are soon going to get into legal
rights like: Do you have the right to cut down a
plant? Do you have the right to cut your lawn
because of what you may do to the oxygen supply?
Then there are other problems of closeness,
restrictions on where you can build and what land
you can clear. Because there are so many people,
the erosion problem comes in. The right to log

your land and thus create floods downstream is
now one that is in question.

Notestein: One can go on with this kind of list forever,
but there is another side to the coin. I don't see
where we are getting.

Ehrlich: What is the other side of the coin?

Notestein: There are very great advantages in the
richness of living in a community that is large
enough to have people that we can talk to over a
wide range, a lot of intellectual interchange. I
don't want to go back to the Middle West where I
grew up. I much prefer living near New York
City.

Taylor: We are saying that high population densities
mean more controls.

Notestein: I agree, but that is not necessarily a loss
in the calculus, so you could make a list and I
would agree with your list, but then there is a
whole other list.

Ehrlich: Then we ought to set up the calculus and ask
what we have lost vs. what we have gained at
various concentrations and look at those trends
and see where the lines either have crossed or
are going to cross. I think you could argue that
the losses have well out-weighed the gains for the
last twenty years. I don't think the intellectual
life of New York, for instance, was any poorer in
1950, or of the country as a whole was any poorer

in 1950 than it is today, or not substantially, whereas I think on the other side we have gone a very long way and very rapidly.

Harkavy: I wonder if I can assert the right to take a coffee break.

(Coffee break.)

Harkavy: We keep losing people all the time. I hope this is a good sign, illustrating what happens to the population curve, but, Mr. Bernstein, would you finish up, please, and then we'll hear from Lyle Saunders.

Bernstein: When you so appropriately called time so that the clinch in which Professor Ehrlich and I were locked could be broken, I think it gave us an opportunity for a new start. The exchange we had indicates that we ought to define those liberties that we think are essential and important, and those which are simply inconveniences.

It seems important to decide what liberties are important, that we must be concerned with in relation to future population growth, and those inconveniences that are already upon us because of what has occurred.

Slobodkin: How do you tell the difference between a liberty and an inconvenience? Is it a legal distinction?

Bernstein: I don't think it is a legal distinction. I am willing to admit other non-specialists into it.

I think the right not to be incarcerated without due process is a basic liberty. I think the ability to fling garbage around is an inconvenience.

Slobodkin: The purpose of the question was to lead to another question. That is, we are talking in terms terms of the existing legal system, discussing how does the existing legal system deal with existing problems of density of population. I am asking what new legal restrictions will have to be created and what will be the impact of these legal restrictions on the general legal structure as population becomes more dense.

Zuckerman: In the United States?

Slobodkin: In the United States.

Zuckerman: It seems to me you are having a little domestic dispute.

Slobodkin: May I answer that? Given any country, you have a legal system that exists at the moment. All of these legal systems will have to be modified to some degree under the pressure of population. The precise path of modification will obviously depend on whatever the country has in its legal system to permit modification of the laws, and whatever guarantees, and so forth, it wants to preserve; but the ultimate problem of having to change one's legal system because population is squeezing things together is a global one. Is that fair enough?

Zuckerman: Not to me, I am afraid. We have a House of Commons which sits, trying to change the law every week or so, and this has been going on for endlessly. The so-called liberties of the individual are entrusted to our Home Secretary and our poor Home Secretary has to give up some of those liberties all the time. Our housing laws, our traffic laws, all of these things are intrusions on your personal liberty, like your point about garbage.

Slobodkin: In that case, with reference to the British legal system as you have outlined it, and your outline constitutes my full knowledge of it at the moment, there is a set of changes that are in fact occurring under this kind of pressure. It is those I am referring to.

Ritchie-Calder: There is a law of convenience, which is your matter of garbage disposal. I maintain there is a difference between fundamental rights and accommodations and laws of convenience, where you just have to accept the situation and modify it accordingly.

Bernstein: I think you are assuming that all the changes that accompany population growth will be bad.

Slobodkin: It was not my assumption.

Bernstein: I got that implication from it, then, and while I share the apprehension, it may not necessarily be so. For example, we have a court system that is not ideal, a system of individual representation that has left an enormous number of people unrepresented. With the pressure of population, we are now in the process of recognizing wider rights to representation and the legal system is being modified for the better.

One of our problems will be to supply sufficient lawyers to meet these newly recognized rights, and that may just press us further to rationalize our system of representation so that it is better than it has been. Large populations to be served need not mean catastrophe; but I think there are some areas where already the problems of crowding may be indicted as a source of more than inconvenience.

For example, and I don't think this is verifiable on the current data but it might be a proper subject of investigation, obviously we have grave crowding (I would say overcrowding) in our public school system. There seems to have been a decided extension of the use of corporal punishment in the schools. I consider that a very serious limitation on private rights and, in the way the system operates, there is not due process for children in those disciplinary situations. I would say that the pressure of numbers there apparently has elevated the requirements of imposing discipline over the imparting of education, and here you have an illustration of a probably deleterious effect of crowding.

I mentioned the longevity problem and I would like to put it to the demographers present whether, if longevity should improve—and I think, again referring to domestic problems, our publicly sponsored medical systems should have some impact upon that—whether they regard that as a serious population factor? If it were to become so, I think you might have some problems, which I have outlined, as to the extent of medical services that will be available to the older non-productive members of society, who are often non-productive because we don't permit them to be productive.

Notestein: There is a fairly simple answer here. I think if the birth rate is high enough to give you a 2 percent expansion, then the achievement of immortality would do very little to the age distribution, to the proportionate distribution of age. Obviously, if your birth rates are low enough so that there is very little input and a very slow rate of increase, like a quarter of 1 percent, then the achievement of immortality would lead to an indefinitely old population.

Coming down to the less ridiculous than immortality, there is an indication (I think a great deal) of a slowing-up of the improvement of expectation of life. As people move to spare parts and the conquest of immunological barriers, we can get some change in life-expectancy. It is going to be very much a function of the birth rate and the proportion of the people in the older ages that will reflect this. If the birth rate is high, the proportion of old folks will be small.

Slobodkin: You are referring to the function of the birth rate as a mathematical fact?

Notestein: That is right.

Bernstein: I was raising the question as to whether
   you anticipate that this would create a density
   problem to the point that the elderly would begin
   to look less and less attractive as current members of society.

Notestein: As a density problem, not in forty years
   or so. Ultimately, any rate of growth has no
   upper limit.

Bernstein: I discussed the principle of equal protection of the law that is a constitutional concept,
   which is not a self-evident one. Equal protection
   of the law does not mean that every member of
   society has to be treated in exactly the same way.
   What it does mean is hard to say with precision
   because the Supreme Court of the United States
   has been something less than precise. What it
   means in gross is that any classification for
   special treatment has to have some rational relationship to a permissible goal. That is not the
   classical formulation, by any means, because the
   classical formulation keeps changing. Where you
   have attempts at economic regulation, the courts
   have been very indulgent and there is a presumption of regularity. As the right which is being
   affected seems to be one of a more critical nature,
   one more basic to our kind of free society, the
   courts are less and less indulgent of the legislative,
   less and less disposed to presume regularity, to
   presume validity, and much more questioning.
   So, in the birth control case, the court looked at

this newly-constructed right to privacy—and I personally consider it a legal novelty—and said that the burden was upon the proponents of the legislation to demonstrate its necessity, which was, I must say, an entirely novel way of formulating the equal protection doctrine. It is the only instance I know where the proponents were called upon to justify this special treatment because it challenged what the court said was such a basic right.

You can see that there is a tremendous amount of flexibility and unpredictability in the area of equal protection. I think one can say, what I have said diffusely in my written comments, that the courts are less jealous of the protection of rights to the extent that they share the apprehensions which moved the legislature, or the executive. If the public action that has been taken seems justified by a serious threat to some basic aspect of society, then the courts are much more indulgent. If that seems like subjectivity, make the most of it.

Shelesnyak: May I ask a question? There is a group in this conference that is very interested in the problem of birth control and population regulation. One of the objectives of this dialogue is to try to incite or induce or elicit activity from professionals outside our own coterie. Do you as a representative of the legal profession, see a role or a mission that you or your profession could play, an active role with respect to both the regulation of the growth curve from the legal point of view; secondarily, to the problems of just working with the legal aspects of the implications of the already existing ten to twenty years of population growth?

Bernstein: I think the legal profession will inevitably become involved in dealing with the consequences. The question always is: To what extent will problems be anticipated and planned for in some reasonably rational way, and to what extent will attempted ameliorations or solutions be the work of short-order cooks? We lawyers tend to be short-order cooks.

Shelesnyak: You have no classification of preventive law, like preventive medicine?

Bernstein: Well, no, but I would say that there tends to be ---

Ehrlich: The zoning laws have been an important area.

Bernstein: Yes, but in the sense of seeking out problems and developing long-term solutions, I would say my profession has been somewhat deficient. That doesn't mean that there aren't quite a number of people, academics, who are concerned with anticipating problems and proposing solutions long in advance of the arrival of the critical moment, but lawyers tend not to operate in that fashion.

Shelesnyak: Do you know of any effective technique by which we could get members of the legal profession to join our club, so to speak?

Zuckerman: Are you talking about the legal profession
of the world or the legal profession of the United
States, because the situation varies so greatly.
You have one set of laws. England has another.
Germany has a third. To give you three illustrations straightaway. A big case is now going on in
the Federal Republic of Germany at the present
about the thalidomide tragedy, and all sorts of
expert witnesses are being called to protect the
people who have been indicted for the offense of
introducing the drug. Heaven alone knows how
that trial will come out, but I am quite certain
that in the United States it would come out differently.

My second example is this. Some years ago
I was sent to the United States to consult with
people about the introduction of estrogens, stilbesterol it was, into animal feeding substances to
increase the conversion rate. I discussed the
matter with the FDA in Washington, and I then
went out to Colorado where the work had, as it
were, its basis. The professor concerned is
now dead so I may tell this story. He said, "The
FDA are making a fuss about nothing. This is
going to go on, and what's more," he said at the
end of the day, "it will go on so long as our legal
costs do not exceed the profits we are making
from this single end use of stilbesterol."

My third illustration is an English one. I
was called in some years ago to consider the
banning of two agricultural chemicals, Aldrin and
Dieldrin. This possibility was powerfully opposed
by the principle company concerned, but it finally
gave up. But, we haven't yet got any statutory

regulation to deal with this sort of thing. They
finally gave up, yes, but they still export the
Aldrin and Dieldrin that they produce and sell
in overseas markets, where the legal restrictions
are not the same as in the United Kingdom.

I am mentioning these things because the complexities are such that it doesn't seem to me that
any legal changes that you may make in the United
States can affect the world problem of population
that we are discussing.

Shelesnyak: Except as a particular example of a
particular situation. Mr. Bernstein might
have come back, saying that since we are discussing global population, it may be an area for international lawyers to exercise some influence.

Richie-Calder: Certainly the International Commission of Jurists is concerned about population
problems. There is McBride's outfit in Geneva.
He is concerned with this.

Bernstein: I would say that in the teaching and training of the legal profession, there is a great
deficiency of interest in the operation of the social
sciences in general, and I think comparative lack
of attention to population problems is only one of
the manifestations of that deficiency. There are
places where this isn't so, but they are a minority
of cases.

I think it would be valuable to stimulate those
members of the legal academic community who
have an interest and induce others to take an interest in the interaction with social sciences and law.

Law should not be looked upon as something that takes place after all the social science experts have come up with proposals.

Taylor: India is a country that will be faced with the problem of holding 500 million people together without imposing onerous controls in a culture where they have not had them.   To talk about it even in terms of Europe is relatively unrealistic.

Harkavy: I think a lot of the discussion on social control of population growth will involve various sorts of infringements on people's liberties or conveniences. It seems to me that this is something that needs to be thought about systematically by legal scholars in India, as well as in the United Kingdom and the United States, in the context of their own legal history.

Taylor: But they are not doing it.   Are they doing it?

Harkavy: No, to the best of my knowledge social control of population growth is a brand new field. Concentrated study really hasn't started, but I think we are at the beginning of something.   After all, the "population explosion" is something that we only realized was with us in the early 1950s.

Notestein: It has been exploding more rapidly since then.

Taylor: The immigration into California is picayune, really, compared with India.

Notestein: I suppose that one of the real reasons that India hasn't pursued this very much is that India

is a country of 500 million people with a national
budget for socialist development, defense, and
so forth, that was, the last time I looked, something like New York State plus New York City—
for everyting. You can't talk about instituting
and administering social controls when you have
got that sort of a resource base. They can't
collect their taxes, much less put money into a
lot of fancy controls. It is unrealistic.

Ritchie-Calder: I would say that I do commend you,
     Shelly, and everybody else: you ought to get the
     International Commission interested in this area.

Chamberlain: Isn't there another aspect of this? We
     can talk about social controls to inhibit popula-
     tion growth but, realistically looking at the rising
     populations and recognizing that these are going
     to continue for some time. It seems to me that
     the potential for social consequences, just in a
     purely objective exmination of what these might
     be, may be one way of calling attention to the
     consequences of a phenomenon which you are try-
     ing to control. It may be an essential aspect for
     alerting more people in India to what is going on
     within their society, or even within our own
     society. It seems to me that this is an area for
     examination that should be of tremendous inter-
     est to social scientists, whether or not they are
     concerned with controlling the population, simply
     as an objective phenomenon for observation and
     analysis.

Notestein: Of course, there is a huge literature on it already. You can say people won't read it because it is badly written or for lack of interest.

Chamberlain: I am interested in hearing you say that, because I have been trying to discover this literature and I haven't been able to identify it. I really would appreciate it if someone would tell me where it is.

Notestein: Let's get back to the European literature. There is the British Royal Commission of the 1940's, mostly concerned with population decline. There is a Swedish Commission on Sex, some sixteen or seventeen volumes. There is a Danish Commission. There is an American Commission of the middle thirties. There are books like Economics of Declining Population and Law and Contemporary Business. There is Determinants and Consequences of Population Change, a summary of the literature in the United Nations, a huge volume that is being rewritten. There is no UN Commission reports that bear on this one way or another.

Ehrlich: But there is a communication problem because they haven't gotten through to the people they ought to be getting through to.

Notestein: This question is always raised; because the books are not read, they must be badly written.

Ehrlich: No, I don't think that is true at all, but they may be designed for the wrong audience.

Notestein: They often are. There is some patching
   to do, but there is a very large literature. You
   were talking a moment ago, sir, basically about
   the economies of scale. There is quite a literature on the economies of scale and the problems
   of diminishing returns. A great deal is known.
   I think one of the very interesting things in the
   case of India, by the way where I have watched
   this situation develop, is what the UN did do in
   early 1946. The UN Commission on Population
   began to take a different position. Before 1946,
   it was simply thought that white people in the
   world were holding the empty lands, where as the
   Indians wanted the right to migrate. The U.N.
   suddenly began to see that they could use India's
   population problem as an argument for economic
   development. They were not willing then to go
   the next step; cutting the birth rate, but I thought
   it was a great shift when they suddenly saw the
   importance of economic development for their
   home population.

   Then we come along a little later, when the five-
   year plans fail, and they say that they will have 8
   million new jobs, but they forget that in the meantime
   they have 15 million more people; therefore, they
   didn't solve their unemployment problem after all.
   When this begins to percolate then the government
   gets excited about it. Frankly, the European countries did not do much to arouse interest. It was politically fortunate that the Catholic countries of Europe
   were saying they wouldn't help because birth control
   is immoral, and India, Pakistan, and the Philippines
   didn't understand what was wrong.

In the international marketplace, it wasn't the
white man trying to push off family planning onto
the dark-skinned people. It was the dark-skinned
people asking for help, and the white people holding back, talking about immorality. This was a
very fortunate tactical position; so there has
really been a very great and growing growth of
awareness.

Chamberlain: I suppose it comes down to the kind of
     social consequences or economic consequences,
     and in some respects you can say that with rising
     population outdistancing economic growth or indus-
     trial growth, you can identify quite readily cer-
     tain problems like unemployment, lowered per-
     capita income, education, and so on; these kinds
     of things you can more readily identify.

Notestein: Shortage of water.

Chamberlain: But then there is another range of
     consequences which strike me as being in some
     respects more fundamental, more intriguing, and
     much more difficult to deal with: Is there a
     change in the character of government that accom-
     panies a rising population? Is it possible, is it
     likely, can it be established that the kind of gov-
     ernment that is suited to a population of given
     size is simply unsuitable to a larger population?

Notestein: It is not quite clear that you would have a
     more rigid government in a declining system than
     you would in an expanding system. There are
     whole books on this subject.

Chamberlain: But I think there is a range of problems that get into this.

Notestein: By the way, I am very much worried about this strain of compulsion that I hear coming into your discussion. I happen to be for family planning and very much against social compulsion in this area.

Ehrlich: But you must balance it against the other compulsions of being hungry, and so on.

Notestein: That is right. I understand that, but I have been listening to you talk for a long time about that while I am worried about the idea of compulsion that seems to me more important.

Ehrlich: I am worried about that, too. But, I would say the reason I am so highly worried about the time factor is that I am afraid the level of compulsion requested—and I have talked to an awful lot of people in the United States who are already saying, "Let's compel people." I am really at the desperation level now in trying to keep the level of compulsion down. We must fight the people who want a law for only two children; to keep the Blacks from breeding; and so on. We ought to work against these.

Notestein: What most of these people are saying is related to the penalties of prosperity and not population, but they are calling it population. It's the idea of getting some poverty to get rid of a lot of pollution. I am not very much for poverty, either.

Slobodkin: I want clarification from a group of experts, since it matters how I design my own thinking. The distinction came up between legal rights and personal rights and personal desires, and I would like to get them clarified in some sense.

There is a range of things that I might want to do. This includes keeping goats, shooting guns out of my window, having four Malamutes instead of one, and having three horses when the zoning permits me to have two. There are a series of things that I absolutely need. I need a certain amount of air to breathe and a certain quality of water. It needn't be the best.

And of course there is ample evidence, I think, on the relative mortality rates of children in slums, for example, that they are higher. Again, someone can correct me on this but I get the impression that the life expectancy is related to economic level in America at the moment.

Bernstein: Among other things.

Slobodkin: Well, yes, but a large component of it is economic level.

Notestein: Among other things.

Slobodkin: At any rate, I have these following desires. I have certain pharmacological needs in a sense of water, air, food, and so forth, and somewhere in between is a legal system which restricts my activities so that they are narrower than my desires, but not so that they are narrower than

my pharmacological or biological needs. The
problem that I am worrying about is that the
critical distance between the legal restrictions on
my activities and what I absolutely need pharma-
cologically, tends to get narrower with population pressures, possibly independent of the
traffic jam delaying me but the fact that the traffic
jam alters the air I breathe, this kind of problem.

I was hoping that I would get some sense of
how the legal system can be adjusted or modified,
or whether there is any theory of how to do this,
to make sure it stays outside the pharmacological
limit. Dr. Notestein, as an ecologist, gave me
an example a moment ago when he said that they
attempted to set a legal limit for DDT in food-
stuffs and found that before it was actually en-
forced, analyses of human milk showed that
mothers were already secreting a product which
was illegal in interstate commerce.

I am asking if there is a tangible question
here: How do you translate it into a question?
It becomes worth translating into a question because all our opinions don't matter unless we can
find a handle on the social mechanism. One of the
handles we have on the social mechanism is the
legal system, and somehow the legal system has
to take cognizance of the kinds of pressures that
I very crudely outlined here. I would appreciate
any comments on that or any clarification. If I
am wrong, tell me why I am wrong.

Harkavy: It is a very intriguing formulation. Do you
want to comment on that, Mr. Bernstein?

Bernstein: I am a little unclear on a few aspects of
    it. When you say, if I can reproduce it, that the
    legal system can intervene in certain areas but
    not in the pharmacological area ---

Slobodkin: No, the legal system limits my total
    activity in the ways indicated, but it protects me
    against deterioration—I cannot legally be bound
    to live in air that I can't breathe, drink water
    that will poison me, or be forced to die somehow
    because of a deteriorating world around me. I
    cannot be confined to this legally.
        The legal system has to leave me some room
    between the biological and pharmacological limits
    that constrain my life and my desires. It doesn't
    have to give me all my desires, but I am curious
    about the freedom that I have available between
    these pharmacological limits and the legal limits
    getting somewhat narrower. This is a confusing
    concept, as I say it.

Chamberlain: You are really assuming here equal
    protection of the law, to come back to Mert
    Bernstein's point, because you could have your
    pharmacological needs protected by law if you
    are willing to shortcircuit somebody else's, and
    here you get maldistribution or some kind of
    classified distribution of the resources.

Slobodkin: Let us leave distribution problems aside
    for the moment and consider that for the total
    population this space is getting narrower. For
    certain fractions of the population—children in
    Harlem, for example—it is damned narrow at the

moment, and when it gets too narrow we are
facing an explosive situation, and somehow the
law has to respond to this if the environment
doesn't.

Notestein: By the way, might I suggest that probably
you will find that this is a function of size, but
it is a rather complex function in the relation of
change. A declining population will not work in
the opposite direction.

Slobodkin: Does that change the problem?

Notestein: No, it just says that the mode of change is
another dimension in addition to the size, the
rate of change, and they are not working in the
same direction. They are probably curvilinear.
There will be more legal interference in a declining system than in a system of somewhat slow
growth, and I suspect more in very rapid growth.

Slobodkin: I am disturbed by the legal interference,
but I am disturbed by the legal interference in a
particular way. What mechanisms within existing
law and what mechanisms within the construction
of laws exist for taking cognizance of this constraint?

Zuckerman: Why should one assume rationality? It
seems astonishing that societies should be assumed to be logical. In the United Kingdom there
once was a window tax (you can see its effects on
the eighteenth century and early-nineteenth-
century houses). At the same time, there were

"Open Lights" notices on houses; some people had a right to prevent others building in their line of vision. To the best of my knowledge, "Open Lights" continues to this very day.

Slobodkin: You are saying that this system can't be rational.

Zuckerman: I am surprised that you think it ought to be rational.

Taylor: Do you think the window tax is good?

Slobodkin: Is it the sense of the meeting that it ought to be irrational?

Zuckerman: I didn't suggest it is the sense of the meeting.

Bernstein: I think you are asking that the system be foolproof and that you have a constitutional guarantee to a foolproof system.

Slobodkin: I am asking what mechanisms exist.

Bernstein: I regret to report that we don't have in the legal system a mechanism to give you what you desire.

Ehrlich: He didn't ask for that. He asked what approach should you make to the system to try to get it to accommodate to this narrowing gap. I don't see any way that he has requested a totally rational system or a perfect or foolproof system.

Ritchie-Calder: I am sorry I have to follow Sir Solly
    in quoting certain instances, but the continual
    battle in Britain is between those who are trying
    to invade, on this argument, the right of people
    to fresh air, the right to have water at other
    people's expense. What we are really talking
    about, surely, is the fact that the pressures of
    population of one kind or another, if not properly
    handled, are going to make more and more de-
    mands and restrictions on the availability of
    these things; but surely this is a mechanism which
    must come out of the social requirements of the
    situation. You start us off, as you say, with an
    absolute right to all the fresh air and fresh water
    and everything else—that is an absolute right, but
    surely this is a legislative process; it is not a
    lawyer's process.

Slobodkin: I am asking the nearest approach.

Ritchie-Calder: I want to make the point that it must
    accommodate itself to the social awareness of the
    needs. Sir Solly refers to the House of Commons
    but he has forgotten the House of Lords; we sit
    until eleven o'clock at night trying to protect just
    this kind of thing.
        Of course we see the pressure, every hour
    of the day it gets worse and worse, and it is an
    element of the density of the population and the
    requirements of a denser population, whether it
    is industrial water or what it may be.

Bernstein: But some of the things that have been put
    forward here as liberties have really been in-
    vasions of other people's rights.

Zuckerman: Always.

Bernstein: The right to dump your garbage in the street is really the right to make Lake Erie and other bodies unusable.

Ehrlich: Which is an area where the legal system really obviously needs a lot more interest of some sort. The whole area of pollution abatement, I think, is one example.

Bernstein: Which is an interference with what you formerly defined as a liberty.

Ehrlich: I'm sorry, there was very loose usage there. I was trying to get to things that we do or did that we can no longer do because of the population pressures that are the concern of the legal profession.

Harkavy: I want to interrupt this with a poem. The poem goes as follows:

> Yesterday from dark to morn,
> Ten thousand babies were not born;
> Like autumn leaves the non-born fall,
> I wonder where we'll put them all.

I want to present the author of that poem, Lyle Saunders.

Saunders: It just happens on this occasion I brought my papers because I have another poem for you. This one is entitled, "The Population Conference

in the Perspective of History," and it goes like
this:

> They sparkled with wisdom and mirth
> And argued for all they were worth
> For a couple of days;
> Then they went on their ways,
> And never prevented a birth.

(Applause)

Ehrlich: I move that that be reproduced on the first
page of the proceedings of the Conference. It
should not be lost to posterity, if there is one.

Saunders: Because it won't get on the record any
other way, I would like to make the observation
that this discussion is being conducted exclusively
by males; that the female sex is represented here
by a token group and that they have remained
discreetly silent through all of this.

I have a private cliché that I bore my colleagues with on many occasions. It goes like
this: Conferences are occasions where people
contribute their private confusion to the public
clarity. I used to think this was true. Now that
I am attending interdisciplinary conferences I
think it is the other way around: that people here
contribute their private clarity to the public confusion.

I sometimes wonder if an overabundance of
ideas is not probably as bad as an overabundance
of babies. In the discussion yesterday we were
concerned very largely with a time span of twenty
to thirty years and our main theme seemed to be

how to cope with and adapt to the population in-crease that seems almost inevitable in that period.

Today we are supposed to be considering an aspect of the problem where the time period is now and the issue is how are we going to prevent population increase, not how do we adapt to it.

If we took a poll of the people in the room and if we were careful to phrase our question most judiciously, I think we might have an accord that population reduction is a good thing, that we ought to try harder to get it, and that the most feasible strategy might be to approach it through trying to decrease fertility rather than through some of the other alternatives, such as increasing the death rate or trying to work out some plan of immigration. At lunch yesterday Kingsley Davis said that we all know what we want to do but we don't know why and we don't know how, and this is a lovely description of the state of mind that I brought to the conference and I am afraid I am going to take away with me.

Yesterday's discussions, I think, were some evidence that we do know some answers or some reasons for the why. Today's discussions have indicated that we have some notions about how.

I would like to know several things. The present rate of population growth can't continue indefinitely. From the figures that Kingsley Davis presented yesterday, it would look as if certain aspects of it can't continue very long. You remember a popular song a few years ago, "Something's Got to Give," and something prob-ably will give.

At the present, we have some alternatives
about what is going to have to give. We may not
have these alternatives very long. Maybe we
won't mind what happens if we don't accept any
of the alternatives. One of the choices we have is
to do nothing, I suppose. If we should do nothing
or not do very much, perhaps the consequences
won't bother our posterity as much as we think
they would bother us. I, for example, don't miss
the brontosaurus very much and get along very
well in a world that doesn't have brontosauri,
since I've never known one. This is why I'm not
troubled by the fact that he is not here. I suspect
that my grandchildren can very well get along by
reading about steak in the encyclopedia and by
looking at grass in a museum. It won't bother
them any more than not knowing the brontosaurus
bothers me.

If fertility reduction is going to be achieved
by rational policies and programs, as we would
like to have it done, a series of more or less
independent undertakings are going to have to be
carried on in national political, social, and cultural contexts. This means that we are going to
have to have not one approach to the problem but
a great many approaches. In fact, we already
have that.

This means that we must cope with national
differences. We must cope with a great variety
of political forms. We must cope with a great
many varieties of culture and cultural values, and
we are going to have to be ingenious in devising
forms that apply in each of the indicated situations. It makes our problem a great deal harder,

particularly when we talk about "we", meaning
this particular small group of people or a group
of people here or outside in a given country who
are interested in helping, or trying to see that a
country comes to accept and to begin to move
toward doing something about its population
growth.

Another point is that governments are
probably the only agencies that have enough mus-
cle to deal with the problem. We do go along part
of the way with voluntary help. Voluntary family
planning organizations have certainly done notable
work in opening up the topic in many countries,
in beginning to make it respectable, and in starting to get an awareness of what the problem is,
but they don't have the organizational capability
and they don't have the resources to do what needs
to be done.

A fourth general point is that perhaps a
majority of the people of the world have never
heard of the population problem and don't know it
exists. For every thousand of us who are very
much concerned about it, there are probably 10
million who haven't the slightest awareness that
this is a problem.

Taylor: You contradicted yourself, sir. You said it
didn't matter if your grandchildren didn't know
about grass except in the museum so, all right,
it doesn't matter that an uneducated population
doesn't know about education. Isn't there an
absolute value whereby you can say that education
is good rather than say there are populations
where it doesn't matter because they don't know

about it? If you really stand on this position, then you can't take the proposition that you just made.

Saunders: This proposition is just a simple statement of what I would believe to be a fact, that they don't know about it, and I would make no judgment as to whether this is good or not.

Taylor: You can't assert an absolute value after having asserted a relative position.

Saunders: Have I done that?

Taylor: Would you repeat your last assertion?

Saunders: Yes, that the majority of people in the world don't know that there is a population crisis.

Taylor: So, it doesn't matter, like the people who don't know about education?

Saunders: I think to them it doesn't matter. This is the point.

Taylor: Well, they don't know about the population problem, so that doesn't matter either. This is simply not a logically coherent position, if I may say so.

Zuckerman: The people in Hiroshima didn't know the bomb was going to drop the day before it did.

Saunders: The difference is, I think, that the people in Hiroshima, had they known the bomb was going

to drop, probably couldn't have done anything
about it. But if the people in the world knew
something more about the population explosion,
perhaps they could do something.

Ehrlich: Many more could have gotten out of town,
or very much larger numbers of them.

Zuckerman: I don't see any contradiction in your
statement of a fact and what you stated about the
brontosaurus.

Saunders: Both I and the brontosaurus are happy about
this.
          Around the world—and this point was made
by Ron Freedman—a great many people have more
children than they claim they want. Whether what
they say represents anything real or not is argu-
able, but surveys done in forty or more countries
show the same thing monotonously: that, by and
large, people have more children than they say
they want when they are questioned. A considerable number of the people questioned from time-
to-time have indicated an interest in learning how
to control births, so there is some receptivity
there, and the evidence from the countries which
have begun to adopt programs indicates that when
contraceptives are offered under acceptable conditions, they will be used by some proportion of
the population.
          A sixth point is that probably no country any-
where in the world has yet faced the question of
what they are willing to pay to bring the growth
rate down, and I think along with this, is the fact

that for some countries, consideration of it probably can't be postponed very much longer. What is happening, what has begun to happen in India, it seems to me, is an indication of the fact that a government may be moving, or a part of a government may be moving, toward the position where they are beginning, at least, to think about what they are willing to do in order to get the population reduced—the kind of thing that happened in Maharashtra.

One might also look at some earlier evidence. The beginning of an incentive movement is the beginning of an approach to a question like this. Somebody once said that graft begins with a cigar. Coercion probably begins with the first small incentive: a free contraception, a free ride to the clinic, a free service, and it goes from there in very small and gradual steps on up to the kinds of infringement on individual liberties that we were talking about. We are probably not going in a single step from a state of complete individual freedom in the matter of how many children we are going to have to complete control by the state. It will be a long series of very small steps and the distance between these two positions is very great. I think we have just begun to put our feet on the road and if population growth continues in some areas as it has in the past, we may take some more steps in that direction.

It is not improbable that in certain countries, values and institutional arrangements may be strong enough to frustrate our early attempts to bring down fertility. This is related to the question of what we are willing to pay. For example, one of the ways in this area that I think fertility might be brought down effectively would be the worldwide adoption of legalized abortion. Certainly a great many women are using abortion now. Ron Freedman has made the point on past occasions that probably abortion is the most widely used method of regulating birth in the world today. We wouldn't gain much by removing the restrictions on abortion unless substantially more people would use it if it were legal. I would think there would certainly be some margin of increased use. We certainly would make enormous gains in health improvement if abortion were legalized, but that doesn't relate to this particular issue.

At the present, the major emphasis of population programs everywhere is on voluntary regulation through contraception as the preferred means, and with services offered primarily in health facilities. This is what we mean, I think, by family planning. We sometimes get our semantics mixed up and talk about family planning and population control as if they were synonymous. I don't think they are. Family planning, as we know it, is essentially voluntary. It is essentially contraceptive, and, fortunately or unfortunately (I happen to think unfortunately), it is tied up with concepts of health, so almost everywhere it gets turned over for management to the health professions.

In most countries that have programs, the level of effort is inadequate and the proposition that voluntary family planning approach can do the job has not been adequately tested. I think that is

a fair statement.   There are some people who believe that voluntary family planning can't do all
that needs to be done.   They are probably right,
but I would like to see a test of this notion as
early as possible—if it were possible.

I think there is a place where we could test
it now if we somehow had people interested and
the ability to organize it.   I have just come back
from Ghana where I helped in the preparation of
a draft of a population policy for the government
of Ghana.   In the next few months Ghana may join
the group of countries that have population policies
and programs for fertility regulation.   Ghana
doesn't have the disadvantages of the African
countries from the testing point of view that Ron
Freedman talked about earlier.   Ghana has a birth
rate that is around 50 or 52.   Apparently, from
the reports of some demographers, it hasn't
varied in the past twenty years or so.   Ghana has
a relatively low proportion of people living in
urban places.   They have a very low literacy rate.
They have made considerable progress thus far
in getting children into school and now have suc-
ceeded in getting about 60 percent in.

Ghana has competent demographers and
relatively good demographic statistics.   If there
were some way that the Family Planning establishment could get into Ghana, as it starts its
population program, a tremendous input would be
required.   It would be concerned, not just with
establishing family planning clinics, but with
making a complete effort to try to make voluntary
fertility regulation work.   By putting a postpartum
program in every hospital, by introducing family-

life training and sex education in the public schools, establishing the commercial distribution of contraceptives through the Ghana National Trading Corporation, by bringing in private physicians as a part of the program through some kind of a coupon system such as the Population Council has helped to develop, by selling contraceptives through the regular stores, and by starting a full-scale public information program that would be frequent, sustained, and designed to carry the message to everybody in the country. If one went into a country like Ghana and did these and the other things that would be necessary, we might have an opportunity to get a test of what can be done by a full-scale voluntary effort.

Communications are particularly important for family planning. If the majority of the world doesn't know about the problem, obviously one way to begin to do something is to try to inform them. With the possible exception of South Korea, I don't know any country with a national program that has come anywhere near making adequate use of the information and communication facilities in the interest of promoting family planning. The Ministries of Information and Broadcasting are rarely called upon. There are frequently small information programs, organized as part of the family planning effort, but they are largely confined to face-to-face approaches. Again, the principle that you might be able to move people toward an awareness of the problem and toward an acceptance of the need for voluntary fertility regulation through the large and sustained use of public information facilities hasn't been tested, and it ought to be.

One of the things that I am interested in at the present is the possibility of whether or not we could develop something that might be called an international population press service whose function would be to generate stories locally or internationally and to send them to a series of regional or national centers for translation and retransmission to the newspapers of the area, in an effort to see if we couldn't get into the press of the world a great deal more information about the population problem and the possibilities for doing something about it.

Fremont-Smith: You mean programs of how things worked well and how they didn't work?

Saunders: I think it would be mainly news about the problem and about what is happening in the world. I think people in country A don't know what is going on in country B in their region. The decision-making elite, particularly, doesn't know.

Fremont-Smith: Wouldn't it be worthwhile to get case histories of what had worked well, which could be used elsewhere?

Saunders: Yes, if they could be put into journalistic-news context. I think the situation is that the newspapers around the world are receptive, and that if they have access to material, they will use it. They don't have access now because they don't have the resources to get the news and they don't have the staff time to write it. If it comes to them systematically, regularly, with a variety of

materials, presenting a number of aspects of the
problem but not necessarily devoted to trying to
motivate anybody, simply trying to get the problem understood, discussed ---

Fremont-Smith: This kind of feedback of successes
and failures is rarely used when we approach
social problems, and it could be extremely useful.

Saunders: We do have, again, the beginning of a
mechanism to feed it back, at least, to the admin-
istrators in a program that the Population Council
is going to start shortly for supplying information
about events and trends in the field to the adminis-
trators of Family Planning Programs.

Notestein: I think studies in Family Planning have done
a lot of that already, and I think you are talking
about Population Reference Bureau's ideal. This
has been their intention. You may not think they
are doing it well.

Saunders: They have done remarkably well, but they
have done it on a limited scale—once a month,
something of this kind. I think much more is
probably needed. Anyhow, we could do a great
deal to move the thing along with some attention
to the communications media and the communications field.
    At the same time, we are not using marketing
nor modern management techniques in population
work, in Family Planning. If we could somehow
find ways to enlist the interest and the skills of

people who are experts at marketing and modern
management techniques, I think we might greatly
strengthen the kinds of programs that we offer and
have a better chance of getting good results.

Frank, I need your judgment on this because
I don't have the slightest idea if it is true but I
think it may be. Is declining fertility a one-
way street ?

Notestein: I think so.

Saunders: If fertility starts to go down and gets a little
momentum, it will continue down. If this is true,
it is a hopeful thing.

Notestein: You have, at least, three illustrations of
countries trying to reverse the trend with little
success. Hitler tried it and he didn't get very
far. Mussolini tired it. The Russians tried it
and the birth rate went down anyhow. I think it
is a difficult trend to reverse until rates get
quite low. It is a one-way continuum.

Saunders: If we could get fertility started down, I
have a feeling that if you can get it down below
40, in the range of 40 to 37, and I have no evidence for it whatsoever, it will continue to come
down.

By the way, I would like to see it go down a
bit further before I would expect it to be automatically continued.

Ehrlich: It had already started down in those countries.
I think this is possible but I wouldn't put my hope
on it.

Saunders: I wouldn't, for another reason. I think when it comes down it will stabilize in the 20's, and as long as the death rates are in the 10's or below the 10's, then this is not good enough, and this is the problem that faces us for the future. Our present problem is to try to knock the present 2 percent rate of population growth down to 1 percent.

Again, I quote Ron Freedman on this. The way from 3 percent to zero goes through 2 and 1. Presently we are concentrating on reducing world population growth from 2 to 1 percent. Even if we succeed, we are going to have a problem that will make this one look small, getting it down from 1 to zero, perhaps.

Another point: at the present time we don't know enough about the social and political arrangements to achieve and support low fertility. Until today I thought that we had gotten the biological sciences, especially endocrinology, committed to the problem. Today's discussion indicates that presently this is a long way from being satisfactory, but we have commitment. We do have an establishment working there, and if we can find funds to keep it up, we are going to have something going on the biological side—at least.

I don't think we have anything like this commitment on the social science side. The social sciences in the United Kingdom, around the world, really have not paid a great deal of attention to the problem of population that we are talking about. They don't devote much time to the consequences of population growth or the means of getting it reduced, and it would be useful if we could find some way to enlist the talents, capability, interest, and body of knowledge of these disciplines.

The issue of "beyond Family Planning" is one that has been cropping up for a year or so. I would hope that a wide-ranging and free-wheeling conference like this might turn up some ideas about it, but the more I heard here today made me a little more certain that Family Planning is better than I thought it was. At least, it is something that is here and now and we can do. There are a great many things that we can do in Family Planning while we are doing these other necessary jobs of finding out what kinds of adjustments in the social and political environment we need to make to achieve and promote low fertility.

Ehrlich: We haven't yet gotten to the issue of "beyond Family Planning." We were stopped when we started talking about it, so I don't see how you could have heard anything on the subject.

Saunders: I heard things like this: that we might try to promote jobs for women.

Ehrlich: There were a couple of suggestions thrown out, but there are lots of others.

Saunders: The death rate; that we might change the fertility span.

Ehrlich: You also put into your discussion of Family
    Planning a lot of things that have sort of been
    classed as beyond Family Planning, like tremen-
    dous education. In other words, Family Planning
    is giving people access to contraceptive material
    so that people can regulate their family size. I
    think that is the core of it. But if you build out
    around it, build a government program behind it,
    add incentive systems, and so on, then you have
    gone beyond Family Planning.

    One of the things that has been most thoroughly
    examined (this is on the cost end) is feasibility
    studies: the feasibility of feeding additional people
    in the world by setting up nuclear reactors, using
    desalted water, using this to create an agricul-
    tural complex, getting minerals and fertilizers
    out of the same desalting process, a very com-
    plicated thing. The people, I believe, at Oak
    Ridge did a large feasibility study. It has been
    widely publicized, skipping the tiny little problems
    of establishing where you will build these. These
    are in the underdeveloped countries. Will you
    put the reactors where people are already buying
    the land or will you put them somewhere else
    and transport people to them, or transport food
    to the people, skipping the cost of training the
    technicians to run them, and running them, and
    so on.

    It was estimated that each nuclear agro-
    industrial complex could feed three million people
    at a cost of 1.5 billion. If you could start it
    tomorrow, you would have to have a $450 billion
    investment by somebody in the next 10 years,
    starting immediately, just to feed the people who
    would be added to the world in the next decade.

If that is the scale of expense being thought of
to feed the people, you could pay $1500 for each
vasectomy and come out ahead. In other words,
there is a big difference in thinking in terms of
giving somebody five dollars or a cheap radio
and whether you could do things with incentive
systems that put in big money. We must try to
get the kind of cost analyses that we can expect
from people in business and economics. Maybe
the real cost of allowing the population to grow
can be shown to be so great that governments
would put big money into paying people to have
vasectomies or other things, or to accept Family
Planning procedures.

Saunders: It seems to me that the preliminary work
has been very small in that direction but it indicates that investment in Family Planning is
probably as good an investment as you can make
in terms of return you get for what you put in;
but one of the questions is how do you get this
information into the heads of the Ministries of
Economic Affairs?

Ehrlich: Nobody wants to pull back, I think, from
Family Planning Programs that are already under
way; even if the government says they will have
Family Planning, and they have three people circulating around the country, that's better than
having no family planning and no circulating people.
It is a matter of how you enhance this and supplement it.

Notestein: All of us agree, but you talk about gim-
   micks and skip the problems of persuading the
   government to take them. This is the real part.

Ehrlich: I am sorry we haven't had more chance to
   discuss this, because I think it is exceedingly
   important.

Saunders: Let's say one thing about government policy.
   I have read the policy statements of a number of
   countries that have had programs and I have
   helped to formulate one or two of them. I don't
   think very much of them because they don't say
   much. They merely make a pious statement
   that population is growing and they intend to recom-
   mend something. They don't do the kind
   of detailed studies of the consequences or the
   necessary alternative procedures that we could
   use. The technical question of how do you get
   the government to consider this kind of thing again
   is a problem for people who are concerned with
   getting population down. We don't know easy
   answers and I think most of us who are in the
   establishment would welcome all the ideas and
   suggestions we possibly could get on how to do it.
        It is a very difficult problem, particularly in
   view of some of the comments that Sol Tax has
   made here, warning us repeatedly that somehow
   the means must be found or the conditions must
   exist in which the developing nations do for themselves, even if we're helping them.
        I often wonder if every government that estab-
   lishes a Family Planning Program from now on
   is going to repeat all the previous mistakes made

by other governments. I am afraid for a time it is going to be so. Indonesia is now teetering on the edge of a national Family Planning Program. They are proceeding almost completely rejecting any outside advice. They have not sent teams to look at what was going on in other countries. They have sent a few people on fellowships to Chicago and other places for short terms of study, but nobody knows how these people are going to fit into the program when they come back.

Ehrlich: Could we start by trying to persuade our government, through the methods we have, to create an example in this country? People do like to imitate us in some parts of the world. At least, they could not say that we want them to do it while we are not even doing it ourselves.

Saunders: You made the point earlier that it hasn't been very long since we had no policy.

Ehrlich: We have been backward in this; we have been far behind the Indians, which is a point a lot of people miss. They talk about how backward the Indian government is.

Notestein: On government policy but not on practice.

Ehrlich: Well, right.

Saunders: Incidentally, speaking of practice, one of the important points that hasn't gotten into the discussion is the fact that a third of the present world population is more or less successfully

limiting its fertility.   There are about a billion
people living in countries that have birth rates in
the low 20's, but that is not good enough.

Ehrlich: But, it is a lot better than 50.

Saunders: It is a lot better than we have around the
        rest of the world.   This was done for the most
        part without formal Family Planning Programs
        and without the two contraceptives that we have
        now, the loop and the Pill.

Ehrlich: And with industrialization, which is very
        difficult.

Saunders: But without the communication facilities
        that are available for getting information around
        rapidly at the present time.
            I think there are a number of ways and let me
        repeat one or two things that are in the Family
        Planning Program where we might get payoff
        from some concerted attention.   We should find
        better ways of getting management techniques,
        perhaps getting the family planning programs out
        ot the Ministries of Health and into some kind of
        managerial structure that will permit them to
        function.   Maybe they can function in some
        Ministries of Health, but so far the experience
        indicated that when they are put in there, they
        don't get under way very fast, unless someone in
        the ministry is keen on it.
            We need to do a lot more on marketing tech-
        niques.   You know about the experiment that is
        starting in India.   It is beginning to go, but very

slowly. We don't know how this experiment is
going to work, but it would look as if, by developing better techniques of marketing, we could get
more information around and more contraceptives
used. This is the point that Barnie Berelson has
made a number of times. It is easier to change
people's behavior than their attitudes, and if you
can change them through marketing techniques
that have been successful in changing behavior in
a lot of other fields, then perhaps it would be
worth trying.

I think we could do a great deal by expanding
communications, both the mass media communications and the face-to-face communications that
are necessary at some points in the system of
getting the service put around.

We need a great deal of expansion, and we
have talked about it today, in the contraceptive
technology, and enormous efforts continue to be
put into that.

The evaluation of Family Planning Programs
is pretty deficient in most parts of the world.
The question of how are we doing seems to be
omitted or put somewhere too far along in a program. Evaluation offers a couple of opportunities. First, it offers tremendous feedback opportunity that a good administrator can use if he
knows what is happening in his organization. He
can correct and improve, making the program
better.

The second broad area where evaluation
would be useful is in scorekeeping, feeding this
kind of information to the people who make decisions about the programs and allocate resources

to the programs. Then they see what they are
getting for their money.

We need a great deal of experimentation with
the delivery of contraceptive services. We have
pretty much tied them to the clinic throughout
the world. We have required people to go through
cumbersome processes to get access to services.
Sometimes we unnecessarily require physical
examinations.

Around the world we tend to require that
people come back to clinics to get renewal supplies. Nobody, so far as I know, except possibly
in Malaysia, is concerned very much with delivery
of supplies at homes on a regular routine basis.
So much could be done there.

We need a great deal more research and experimentation on incentives. You were making
the point, Professor Ehrlich, that if incentives
are high enough, we might get a lot more response.

Ehrlich: We might; we don't know.

Saunders: We don't know and we ought to try it, but
before we start at the top ---

Ehrlich: We shouldn't be starting at fifteen hundred
bucks per vasectomy.

Saunders: We ought to start with something other than
money, perhaps at the same time, but there are
enough programs going on in enough places around
the world, if we had access to them and if we were
ingenious we might set up some experiments and
learn a great deal about incentives.

Notestein: Especially giving incentives to the staff
    that is trying to do the job for you.

Saunders: I think it would be helpful if somehow we
    could get Family Planning defined as not entirely
    a health matter. There are lots of advantages in
    trying to get it accepted, defining it as a health
    matter, but I think the explicit definition of it in
    the area of health may have held back the develop-
    ment a little bit more than otherwise might have
    happened.
        Let's stop at that.

Harkavy: Lyle, I think it is a tribute to that beautiful
    and comprehensive presentation that you drove the
    idea of a tennis court completely out of my head.
    I think the attentiveness at five-thirty, which has
    probably exceeded that of the former two days,
    indicates what a nice job that was.
        There are several points. I know that Bill
    Knox wants to raise some points on the communi-
    cation side tomorrow, and there are others who
    will have a lot to say.
        I would like to urge anybody who has not al-
    ready done so to look at Table 1 on page 40 of
    Barney Berelson's "Beyond Family Planning."
    It outlines the strengths and weaknesses of most
    of the serious suggestions that have been made
    for encouraging fertility reduction outside of
    family planning programs.

        (The conference recessed at five-thirty
    o'clock.)

MONDAY MORNING SESSION
September 30, 1968

The conference reconvened at nine-five o'clock,
Dr. Harkavy presiding.

Harkavy: Why don't we get started? I think we are
probably down to a group that possibly can com-
municate.

The first two days have been spent largely,
and I think appropriately, in a review. I feel
there should be a certain amount of authoritative
exposition of various areas, but this exposition
has left insufficient time for the kind of interaction between people in the population field and the
outsiders that might lead to some new insights.

Lyle Saunders referred to the need to use
press services to get articles on population into
the mass media. Bill Knox indicated he wanted
to react to this idea. He is, you know, an expert
on communications.

Knox: I was asked this morning, as a matter of fact,
whether I considered myself to be an expert on
birth control. I admitted that I had come to this
conference as ignorant of the details of population
planning and birth control as a newborn babe, but
thankfully not as an unwanted one.

377

I have listened to all of these experts in the field and we have now come to the time in the conference when I think my own interests and expertise might have some beneficial input for you. I have been stimulated tremendously by everything I have heard.

I would like to address the problem of communication to see if we can highlight some of the issues that are involved in getting something done to allay your worries. I think it is well then to face up to the fact that what you want to accomplish is a gigantic social revolution, one without parallel in human history since the invention, anyway, of language or of agriculture.

Let's assume that you are right in what you are trying to do and that you have enough right answers, technology, and money to persuade or at least silence the objectors to what you are doing if you turn out to be wrong. The question is: How to bring it about ? I think we can learn something from the experience of the United States and Canada in their efforts to modernize and eventually to industrialize agriculture. These two countries stand in the forefront of those nations that have tried to do something about it on a large scale for many decades.

Furthermore, I chose agriculture because, like parenthood, the acceptance of agricultural innovation has primarily involved individual decision, and agriculture is also a business heavily dependent on fertility, disease and acts of God.

It has taken the U.S. almost one hundred years to get most, but not all, individual farmers practicing a reasonably high level of modern

agricultural technology. Canada has had an analogous agricultural extension service for fifty years,
yet there still are about 40 percent of individual
Canadian farmers yet to be persuaded of the benefits of modern agricultural technology. It has
been a long, slow process, and having the idea of
progress isn't enough.

These were instances of government concern
for the general welfare being implemented through
decisions of individual citizens, a situation quite
analogous to the one that you are concerned about
here, and I want to call your attention to the fact
that although the national governments were concerned about the national welfare (and the international coterie here is concerned about the international welfare), the programs for innovation
were keyed to the individual citizen's welfare:
What was in it for him? And I am persuaded that
parenthood control must similarly be made a
matter of individual welfare. I know of only a few
parents who would deliberately limit their offspring for the national or world good.

A number of powerful forces are acting
against the successful achievement of population
control. Let me mention the ones that can have
some relation to attitude and communication of
attitudes. While there is an immediately critical
problem in the lesser developed countries, the
problem is also of less immediate criticality even
in the industrialized nations.

One, there is an all-pervasive belief that growth
of all kinds—of organisms, of organizations, of individuals, of firms—is essential. It is essential for
strength; it is essential for progress; and it is

essential for vitality. Everyone believes that
growth is important. The growth of population
will inevitably have to come up against and face
squarely this attitude on the part of everybody that
growth is helpful.

There is a belief, therefore—and I believe
Saunders made this point yesterday—that population growth is no problem. There is the belief
that we can do anything—and modern technology
has its share of the guilt, if there is any guilt
here. Modern technology certainly has made it
possible to do almost anything we desire, including going to the moon.

Therefore, there is a prevalent, world-wide
opinion, even in well-informed circles, that
technology will save us again. Population growth,
however, doesn't wait for technology. Not only
must the technology be developed, as I believe it
will, but it must be applied in time.

A third factor, mostly confined to the industrialized world, is an enormous business stake
in babies and children and the inevitable social
benefits that arise from prosperous businesses
serving the needs of babies and children.

There are two other areas about which I will
comment very little, really, because you are
more aware of them than I: first, religious taboos,
which I believe have arisen primarily out of the
results of human history over centuries. I don't
think that some group has deliberately decided to
foist them on people. I think they are expressions
of human experience, really, and so it will be
necessary to combat this particular way of expressing the historical record.

Second, there is the all-powerful sex drive
which we aren't going to do anything about, I
guess, unless we take up some of Shelly's comments or suggestions yesterday—but I am concerned now about its exploitation in the developed
nations by industry, business, and the media.
Will it be similarly exploited in the other nations
as soon as they cross the threshhold into industrialized society?

It is a fact that early sexual expression,
earlier every year it seems, is fostered by the
desires of some industries and the media, operating within their own separate context, their own
system of rewards and penalties, costs and
benefits. The automobile industry is, of course,
a powerful contributor to earlier sexual expression
and it will be very difficult to roll back this trend,
for example, by increasing the age at which people
can drive. There is the counterpart expression
of later sexual expression, maintaining youth well
into the 50's, 60's and 70's—"Stay young. Stay
active." I would guess, unless one becomes completely exhausted by all that, that the inevitable
result will be more babies.

So I can see really a fantastic, gigantic communications problem. Population growth will
slow only when people—individuals—act to slow it.
It will be, as pointed out here, a behavioral
matter. Somebody said that he didn't care what
people's attitudes were; he only cared about how
they behaved. But I see little chance of changing
people's voluntary behavior on this matter without changing first and foremost their value standards, their attitudes. We can change their

behavior compulsorily, using legislation and many
other forms, I guess, but we can't change their
voluntary behavior without first changing their
value standards.

With all that is working against population
control, I think it will require the most professional of value reorientation programs to achieve
your goals. I question seriously any and all
government appeals on behalf of the national welfare. They may help, but they won't be sufficient.
In many instances we are trying to change the
value standard of people who are functionally
illiterate. There are programs, I know, which
take that into account, but there are still a great
many programs using literate techniques to accomplish a job that is primarily for the illiterate.

We must face the question of how the message
is to be delivered. We can have choirs of angels
or men on horseback, the radio, TV, more of the
printed word, or others. I feel that in this area
of parenthood we have been relying more on the
angels than on the printed word, and I believe we
are going to have to use more modern mechanisms
of communication and modern techniques. If you
will just think about it, the use of angels and the
printed word, or radio or TV, allows no response
from the audience. They are all one-way communication streets.

But I can see two rays of hope: first, the
steady improvement in communications capability
at low cost all around the world; and second, the
involvement of businesses which have a profit
stake in birth control.

Here I raise a very serious issue. Are the program objectives best achieved by maximizing the communications projects of government, public health, and other not-for-profit organizations and institutions, which seems to be a trend? I would guess not, at least in the nations which have a good communications infrastructure. An advertisement for a birth control device or product or service will get more attention from people in the developed nations than a hundred editorial items. Furthermore, it is difficult for any government to mount a program which inevitably threatens the profitability of major business segments, but a competing business can do it with much less social conflict.

Getting down to specifics, why aren't contraceptives, either as products, devices, or services, advertised in popular magazines and the mass media? They aren't. Only within the last year have vaginal foams been accepted, provided nothing is said about them in the advertising. It has to be in "good taste." This was done in Look magazine, but still radio, TV, all the other popular magazines, and, I believe, the newspapers (though I do not know) just do not accept these advertisements.

It seems to me that if the provision of contraceptive services were made into a business operation in the industrialized nations, as opposed to a public health-delivered service, you might again have the possibility of building up a profit-oriented—not necessarily a profit-making but profit-oriented—business which could begin to advertise.

If you think about the advertising that we do
see, it is always a healthy baby. Even if the baby
is crying, it is a healthy baby. I think we must
figure out ways to show some scrawny ones, some
very unhealthy babies. Children will have to be
shown in their more natural, untamed state, with
all of the problems that they bring.

I think we must also tie in property and income tax increases with the increase in population.

Let me now leave the area of communication
and touch briefly on this problem as a technological or sociological innovation problem, a problem
in innovation and its spread and dispersion and
adoption within a society. In the last fifteen years
there have been a number of efforts focused on
learning how innovation best takes place within
a society. NASA has pioneered with their Technology Utilization Program. There have also been
studies by the Department of Commerce on technological innovation and how it takes place. European countries are concerned that the United States
can bring about the widespread adoption of a technological innovation faster than European organizational mechanisms permit.

I just point out that in this relatively short
period, we have begun to assemble and evaluate
what we know about the techniques for bringing
about innovation. It involves more, of course,
than just advertising in the mass media which I
have talked about up to now. It involves incentives. It especially involves the forces influencing group behavior, and, of course, it involves
communication technologies.

As a final little point, may I throw in my concern about one of the least required but one of the most serious consequences of population growth—the information overload. Not just verbalized information, but the stimuli that each of us receives from his surroundings every moment, awake or asleep. I feel intuitively that the instability we are experiencing in much of the world is a reaction primarily to information overload. I think we must find better ways of either reacting to it or controlling it, or like an overly stimulated rat we will probably end up dead.

Along this line, the information that you want to convey must compete with all of the other information that is rained down on each individual. Your information, therefore, must be presented in such a way as to give it priority in reception instead of priority in transmission and dissemination. It will be an extremely difficult, time-consuming job.

Harkavy: Thank you very much. May I press you on some points that you have raised?

I had a feeling you referred to the American scene when you spoke of the information overload and the need to advertise contraceptives on TV and the radio. Other things you said were applicable to the developing world. What for Asia—what kinds of techniques in communication would you suggest?

Knox: You can press me but it might be like trying to get blood out of a stone.

I am glad you point out that I was jumping from developed to underdeveloped parts of the world in my discussion. Perhaps those who were confused and didn't know why they were confused have been straightened out by that bit of insight.

I find it very difficult to answer your question specifically on what to do in Asia because I know so little about what actually is done in Asia, or what is possible. I think it is true that in Asia there is relatively little saturation of the media of communication as we, for example, have in the United States. We have one radio station or TV station for every thirty thousand people. We have eighteen hundred newspapers published daily.

You don't find that kind of situation in the underdeveloped countries at all. My comments, then, about the role of advertising and of the private services which would advertise their products or services on TV and radio would be relatively inapplicable in Asia. I just don't know what the Asian mass media communication situation is.

Ross: May I interrupt with a generalization that might be useful; that would be not to put stress on the modern technologies of communication but on the more effective ones, whatever they turn out to be, for that particular corner and style of the world. That is the kind of thing. A colleague is working for modern industry to open up Latin American markets. Essentially for communication, for softening purposes if you will, the technology that he is adopting includes things like comic strips with very few words—self-explanatory.

Ehrlich: Because I have found as little resistance to the idea of community TV viewing on very simple receivers as to anything else, I have looked into this in some depth. As some of you may know, one of the characteristics of primitive people that has always fascinated anthropologists is that if you show them a black and white photograph, they very often don't recognize things unless they have had contact because the photograph contains a whole series of stylized things that we don't realize. The most striking thing about it is the white border. We know that we just disregard that. If you show them a picture in motion, or in color, there is no confusion

When I was with the Eskimoes, I was always fascinated to see that they would sit through any movie, even if it dealt with something so completely out of their context that it was unbelievable to me that there could be anything in it for them at all. I have seen in places in Asia large groups of people sitting around a TV set actually fascinated with what to us would be very, very primitive programming.

I would think that if you could interest anthropologists and communication experts in the very real problems that you have brought up of how to get the message in, that would be a tremendous help; but I think another very important point that you brought out is this necessity of response. I have actually heard serious discussions that maybe the best thing to do would be to use science to invent religions, and perhaps even create miracles, and to get people participating—in other words, to add an element ---

Ross: That's what we do now, isn't it?

Ehrlich: I mean do it Machiavellianly.

Ritchie-Calder: Buy up the witch doctor.

Chamberlain: This really brings in the point that I
     was going to make, because it seems to me that
     your stress was largely on the techniques of com-
     munication and I think that equally we would have
     to give some attention to the message that is being
     communicated. Here we are back to the old ques-
     tion of whether the normal Family Planning
     approach, which I think you largely stressed be-
     cause your emphasis was on selling this to the
     individual, or the individual family—whether that
     is enough.
         In putting together what Shelly Segal was
     telling us the other day and what you are saying
     now, might it not be possible to change some of
     the mores by different messages conveyed through
     your means of communication.
         If now we have techniques by which, through
     implantation or something of that sort, we can
     effectively delay the period during which fertiliza-
     tion takes place, would it not be possible to get
     across the notion that just as voting begins at a
     particular age, 21, childbearing does not begin
     until that point; and even though you may not be
     able to get a voluntary sterilization of a large
     segment of the adult population, because this would
     be an infringement on private matters, we still
     have the notion that the adult takes care of the
     child. Could we develop the idea that it is not an

infringement of personal rights to prevent children from having children—children from bearing children — the girl of 15 or 16 from bearing a child at that age. Postponing the age of having children until at least 21 or 22, even by compulsory means, might be effective.

Slobodkin: Just to throw in a more cheerful approach; the Enna Jettick Company runs ads in the New York Times. They are fascinating ads and I think they are very relevant. They say, "We make shoes for grandmothers," and they have a picture of a very sexy looking woman, sitting on a bar stool, with a long cigarette holder, and the ad says, "Grandmothers nowadays are young, exciting, know how to hold their man," and so forth. There is a general image of the sexual opportunities being extended into time to an age which is relatively innocuous from the population increase standpoint.

Rather than say, "Thou shalt not horse around at an early age," why not offer, through medicine, pills, and other goodies, the possibility of tremendous years and years of sexual activity ahead of you? "There's no hurry," sort of thing.

Ross: It would be pretty hard to sell. You would have a lot of selling to do.

Chamberlain: Why do you have to go that far? What we are saying now is: go ahead and horse around. You don't have to wait, and we are going to make sure it can be done without any sense of danger.

Ross: It is a hard business to sell delayed gratification, sir.

Chamberlain: You don't have to delay gratification, that's the point. With certain techniques, you can have sexual gratification and still society doesn't have to pay the price.

Ehrlich: You have got to get over the not quite hopeless viewpoint that it is a terrible thing that something as lovely as sex is befouled with children, which limits the amount of sexual activity you can have.

Bernstein: What you want is a puberty unfertility rite.

Hoagland: You can argue that just as one goes to a very good restaurant to get French food and other things for the palate, you don't go to that restaurant simply for calories, and this could be applied to sex and children.

Ritchie-Calder: I just want to intervene on one point that was raised by Professor Chamberlain: that is that there are methods, you see, but they are not applied. If the Indians applied the Sharda Act, which prevents child marriage, you could very effectively deal with the lower end of this thing, but nobody does because it is such a common practice. There is no common informant. It is against the law but it must be by common informant and it doesn't work.

       I had an interesting experience in Burma some years ago. The area of Burma, for example, is

an eighth the size of India, but the population of
Burma is a twentieth that of India, and I said to
the Minister of Social Affairs, "How does this
work?" She said, "It is because we have had
women's emancipation in Burma since the Burmese
kings and therefore women are active in trade.
They are women lawyers and everything else. That
postpones the marriage age."

And then, of course, we got into the question
of techniques, which she didn't understand. "I
know what happened," she said, "before the
Narcotics Commission came along. When a
woman had enough children, she put the old man
on opium."

But the thing about the Indian situation is that
you can change the bottom level, you see, very
drastically, but how do you do it? In India there
is a law against child marriage, but it isn't en-
forced.

Chamberlain: You wouldn't have to change that. You
could go ahead and have child marriages. There
simply would not be a product of the marriage
until the age of 21. Couples would have a chance
to adjust to each other, to establish the household,
and not until, let's say, the age of 21 or 22, or
whatever it is, will it be permissible for that
family to have a child.

Shelesnyak: Ritchie-Calder is saying there is a law
that forbids their marriage. You want to suggest
another regulation that they are not supposed to
have children.

Chamberlain: Not as a matter of regulation. Shelly
        Segal has taken care of that. All we have to say
        is that children will have compulsory inoculation,
        like smallpox, an implantation that involuntarily
        takes care of it as far as the person of that age
        is concerned, but voluntarily as far as society is
        concerned. You have accepted that as being part
        of the mores, just as you delay voting and other
        forms of activity.

Shelesnyak: Then you have to make a selection, un-
        less you do it to all children.

Chamberlain: Exactly. It would be done just as voting
        is delayed across the board.
            Shall all female children have this implanta-
        tion of a capsule that Shelly Segal was talking
        about?

Ehrlich: Midwives do most of the deliveries. It would
        be very difficult logistically. That is one of the
        horrors of it. They don't all come into hospitals.
        If they came into hospitals then you would have a
        much simpler problem; but mostly it is out in the
        fields and getting hold of the young females would
        be more difficult.

Zuckerman: Let me as a student of reproductive
        physiology say here and now that if anything like
        that would be suggested for any daughter of mine,
        I would resent it and resist it immediately.

Chamberlain: Why?

Zuckerman: Because we don't know what the effects would be genetically. We don't know what the effects would be on the stock of ova. We don't know a thing about this.

Slobodkin: The Enna Jettick Shoe thing got passed over. Let me come back to it because I think it is important. What I am suggesting is propaganda to the effect that having babies ruins the figure and cuts out a great deal of sexual pleasure—as gentle as that. With modern cosmetics, modern food, and so forth, one can have a long, long, lovely sexual life.

Ritchie-Calder: We are talking about marriages.

Shelesnyak: Ritchie, you say we are talking about something. I would like to know what we are talking about. As I recall, Bill Knox started presenting some aspects of communication from a technical point of view and some questions were raised about the importance of concerning ourselves with the content, the quality of the content, so to speak. I think we are getting off the track now if we are trying to start a program here to work out the types of messages in detail. Perhaps "Energetic Shoes" do it beautifully. I love grandmothers, I can assure you of that, even sexy ones, but I think we are getting off the point, really.

Bernstein: I don't think it is off the point because yesterday we were talking about the desirability, for example, of delaying marriage if we could. Such a course would lead to complex problems such as what would be permissible sexual activity during the pre-conception period. Within our own society, and possibly others, the idea of extramarital relations would be a tremendous hurdle, if you are talking about a strategy or tactic of delaying marriage, and you have to take into account the obstacle of mores against extramarital activity.

Zuckerman: There seem to be a little misunderstanding about what I have just said. I would certainly not be opposed to any measure which would deny, let us say, children or adolescents, sexual gratification that leads to procreation. The thing that I am saying we cannot risk is the physiological repression of the ovary at that stage of development.

Chamberlain: I understand your point but I didn't understand from Shelly Segal's presentation yesterday that there was that degree of danger. This may be a dispute between certain people in the field.

Fisher: I think that Neil Chamberlain's point is possibly the most practical of a large number of the impractical suggestions that I have heard, and we ought not to bog down because the particular way of preventing conception may not have been tested adequately. The idea of delaying conception is a dandy one and there are other ways of promoting it—perhaps not so efficiently—than the implant of a capsule.

I should think that a campaign of birth limitation could be focused strongly in all the media and world press on the idea of delay of conception—not marriage, not sexual activity—but delay of conception as a norm. Emphasize it as a way to promote better family adjustments. In such circumstances, the promotion of contraceptive devices that are thought to be unharmful could be included; then, as the contraception techniques improve or get tested out, the thing could be made binding. I think this is the best idea that has been put forward so far.

Ehrlich: It is also statistically very good. It is one of the most effective things you can do demographically.

Fisher: It goes right to the problem, it seems to me.

Zuckerman: This is the one that worked in Ireland. This is the one that has been thoroughly analyzed. We know all about this.

Fisher: Only it is even better because you don't have to defer marriage and sexual activity within marriage.

Ritchie-Calder: I want to come back to techniques because I feel there is very great danger of misunderstanding this thing when we think in terms of very sophisticated measures of communication. I think what we have been talking about is relevant, even about the grandmothers, but this cannot apply in the areas that we are most deeply

concerned about. I think we have been very backward over the last twenty years in dealing, not
only with this problem, but with most of the problems of technical assistance, in that we really
have not understood the nature of the people with
whom we have been dealing. I have had hundreds
and hundreds of examples of very effective
methods which are entirely localized—they must
be localized, they must come out of the idiom of
the people, they must come out of the nature of
the society—and I think what we have been deficient
in spreading the kind of ideas which would, in fact,
generate themselves in terms of methods in the
countries.

I will give a simple example. In Indonesia
there was a very effective campaign of regional
agricultural instruction that was initiated by a
man who went around as a troubadour. He sang
his instructions and got the people singing the
chorus, and they want around singing the glories
of better grain production. I went with him. This
was extremely effective.

Then I got to India where they were trying to
launch a malaria control scheme. They were
doing the sort of thing we have been talking about
here, even to the point of having large blown-up
plastic models of the Anopheles stephenensis.
They put these models in the midst of children in
a mud hut or a mud school, saying, "This is your
enemy." The children went out and found the
stephenensis in the local pond and it was a friendly
little thing. The people and the doctors back of
this program did not understand that the children
did not comprehend the idea of magnification. It

was rather like our earlier comments about black
and white photographs.

In Mexico, I told them the story of the singing troubadour, and we did this, incidentally, by
transferal of the idea. I asked if there were anything in their culture like the tradition of the singing troubadour, and they told me about the taja.
The taja is a sort of mock-up, a sort of human
Punch and Judy show—two characters that have
ferocious arguments in the village square.

This is what they did. They introduced taja,
with somebody taking the side of the mosquito and
somebody taking the side of the doctor, and in
each case the doctor won.

I think wherever you go you will find this kind
of thing, which is not only the simplest way, the
most direct way in the sense of taking it out to the
people, but the transferal of these ideas. This is
not something you take literally and transfer from
here to there. You have to find the thing that is
the system of communication.

Fisher: You English have the greatest troubadours of
all time in the Beatles, and I made the suggestion
quite seriously last night that if you want to get
quick penetration across cultural barriers, interest the Beatles in the subject of birth control.
They would probably know how to translate this
into the idiom and you won't need to tell them how
to do it. They know how to do this, believe me.
I am for the troubadour idea and I suggest that you
have in your own country the greatest troubadours
perhaps of all time.

Ritchie-Calder: Well, I am not so sure about that.

Fisher: But in the sense of getting a message across.

Ritchie-Calder: As a result of that, we're all on LSD now.

Zuckerman: Neither the Beatles nor any of those young troubadours necessarily share the views we are expressing here. They have a totally different picture of the kind of life they want to see constructed. They are not necessarily concerned about population problems. There have been such transformations in the behavior of the young English child, the adolescent, over the past ten years that nobody could have conceived of them twenty years ago. I do not myself believe that one could easily enlist the aid of the Beatles in turning back a trend which they themselves have created.

Slobodkin: In photographs shown in the New York Times of the student revolution at Columbia University, there is one that shows students in a classroom taking it over. The professors have been driven out; the revolution is in full swing; and on the black board is written: "Judy, remember your Pill."

This appeared a few weeks ago. It demonstrates an interesting identification between the kind of revolution you are talking about and the kind of revolution we have been talking about. These kids are very, very birth control conscious.

Ritchie-Calder: Can we get back to the question of how
    you get through to the underdeveloped countries?
    Everyone is quite right when he says you cannot
    induce people to do something because it is good
    for their country. There is no patriotism in
    population, unless there's a need for armies.
        It is important that, first we ask ourselves:
    What are the limitations of our method? Even if
    you had a satellite over India, you are still sub-
    ject to group listening, to group influences, and
    so on, and when you come down to the alternative it
    is the family influence. I am not talking about the
    parents; it is the group-family influence in places
    like India.
        Women have held up technical development in
    India—no question at all about it. You can encour-
    age men to take up new methods of agriculture but
    nothing happens because the hidden woman cannot
    see the destruction of the one world she knows,
    which is the family group. Until you get through
    to the grandmother—and I think most people who
    have had any experience with techniques knows
    this—the mother, the daughter-in-law, through
    the emancipation of the daughter-in-law, you are
    not going to make any progress.

Ehrlich: First of all, I think things like the Beatles
    are extremely acceptable to a sort of worldwide
    teen culture. If those women ten years from now
    would be grown-up, Beatle-influenced females ---

Ross: What a horrible thought that is!

Ehrlich: As a small fraction of our foreign aid, put a TV set in every village in India. We are putting, what is it, a billion and a half into foreign aid but there are what, 200,000 villages?

Ritchie-Calder: Eight hundred thousand if you come down to it.

Ehrlich: All right, 800,000 villages at a cost of twenty bucks for a TV set.

Ritchie-Calder: Eight hundred thousand sets—how do you maintain them?

Ehrlich: You can make an awfully reliable TV set for $20 now and you could afford to replace them.

Ritchie-Calder: You are not going to get across with black and white.

Saunders: May I point out one thing with regard to this? In India, for example, the radio is presently being used very effectively in terms of the kinds of things we are talking about. They don't have the Beatle song but they have the local equivalent, which is even better. There are certain stock characters similar to Lum and Abner that we used to have here, or Amos and Andy, known to and in a sense reified by the villagers who believe they are real characters, and these people are beginning to introduce this.

Hoagland: Are the villages well electrified so that one has power for TV?

Saunders: The five hundred thousand, no, but there is a considerable audience for radio receptivity in rural areas, so that this is being introduced and used to the extent that the technology permits. As Mr. Knox said, there are some strategy implications that are very broad and very basic, and I wish, instead of discussing the details of these things, we could look at some of this basic strategy.

We have been talking several themes here. One of the themes we have been using is the kind of approaches you need to prevent the first pregnancy, particularly in teen-age girls. We are supporting at the present in Baltimore an experiment to see if the first illegitimate teen-age pregnancy can be prevented. There is a fair amount of interest in preventing the second one but heretofore there has been little interest in preventing the first one.

In the United States (I am not sure of this number but the order of magnitude is right), about one in three teen-age marriages occurs with the bride pregnant at the time of the marriage. In certain of the Baltimore census districts, about one in five of the teen-age girls between 12 and 17 are pregnant at any one time; so this is a very serious problem. We are just now beginning to do something about it, and we are proceeding very, very timidly because we don't have very much of an idea what community reaction will be. That is one level.

Much of what we have been talking about is based on the assumption that births are rational, that children appear because parents want them.

I suggest we don't really know to what extent this is true, and that just as people cause accidents, so do accidents cause people. Here again motivation really does not enter into it. The child comes along as a byproduct of something else, and the something else is a very powerful thing that is going to be very difficult to change but we need to be concerned about it.

Chamberlain: Lyle, are you saying that there is no fear of the unwanted child in these unmarried teen-age girls, that they are unconcerned?

Saunders: There may be. I don't think this has been studied carefully enough to say. We don't know very much about it.

Chamberlain: But, you are saying there is some concern about the second child.

Saunders: Once a girl has had an illegitimate child, then we can argue within our value system that it is an appropriate thing to give her contraceptives.

Ross: Then she is marked and we, as a society, enter and try to do something about it.

Ehrlich: There are some hints that they are relatively unconcerned, for various reasons, which is kind of frightening.

Saunders: On the matter of messages, we have been talking again as if there is only one audience and only one message. As a matter of fact, there are many audiences and each audience requires a different set of messages and probably a different set of procedures. One of the most important audiences are the decision-making elite who have to allocate the funds, dig up the resources, and make the decisions that will make programs possible. For them you need one kind of technique. I don't think the Beatle approach in this case would be the proper one.

There is the whole public in the reproducing ages, which is what we have been talking about for the most part, and they need certain kinds of messages, too—especially in much of the developing world the simple message that it is possible to make a choice in this area and that there are ways in which it can be done.

There are special messages that you need for the people who are on the point of acceptance— information messages about what are the best kinds of contraceptives, what are the most suitable, what are the preferences, how they work, what the risks are, things of this kind. These probably are transmitted best in face-to-face communication, but also there are some other techniques that can be used.

Finally, we need a whole set of messages going around within the Family Planning organizations to the people who work in it so that they all know what is going on, so they are getting proper supervision, encouragement, support, stimulation, and so on. So this part of the communications business is very complex.

One of the points that Mr. Knox made related
to the business stake in children. I think in the
developing world there probably isn't much of a
business stake in the production of children. Nobody has diaper services in the villages of India
or Ghana. People are selling milk products and
things of that kind and they are pushing them. But,
at the present time I don't think there is any resistance from the business community, so in the developing world at this time this is not a major factor.
It may come in later. It may be that to some
extent in urban areas we shouldn't rule it out, but
it won't be a major part of our present strategy.

The business approach was suggested. It is
being done very badly but I think the business
approach is the one that is being used by IPPF
and Family Planning Associations at the present
time. They offer services and they charge for
them. They try not to make a profit but sometimes they do. They operate on the theory that
it is bad for people's character to give them something for nothing, that they appreciate it more if
you charge for it, so they put on a fairly substantial charge. In Ghana the FPA is charging the
equivalent of four American dollars for an IUD
insertion, and four American dollars is probably
one-sixth of a month's salary for some people.
Relatively few people can get help under these
conditions.

I would like to call attention to two big strategy areas and hear some discussion. These relate to the relative merits of an approach using
a one-to-one communication system and one using
a mass connunication system. I think Mr. Knox

used as an illustration the agricultural communications in the United States and Canada, and I
would like to raise the question: Is it conceivable,
at least, that the reason that it has taken so long
and gotten so little results is that they have been
working on a one-to-one, face-to-face approach,
the agricultural extension worker, the home
demonstration worker, and so on, going out and
visiting people in their home and talking to them,
trying to change a person at a time?

I think it is at least plausible that an approach
which recognizes decisions are taken in the context of the community matrix and addresses itself to changing that matrix might have as good a
payoff as this one.

The second strategy point is whether you
start to work on behavior or you start to work on
attitude, and here again I think it is not entirely
clear. The essential theoretical problem is
whether behavior follows attitudes or attitude
change follows behavior? It is not entirely re-
solved but there is a certain plausability in the
notion that if you change behavior, the appropriate
attitudes will follow.

These are, I think, the kinds of strategy issues
that we should consider.

Ross: May I add one other one, commented on only
in passing, that has been bothering me. I was
sitting here daydreaming that I was with a group
that was plotting a new world revolution and that
our session was a meeting of its general staff.
At one moment I became confused by the continuous daylight arrangements of this room. I looked

at all the generals and political leaders, plotting
this revolution, and I was one of them. I worried
about where we came from and who we are. One
characteristic, which has impressed me continuously and reached a peak this morning, was that
all of us are from one part of the human population. I would like now to play the role of a G2 and
to indicate for strategic purposes the critical
soft, non-visible, most important target audience
for action.

We have been talking as if all we have to do is
shell a whole area. I would like to identify for you
the world force that is emerging and on which my
hopes for change in a desirable direction will
occur. I refer, of course, to the unrepresented
group in this audience, women with their controlling role. This control is exercised in an
interactive, subtle, and frequently in a most
determining way in all of human affairs. The
generals sit around thinking they are in control,
particularly in the area of sexual activity and
reproduction.

So, I would offer for strategic purposes, a
specialized half of the world as a target. I think
the more important half of the world, if you will.
With all of the shadings and meanings that those
of you who are familiar with Asia know, you can
perhaps interpret better for such settings. As I
listened, I got a feel of the difference between
the situations, in Burma and India, and you know
the evidence far better than I do.

So I would urge us, plotting the revolution,
to pay special attention as to where we apply our
energy, in what specific form, and to what target.

Ritchie-Calder: May I follow that one, please? I
     want to reinforce it as strongly as I can. I will
     give you one example of a social revolution, in
     Afghanistan. It started with a glass of UNICEF
     milk in 1952, when we got the women to come in
     their chadares, to the gynecologic and pediatric
     clinic. Within months the women had discovered
     that they were important, because the women
     who were treating them were professional women.
     They had never realized a woman could enter pro-
     fessional life.

          The second stage was that they themselves
     became important; that is to say, they began to
     be treated not just as childbearing machines but
     seriously as people.

          The result of that over the years has been
     quite extraordinary. In measurable terms I
     don't know how far it has changed the actual
     structure of Afghanistan but I can tell you that
     within ten years the King of Afghanistan was in a
     position (his predecessor having lost his throne
     because he unveiled women) to tell the women
     they could abandon the chadare. The result of
     this has been quite extraordinary.

          The instrument of social change in the vil-
     lages now, where there are better wells, where
     there is better housing, where there is family
     planning if you ever get that far, is the woman.
     She is the instrument of this whole revolution,
     without question.

Ehrlich: In the United States women are showing
     signs, for instance, of finally doing something
     about laws on abortion. There is a very active
     group in California.

Ritchie-Calder: We have done that in Britain, sir.
The men did that.

Ehrlich: Men made the original laws.

Marcus: To return for a moment to the comments
that were made about reservations on the widespread use of contraceptive implants for early
fertility control (or for fertility control at any age),
do we have time to postpone the application of
such techniques merely because we are uncertain
about the possible medical dangers or genetic
dangers? Even if we had a complete awareness
and detailed knowledge of exactly what those dangers were and what could be expected from the use
of these techniques, would we hesitate to use them?
In other areas, such as, the use of certain antibiotics, we don't hesitate to use them in spite of
well-known dangers.
    As the urgency of the problem of increasing
population becomes more and more immediate,
inevitably our concepts of morality and our reservation about the application of various means and
levels of acceptability will have to change. I am
not saying that we shouldn't test, but can we afford to postpone the use of existing techniques
while testing?

Hoagland: I was thinking along the same lines. If
you consider a 2 percent growth rate, which we
are concerned about, continuing, in 35 years
there will be 7 billion people in 70 years 14 billion,
and in 105 years 28 billion, and it seems to me
that by the time that has happened, or even before,

there will be so much pollution, so much misery and illness, so much stress of trying to adjust and live with this condition, that there will be a public demand to do something about it, regardless of where it is from. Then I think there will be insistence on the part of governments to protect the people and regulate the population growth.

I have been interested in the effects of stress on animals. We have done a study of stress at the Worcester Foundation in terms of responses of the adrenal cortex to stressful situations, ranging over a great variety of phenomena in various animals, including man. We have demonstrated that the stress of crowding is a very real thing. The behavior of animals under crowded conditions I have reviewed briefly in the Bulletin of the Atomic Scientist. There is a considerable literature on the effects of crowding of animals and how far it can be extrapolated to considerations of stress and crowding and disturbances in human behavior. There is again evidence that under really severe crowding, there are increases in a variety of illnesses, and the length of life is shortened. This applies particularly in men who compete so intensely in modern society.

We have a parallel situation, I think, in some of the contests in animal societies where crowding breaks down the social organization of animals in their hierarchies and in defense of their respective territories. With man we have not only geographical territories but also ideological, political, and religious territories to defend. Defense of job status and roles in various human social hierarchies is stressful.

I think we would have great difficulty in showing that crowding per se in present urban levels has any significant effect on increasing death rates and thus lowering human population growth. However, the crowding in concentration camps made the stress syndrome play a direct role in producing deaths and lowering the population. Here, of course, crowding was extreme.

If the present growth rate continues, I think it probable that we will have a nuclear war that will reduce the population. Hopefully without nuclear war and before 140 years from now when the world population would be 56 billion (at a continuing 2 percent growth rate) we will be forced to put through compulsory regulations to prohibit further growth. So I think that excessive population growth will take care of itself in a catastrophic way if we don't find an earlier and more humane solution.

Harkavy: The question has been asked, What kind of advice do we as Americans in a philanthropic institution give to our opposite numbers overseas with regard to contraceptive safety? We send all relevant information to people overseas and urge them to share this material with the medical authorities in the host country, so that the latter can formulate policy on the basis of all the facts. In other words, we would feel it unethical for us to know something that we don't share with the responsible medical authorities in countries where we work.

Ehrlich: Let me support Dr. Marcus on this question
of ethics, and so on. Your position is a very
difficult one, but I am totally in sympathy with it.
It continues to appal me that people place this
tremendous emphasis on the safety of methods.
If Dr. Shelesnyak's suggestions are taken in
India, might that injure people there. Would we
do it for our own children here ?

Only in this area do we have this kind of concern. We have no concern about the fact that we
feed our children here a diet which is inaccessible
to 90 percent of the children of the world. We
have other standards of living in this country that
are beyond most other parts of the world; we get
protein from the protein-poor people of South
America; we are able to afford to raise beef in
Asia and transport it all the way across the world
to eat.

It has been estimated that we consume almost
50 percent of the world's natural resources every
year. In other words, we don't have all of these
standards of safety and consideration for the other
people in the world. I would say that I would not
want my daughter or wife to go on the Pill, because I don't think it is all that safe; but from the
point of view of the Indian situation today, one
which we have helped to create, better they should
all be on the Pill even if the Pill killed one out
of twenty-five of the women than to allow the kind
of situation that is developing there now.

In other words, I don't understand why the concern for what we would do in our incredibly unique

society in time and in space should prevent us
from looking at solutions in these other countries
where the situation is not parallel.

Shelesnyak: I believe there is a more fundamental
question to which we should address ourselves.
I, for one, don't know how to solve it. I mentioned it fleetingly yesterday. When it comes to
contraceptive techniques, the public demands two
things: perfect 100 percent effectiveness; and
second, absolutely no side effects. There is
nothing that I know of that is prescribed or
bought which can fill this set of criteria. Just
plain, ordinary, delicious, pure water can be
lethal under certain circumstances. But when it
comes to contraceptives, it has to be absolutely
perfect in every respect. Nobody ever says stop
taking aspirin because it may do damage. Get
rid of all the televisions because of the possible
radiation effects. This is a fact. Is there anything we can do about this? Is there anything we
can do to persuade the public at large to accept
the same reasonable degree of risk in life when
it comes to contraceptive agents that they accept
without question in other areas?

Knox: The medical profession, I think, is somewhat
at the root of a lot of this: the idea of good health
as being an inalienable human right.

Marcus: In America.

Shelesnyak: And England.

Zuckerman: Not to the same extent as in the United States.

Knox: -- and the fact that everything must, therefore, be absolutely free from side effects. It is a very unusual situation.

Shelesnyak: Bill, they don't insist on it when they get medication for other things.

Knox: The trend is in that direction. Increasingly, FDA insists on the same guarantees of freedom from side-effects in non-contraceptive drugs as well.

Hoagland: Some doctors, when they have patients on the Pill, one of whom dies, tend to write a paper about it and this gets headline billing by the press. I agree with you, Paul, and I am surprised at Bud's reaction to it.

Ehrlich: He has a special problem.

Hoagland: I have recommended to my daughters and daughters-in-law the use of the Pill. I have not had any hesitation about it. Clarence Faust of the Ford Foundation was an early supporter of Pincus work on the pill. He said, as did you, that even if there is a certain amount of deleterious side effect from them, they ought to be used because they can be so exceedingly important in controlling runaway populations.

I really think that Shelly put his finger on the problem. It is a very strange reaction in which it seems to be the ambition of some physicians to show that the Pill is a deadly poison.

Ehrlich: The medical profession is against contraception and against abortion. Don't kid yourself. In California we managed, with help from a very few dedicated doctors like Dick Lee, to get the abortion law changed to a semi-sane one, and in the first six months the concentration of abortions being done by about five guys in the state was about one-third. Many doctors will still not give an abortion because they have been trained not to do it.

Zuckerman: Let's get this thing in proportion. I think all these sweeping statements about doctors simply should be rejected—and I am not speaking now as an M.D., which I also happen to be— nor am I suggesting, nor would any doctor urge that no therapy should be engaged in if it carries any risk. But yesterday when Shelly Segal was talking, he told us that in the sample of people who had been studied, 38 percent showed changes in their glucose tolerance. He was discussing a pre-diabetic condition which results from contraceptive treatment.

The Pill has been going for just a few years. He never mentioned, incidentally, the major concern in the United Kingdom, thrombosis, which probably is a triviality. But I was immensely struck that there were many millions using the Pill.

Hoagland: Twelve to fifteen million.

Zuckerman: Twelve to fifteen million are using the
    Pill.
        Let them go on using the Pill and let us wait
    five years and find out whether, as a result of
    using the Pill, something happens as a conse-
    quence of the pre-diabetic condition.
        I do not for one second suggest that we should
    not try methods which carry risks, but there is
    a choice. There are options before us. If we
    could get every adolescent boy who is responsible
    for the one in five illegitimate pregnancies in
    Baltimore to use condoms, that would be good
    enough without running into all these extravagances
    that carry risks with which we cannot deal. Even
    in India—from this paper sent to me yesterday—
    I read that there is a big turn to the condom,
    which we know is not dangerous.

Ehrlich: But it is not working.

Zuckerman: Let's not be black and white about this
    particular thing.

Ehrlich: I wasn't suggesting that the Pill is even a
    method of choice, but any decision like this I
    still feel must be weighed against the environ-
    mental and the disease consequences on the other
    side, which I think you seriously underestimate.

Zuckerman: In 1955 at the Tokyo Conference I sug-
    gested that instead of focusing on every individual
    act that might lead to procreation, we ought to

concern ourselves with general methods that
might reduce the chances of a mating act becoming fruitful. I suggested the illustration that
one can reduce the stock of oocytes, finite stock,
by means of measured doses of radiation. We
have done this and proven that it reduces overall
fertility in the rat. But, I don't know what radiation would do to the oocytes remaining in the
human ovary after radiation. That is why I am
nervous about advocating such a method—from
the point of view of the next generation of young
who emerge from the remaining stock of oocytes
after the mothers' ovaries have been dealt with.

We don't know what happens when you suppress an ovary, how you increase the rate of
atresia, whether the oocytes that become atretic
are selected, what the remainder of the oocyte
population is. I wish we did know these things
and we did have safe methods. And I am not suggesting for one second that risks should not be
taken; but, there are certain risks that I would
not advise.

As I picked up the thread of what I think Bud
was saying, I find it is a view that I share completely. The responsibility in the end is not that
of the propagandist. The responsibility has got
to be that of the people who accept the propaganda
and are prepared to use the methods.

Harkavy: We have left out one of the presentations
that we had in mind, namely, that of Dr. Slobodkin,
but we have been talking a lot of amateur ecology
up to this point. Are there some remarks that
you want to get in now?

Slobodkin: Let me do a few things. First of all, I
    am not going to go through the whole horror story
    of ecology. We know the story. The air stinks.
    The water stinks. This has been summarized by
    Tom Lehrer in his lovely song on pollution.

    There are a couple of general things that do
    come of it that are immediately relevant and I
    am confining myself to things that are relevant
    from, I believe, an operational standpoint, not
    a descriptive or an emotional standpoint. We are
    concerned with a system of global regulations or
    persuasions. Similar problems have arisen in
    less loaded ecological contexts, for example, the
    regulation of fisheries where you have to have
    laws that will be enforceable and not too repugnant
    to persuade fishermen to avoid destroying their
    own livelihood.

    One thing that has become clear of a very
    simple kind, that took a long time to get clear, is
    that you must formulate regulations in the form
    of intensive variables rather than extensive vari-
    ables. To make the distinction clear, when I
    enter a bathtub, the total heat content of the bath-
    tub doesn't concern me. I can describe the total
    heat in the tub and there is much more heat in a
    large swimming pool full of ice cubes than in a
    small tub of warm water. What concerns me is
    the temperature at my skin, the intensive variables
    in the situation. It turns out that fishery regu-
    lations, couched in the form that this country must
    take no more than $\underline{n}$ kilo-tons of fish from the
    ocean, are completely unenforceable. The only
    regulation that make any sense to the fisherman
    or to the enforcing agency are those which have

meaning every time a fish meets a fisherman; for example, a regulation that net size shall not be smaller than so much. This is the junction where the problem occurs.

In the same sense, regulations or recommendations relating to population control must have meaning when a man meets a woman, in a very real sense, and if they cannot be translated into those terms, we are talking a kind of nonsense and substituting intention for action. This is one general principle.

Bernstein: May I interrupt there? It seems to me that this is not a very valid principle because, while you have a competitive factor, we are looking after all the women of the world and when somebody elsewhere has a child, it doesn't have an effect upon our ego or our income, whereas in fishing you have a competitive factor that gives you a large force for uniform requirements on all fishing nations. I fail to see the relevancy.

Slobodkin: Let's take fishing where we are safe. In fact, a competitive factor exists in people, too, if your kids are trying to get to college—you know what I am talking about.

Bernstein: It would have to be worldwide, though.

Slobodkin: Worldwide it also exists. I am trying to avoid belaboring that issue; that is, if there are enough people miserable enough anywhere in the world—John Donne summarized it and it is in the literature. I can document John Donne's sermon, but why bother? Is that fair?

Bernstein: I think it is a hell of a leap from John
    Donne to your proposition.

Slobodkin: O, dear! In fact, I find it difficult to
    answer you in the time limitation. I think we can
    say that those fishery regulations or control
    regulations that were not phrased in terms of
    intensive variables have resulted in the destruc-
    tion of fisheries completely. We can say further
    that any law which says: Mississippi, for example,
    should not have more than n children is an un-
    enforceable law, or even a recommendation that
    says Mississippi should not have more than n
    children is an inoperable recommendation. Does
    that make sense?

Bernstein: Not completely, because there isn't that
    degree of mobility. There are lots of things that
    Mississippi can do about childbearing that might
    be effective. Not everybody can dash off to ad-
    joining states. Not all people have the opportunity.

Fisher: In the case of the fishery you have to know
    how big the mesh in the net should be; and there
    must be an overall notion of what tonnage of fish
    can be taken that would be consistent with certain
    conservation principles. On the other hand, you
    can't start with the size of the mesh without having
    the other, for you have to have both as they are
    different levels. One is more general, one is
    more operational, and so with the babies in Missis-
    sippi.

Slobodkin: Good. In fact, one is a policy statement.
    One is turning a policy into operational form.

The policy can be over a broad area and this is
decided on other grounds, presumably on rational
or political grounds.

Making the regulation or the recommendation
operational involves translating it into the actual
intensive variable form where a man meets a
woman, or a fisherman meets a fish, or a fish
meets a man. On a certain level is the problem
how to decide the policy first. Then how do you
make it operational?

Again, sticking to ecological problems, you
have a hierarchy of decisions that have to be
made (some of the decisions to be made) by
responsible officials depend on information which
must be provided from completely different kinds
of officials.

We have practical problems, recognized as
practical problems by the mass of people, or by
the governing elite, or by someone else. You
have to recognize this as a problem and decide
that we must do thus and so about it.

In order either to recognize it or decide
what to do about it, one must have available a
feed-in of "scientific information," and I will put
"scientific" in quotes for reasons which I think
will be clear in a moment. The idea here is that
we would not be worrying about the population
problem at all unless we were worried about its
ecological consequences in a sense—that is, the
quality of life is dependent on the number of people,
and if there was no evidence whatsoever of a
deterioration in the quality of life for people as
a function of the total number of people, this
problem would not exist.

Therefore, we have a problem related to what we know about the quality of people's lives and what we can do about it, a kind of information required by whoever is making the regulation to deal with the actual practical problem.

What kind of information do you require? You require census information, low intellectual level information, the fact that so-and-so is hungry, the fact that this-and-this river is bad, and so forth. This is information of a curiously empirical kind that does not involve any firm scientific foundation. You know that things are bad with the intuitive sense of what bad means, and which requires no particular intellectual elegance. So you have what one might call first order observational information. We have been talking mainly on this level.

To have our concern meaningful and practical, we require, in particular, first-order observation. It has come up in the discussion that, to a large extent, we don't have all of the first-order information that we would like. We have some, enough to know there is more to be had and important to have the remainder.

In order to get better first-order information (and this outline isn't going to be completely logical; I don't have time to restructure what I was going to say), to construct or to get the proper information, we require certain censusing techniques, bioengineering techniques, and so forth.

We are operating at several levels, namely, information is being fed in to permit decision-- information about the world. Information is also being fed in on the same set of pathways or the

same kind of pathways how to affect the world,
so that when we are talking here about engineering,
we are talking about how you engineer a census
program. We also mean how you engineer an
intrauterine device. The man who does the job
of engineering the census program or the man
who does the job of engineering the intrauterine
device needn't be a demographic expert nor an
expert in biochemistry. He is fed certain information from two sources. He is told what is
needed on a policy level. He is also told what he
ought to know to get the job done, from a scientific
level.

So, the engineer provides either the first-
order technique or the first-order observation
which permits the policy-maker to modify his
activity. The policymaker, of course, is in a
political context that I haven't mentioned.

On the level of fundamental science, the
population problem in its broadest sense involves
two utterly disparate things. One is the physiology
of reproduction and perhaps certain aspects of
very fancy theoretical sociology and anthropology;
also a theory of evolution that tells you what you
might do to the environment if you are mucking
it up. These all have to come in, to feed in, so
what we are getting is a census system involving
different degrees of technical depth, different degrees of intellectual depth, and a series of such
channels, one starting with ecological theory,
meteorological theory, and so forth; one starting
with biochemical theory, all feeding up to decision-
makers who in turn are receiving their orders—
and they are orders—from a set of political

constraints and a set of sociological circumstances. To make the problem complete, on every one of these levels we have gaps. We simply don't know. That is, the decision-makers, as I understand it, have a feel for what their constituency, whatever it is, wants them to do, but it isn't spelled out.

Saunders: And it is sometimes wrong.

Slobodkin: It is sometimes wrong. Also, the decision-maker doesn't have the information on all these levels that he must have if he is going success-fully to do what his constituency really wants done, if he can find out what that is.

    Correspondingly, the engineer has relatively clear orders, perhaps not, but he doesn't have the fundamental knowledge that he requires to do his job, and on every level there are these gaps. On every level there is an absolute urgency. The decisions of the decision-maker, as we have seen in connection with the Pill, for example, cannot wait on the final word from the biochemist; nor can the direction of the biochemist wait for a valid statement of what he ought to do from the political decision-maker, so the approach that has to be taken is to avoid the kind of statement that I have heard in the last several days, "That is beside the point." It is startling how much is to the point here. All of these pieces have to hap-pen at once; they all have to be fed in at the same time, and they all have to be fed in immediately. We cannot, in practice, wait for this to be ab-solutely firm and then go on to the next thing.

Harkavy: Thanks very much.   That was an interesting exposition.

SUMMATION
SIR SOLLY ZUCKERMAN

THE FIRST CONFERENCE ON POPULATION
Princeton, New Jersey
September 27-30, 1968

Let me begin by saying that I owe the privilege
and the burden of summing-up our discussions to a
mistaken view of what constituted the head of the table.
I sat in this chair believing that Dr. Harkavy and you,
Dr. Shelesnyak, would place yourselves at the central
point of the horse-shoe. The fact that I ended up sitting at the side of Shelly made him impose this task
upon me. If somebody else had been sitting where I
am, I have no doubt he would now be doing this.

Nonetheless, the opportunity of providing a summing-up of our discussions of the past several days
does afford me the opportunity to see if the objectives
we were all invited to state at the start, about what
we individually expected to get out of the conference,
have in my case been satisfied. I do not recall my
exact words, but I seem to remember that I said I
would first like to learn in the days before us whether
there was a population problem; and second, whether,
if there were a problem, we were concerned with a
single problem, relating to the whole human species,

425

or whether we were dealing with a series of separate population problems.

I wanted to discover, too, if we knew enough
about the whole problem of limiting population-
growth either to encourage or to impose restric-
tive measures on human breeding, in a general
way or in a directed way.

Then I said I hoped the meeting would show
that we all realized the realities of political and
institutional controls, and what national and
cultural interests are involved in different countries—because these things are not always the
same. I reflected that I have taken part in discussions on population growth for many years,
but that today I occupy an official position that
could impose on me the obligation to provide a
sophisticated answer to the questions: What is
the population problem and what does it mean to
the United Kingdon, and what should we do about
it?

When we began, I described myself as a natural
scientist who had specialized in the physiology of
reproduction. I also added that I was a politician.
I certainly did not mean a politician in the ordinary
electoral sense; I meant that I am concerned with
the political process. I also tried to remind you—
perhaps I didn't explain the point sufficiently—that
we have been talking politics at this meeting; we
have not been talking pure science. We are talking
about action programs. We are talking about social
problems that are seen differently, through different eyes, and for which we all can suggest solutions—but solutions which don't necessarily coin-
cide one with the other. We have to stand up

and be counted when we talk about population, whether we are active propagandists for limitation or whether we are on the other side.

As Dr. Harkavy indicated, I can't possibly make a résumé of the two and a half days of talk. I can't refer to people by name, and I don't propose to; I shan't be comprehensive, and I may not do justice to everybody. I certainly must select, and it is quite clear in my own mind that if somebody else were doing the job, his summing-up would be different from mine.

He might, for example, prefer not to take my view about what the central emphasis of our discussion should have been. I myself am concerned with action, for the simple reason that if sensible action is not taken now, those who have to propose action twenty years from now will have a much more difficult problem to deal with. We live in a period of rapid change. Issues new to some of us may have been raised during this conference. But, we should first ask ourselves—and particularly those who have been studying the problem of population over, say, the past twenty years— whether the picture of the population explosion that we had in mind in the late 40's and the fears that we were sensing at the time, have been realized.

The answer is that so far as global population growth is concerned, the picture has been realized. I remember the estimates and projections that we discussed at the first UN conference on the subject. World population has grown very much faster than people supposed it would at that time. On the other hand, the explosion has not been as

shattering as people had expected. The peoples
of the world have accepted the fact of rapid population growth: they are living with it; and they are
adjusting to it. So far as the present is concerned,
I ask what new fears are we envisaging, and how
are we going to accommodate to them?

In the long term, by say the year 5000, I
accept that all fossil fuels may have been exhausted.
I accept that even by the year 2000 the world will
look very different from what it does now—with a
population of 7 billion—if it becomes 7 billion.
Equally, I am tolerably confident, because of my
own awareness of the changes that have occured over
the years, that human institutions different from
those that now regulate our social lives will
emerge over the intervening period. When one
reflects on the ultimate population catastrophe
about which some people talk, one must ask
whether our species as a whole is still in the position of the animal, and of those few human groups
of hunters and foodgatherers who still live a life
similar to that of the animal; whether with our
technological miracles we are creating an environment incompatible with continued human survival,
an environment to which we cannot adapt; or
whether we will be able to transform that environment in such a way that the much bigger population which the world will see tomorrow will be
able to survive. We have heard much about the
way we pollute our environment. But, we know
that pollution also occurs in the animal world.
The beaver, for example, is responsible for a
great deal of erosion, but he lives in a biosphere
in which the trees that he destroys are adapted for
survival just as much as is the beaver.

We know that certain primitive peoples, for example the Kalahari bushmen of South Africa, still live the simple lives of foodgatherers and hunters, in the same way as does an animal species. That kind of life could go on idefinitely. It is not provoking the kind of environmental erosion and pollution that industrialized man seems to be doing. The question is whether the consequence of unrestrained population growth associated with industrialization will be the creation of an environment to which we cannot adapt. That is a basic question which underlies much of the discussion of this meeting. It has cropped up implicitly time after time.

Equally, I think, what has emerged is that all people want to avert the political disasters which could occur as a consequence of uninhibited population growth. We don't want plague and pestilence; we don't want large-scale massacres; we don't want poverty, and we wish to see any kind of hardship reduced. We all want to encourage a better world. And, we know that the economic and political problems of the underdeveloped countries will be more easily dealt with if rates of population growth are lower.

What then have we learned from this meeting about what needs to be done to avert the unwanted consequences of unrestrained population growth and to encourage a favorable outcome? What have we learned about the facts of the situation? For the answers I now turn to the program we have followed, a program which I think was very well arranged.

We discussed the question of the likely size of the world population, now 3.2 billion, and the

question of the population of different parts of the
world by the year 2000. Dr. Notestein told us
that the figure for the world will fall somewhere
between the limits of 4. 5 and 7. 5 billion. Those
are the best estimates for lower and upper limits,
4. 5 being an absolute minimum that assumes all
potential parents now alive do no more than reproduce themselves. We know, too, that with a
net reproduction rate of 2. 4, world population
doubles in a period of twenty-five years. We
learned that in the underdeveloped parts of the
world, where population is growing most rapidly,
there isn't the same age distribution in the breeding stock as exists in the more developed parts of
the world. There are more in the younger age-
groups, meaning more breeding couples for the
years ahead.

Reference was made to various discontinuities
that might affect the projections we make about
population growth—for example, the possibility
of nuclear war. I think it was Professor Ehrlich
who suggested that the likelihood of nuclear war
would increase as world population grew—because
of growing tensions. That is a generalization
which, must confess, I find rather difficult to
accept. Nuclear weapons are dangerous enough
without bringing in the population problem. And
there are a lot of countervailing political pressures. Equally, I am personally dubious about
those plagues which it was suggested might spread
because of Bacteriological Warfare Laboratories
starting to spill some of their products. These
were the kind of discontinuities that were referred
to in our discussions.

We heard about the errors that constantly beset our straightforward predictions. There have been considerable errors over the past twenty years. In fact, practically every estimate about population growth has been an underestimate. Underestimating has come about mainly because mortality rates have been falling faster than people supposed. The basic uncertainty about forecasting population trends was, of course, epitomised in the 30's by the publication of two conflicting books, more or less simultaneously: The Twilight of Parenthood by Enid Charles, and No Standing Room by E. A. Ross.

We were reminded that a learned Royal Commission on Population sat for several years in England, reporting shortly after the conclusion of the Second World War, and that most of its estimates turned out to be wrong. But they were highly important estimates for the United Kingdom, because it was on their basis that the first postwar plans for the expansion of our schools, our hospitals, and so on, had to be based.

In spite of our disappointing experience with projections, we cannot escape them. Estimates and predictions of population growth are absolutely necessary to carry on. Without them we cannot begin to plan our cities (regardless of the deficiencies of planning); we cannot plan our schools, our hospitals, our road systems, and so on. It doesn't seem fatal to me if the new cities we plan on the basis of these projections turn out to be obsolete twenty years from now. There seemed to be a note in some of our discussions that this possibility constituted disaster. But, which city is now

adequate for the particular circumstances in which
we operate? What cities of the seventeenth century were adequate to the population of the nineteenth? These things happen all the time. We
are never going to be able to plan for a permanent
kind of human society. Transformation is of the
essence of things.

It is for that reason that I would remind you
of some things that emerged clearly from our
first two discussions: first, we need better data
than we now have about the existing stock of
people in different countries; second, we need
far better data about birth rates not only within different countries, but in different parts of the
same country; and, third, we need to know more
about the changes that are taking place in birth
rates, and I would add, in mortality rates.

Much of our talk focused on the need for better
information about changing trends in family and
mating habits. Equally we could do with better
analyses than we now have about the changes that
have occurred in fertility trends over the ages.
I don't believe as much has been done in this field
of research as might be done. Such analyses
could provide us with a better understanding than
we now have of the particular variables that have
been the most important in transforming family
habits and the size of population in particular
countries. But clearly work of this kind is possible only when registers of births and deaths in
particular communities are available over a long
period.

So much for the predictions about population
increases which we have been discussing. The

broad conclusion is that the world's population
will increase considerably. The traditional way
to confront this fact is, of course, to assume
that population will increase so fast that all the
resources on which mankind draws in order to
keep alive would soon be exhausted. But this
meeting has also concluded that in global terms,
so far as the world as a whole is concerned, the
old Malthusian proposition that land is going to be
a limiting factor on population growth no longer
applies. Through the modernization of agriculture,
it is possible to envisage an increase in the output of food which could, in theory, satisfy any size
of human population—even, if I followed the discussion correctly, a human population of 7.5
billion by the year 2000.

Food, it was urged, is thus no longer a constraint on population size. This is due the successes achieved by agricultural scientists in
devising new breeds of food crops, better and
cheaper fertilizers, and in providing a better
understanding of the uses of water and of the value
of modern pesticides, herbicides, and so on. I
was immensely impressed to learn that Haber's
discovery of nitrogen fixation had, in effect,
halved the cost of a unit yield of crops by the time
the First World War ended, and that in the past
few years it has halved it again.

We were also told, if I remember correctly,
that with respect to fertilizer and pesticide usage
the annual input into an acre of land in countries
such as India, countries which have recently
enjoyed a phenomenal increase in their production
of food stuffs, is considerably below what is regarded as the optimum in the United States.

But, we were also reminded—and this is
important—that the modernization of agriculture
brings in its train inevitable and often unmanage-
able social problems. First, that concentration
of production carries the risk of overwhelming
catastrophe due to a failure of crops, leading to
major overall losses in output. This risk does
not apply when production, instead of being concentrated in one area which has been highly cap-
italized and modernized, is distributed between
large numbers of small farmers over a much
wider area. Second, it was suggested that
the modernization of agriculture in more favorable
areas of India, such as the Ganges plains in the
north, and the extensive rice bowls in the south,
will mean that the chosen regions will, for a short
time, be able to absorb new labor from the vast
Deccan, we would end up with a situation in which
the millions who live there find themselves in
increasing difficulties due to the impossibility,
because of environmental disadvantages, of increasing their own productivity in agriculture or
of finding alternative employment through industrialization.

We learned about the difficulties of converting food surpluses, produced in the favored capi-
talized areas, into mobile resources, into real
income, and about the danger of countries, for that
and other reasons, reverting to cheap food policies.
Our attention was also drawn to the important consideration that it is meaningless to talk about increasing food production in purely global terms.
A superfluity of food in the world-at-large is not
a sufficient condition for the elimination of world

hunger, any more than is the modernization of
agriculture necessarily synonymous with the right
balance of nutritional requirements for a given
population. We were warned about the effects of
consumer demand and preference on the way the
farmer plans his production.

As a result of all these things, the modernization of agriculture in a country like India is not
an unmixed blessing. It leads to differential advantages and disadvantages among parts of the
country. When agriculture is modernized at the
same or at a different pace in different countries,
the trading advantages they enjoy with respect to
each other also become transformed. All this
can lead to new inequalities, to serious problems
of displacement, to internal migration, and to
other difficulties that can stimulate political unrest. And, if food surpluses in favored regions
cannot be transformed into monetary surpluses,
there could be a major shortage of capital to provide the opportunity for new work in depressed
agricultural areas.

We then touched on the urban problem. I
was greatly interested to learn yesterday that,
in general, the cities of the underdeveloped world
do not need underused and displaced agricultural
labor. Their populations are now reproducing at
a rate sufficient to keep pace with their increasing
labor demands. So each country concerned—and
this is presumably a world problem—will have to
face problems as it modernizes its agriculture
and as its population grows. In the life of each
developing country there will come a time when it
must face the political problem of balancing the

advantages of modernizing its agriculture against
the deleterious social consequences of doing so.
But, again, no politician need suppose that—in
theory at least—it will not be possible to produce
enough food, by and large, to match population
growth. Here I am thinking about India particularly; that was the illustration we were given.

Someone asked what agricultural policies
would be most conducive to the control of population growth; but we did not get a clear answer to
that question. Since we did not, it seems to
suggest that this issue cannot be viewed in isolation. One cannot conceive of the modernization
of agriculture occurring as a single program of
development in some large country. Educational
levels are rising at the same time. Knowledge of
birth control spreads. Alternative opportunities
for the employment of women—a very important
matter so far as controlling the rate of population
growth—would also occur, or should occur, as
new technology is introduced to modernize agriculture.

It seems clear that the modernization of
agriculture is not an operation that can or should
proceed independently of general rural development plans. And rural development plans, of
course, are plans that have to be made by the
people on the spot, by the people belonging to the
country transforming itself, because only they
can see that these plans are successfully and
happily implemented. Even the United Kingdom,
a country which enjoys all the dubious advantages
of advanced development and apparent overpopulation, experiences enormous difficulty in seeing

that its regional development plans are carried
into effect.

Another point that struck me when we were
discussing these things was the importance of
seeing to the generation of capital. The less a
country is able to transform its food and other
primary product surplusses into exchange commodities, the more will it have to seek capital
from outside.

So much for the idea that population growth
can outstrip the possibilities of food production.
When we came to the question of hard resources,
we learned much the same story. Theoretically
there is no reason to suppose that population will
exceed, by the year 2000, the physical resources
necessary to satisfy demand. From the purely
global and theoretical point of view, forgetting
about the differing circumstances of different
countries, there is no problem about water, about
energy supplies, about minerals, about metals,
for advancing technology will provide the necessary
solutions. It has done so in the past, and there is
no reason to suppose that it will not do so up to
the year 2000. We are apt to lose sight of the fact
that materials are often interchangeable, and that
interchangeability occurs at different rates in
different parts of the world. The Americans,
for example, are ahead of the United Kingdom in
things like this paper cup. But because we do not
have as much copper and lead available as you have
in the United States, it is possible that we in the
U. K. went in for plastic drainpipes in a big way
before you did. Our new building programs,
housing programs, are based upon cheaper, and

what some people over here regard as better
designs, and upon better materials than those
which are in common use in the U.S.A.

But, I should remind you that while it may
be true that there is no need to fear that we shall
run out of hard resources and energy supplies in
relation to the predicted growth of population up
to the year 2000, everything we are doing at this
moment in major investment programs is determining the stage for tomorrow. For example,
in the United Kingdom we have to plan our energy
supplies well ahead. Although for the last year
or so we have been tapping the natural gas in the
bed of the North Sea, we, in fact, did not know
about natural gas long enough for the plans we
had already laid for our coal industry and for our
nuclear power to be significantly affected, given
that they needed to be because of this new factor.
To revise vast national plans is easier said than
done. There is considerable momentum in social
and economic decisions that have already been
taken. But above all, let us remember that what
the advanced countries can look forward to in
their enjoyment of hard resources in the years
ahead is hardly the same prospect that faces the
developing countries of the world.

Another major consideration that we have to
remember is that as we provide the increasing
volume of raw materials that will be called for
by the year 2000, their consumption will add to
the general problems of pollution which we have
been discussing, and to which I shall return a
bit later. I am talking about the year 2000: I am
not talking about eternity. I am talking about the

year 2000 because what happens in the years between now and then may well be affected by the
advice and propaganda emanating from experts
in this group.

We then discussed living space, hearing much
about overcrowding. We heard what was to me a
fantastic story about the growth of cities: that in
about fifty years, cities of over one million inhabitants will hold 50 per cent of the world's population. A city of a billion inhabitants—an agglomeration of a billion people—can also be imagined
as existing by the time world population has
reached 15 billion. This is an amazing thought in
light of one's own preferences in the field of
esthetics and amenities. The trend to increasing
urbanization is happening now, and seems relent-
less. We were told—and I know it to be a fact in
the United Kingdom—that most people prefer to
live in big cities. There are also irresistible
structural and economic forces that impel them
to do so. The prospect, to me, is a most astonishing thing. I live in a city because that is where
I work; but whenever I can, I flee to the country.
That, apparently, is becoming an eccentric taste.
Try, for example, to get a secretary to leave the
city to come and work in the glorious environment of a marvelous countryside, provided with
far better accommodation than can be enjoyed in
the city, with a salary that is even bigger than
they get in the city, they still prefer the city.
This is happening in the United Kingdom at the
present.

We all accepted at the start of our discussions
that unrestrained population growth entails, both

directly and indirectly, the risk of political instability. When we were discussing the issue of
big cities yesterday, I asked the question, "What
is wrong with big cities?" We were told that big
cities are centers of political unrest. But, I
must ask again now, what is new about this? Big
cities have always been centers of political unrest. It wasn't, and isn't, always a village
Hambden who began or begins the attack on the
Crown, or the modern equivalent of the Crown.
Cities have always provided better possibilities
for political discussion, and political discussion
can lead to major upheavals.

The countries of the world are in imbalance
now. It is an imbalance that cannot but continue
and increase for many years to come. Some feel
a sharp disparity between the growth of resources
and the growth of population. For years it has
been a commonplace view, perhaps too simple a
view, that the rich will get richer, and the poor
poorer. At this meeting we have asked whether
we could ever assume that the rate of population
growth in India could be so retarded that the
average level of welfare, the average standard of
living would not deteriorate. There is nothing
qualitatively new about this problem. Let's not
lose sight of this fact. Social disparities have
always been with us. They existed in the six-
teenth century, in the seventeenth, in the eighteenth and the nineteenth, as they do today. But
there has always been an effort to reduce them
and to improve conditions.

Admittedly the spur to action is greater now
than it has ever been. We all know that the clock

is not going to be turned back, that the drive for
modernization—for transistor sets, for motor
cars and all the rest of it—will continue. We
know that death rates are going to continue to fall.
We can't legislate for nuclear disaster or for
plague. All countries will, therefore, press on,
on as broad a front as possible, and to the best of
their abilities, in trying to match the growth of
such resources as they are able to command to
the growth of their population. They will try to
limit births. They will try to improve educational
programs. They will take whatever steps they
can to improve their standards of living. And
from what we have been told—and I have been much
comforted by this—while family planning programs
of a broad national kind are only a recent development—as Professor Berelson's paper says (and
I am very sorry he wasn't here because I was
greatly impressed by what he wrote)—when they
are properly planned and properly implemented,
they have a high prospect of success.

We heard—it was new to me and will, I hope,
be the subject for further inquiry and research—
that once a reduction in net reproduction rates
begins (I think Professor Ehrlich expressed some
doubt about this), the trend is irreversible. Unless I misunderstood, that was claimed. If this
is the case, I would like to know the evidence on
which it is based; it is a matter of immense importance.

But while national family planning programs
can succeed—they seem to have had a remarkable
success in countries like Taiwan—there are a
variety of obstacles to the spread of knowledge

about birth control procedures, particularly in
illiterate and impoverished societies. There are
a vast number of institutional and cultural barriers.
I was much surprised that during the whole of our
discussion nobody drew attention to the recent
Papal Encyclical about birth control that has
caused so much discussion—certainly in the newspapers of the United Kingdom.

Apart from the institutional barriers which
oppose the spread of knowledge about birth control, there are the educational and social barriers
which have the same effect. I imagine that it
was for these reasons that some of us here were
unready to conclude that what has happened recently to birthrates in Taiwan and Korea will
necessarily be repeated in India and in other parts
of the world where the problem of population
growth is acute.

There also seemed to be a bit of doubt in
some of our minds about what in fact did cause
the rate of growth of population in, let us say,
Taiwan to fall. One view was that it would have
fallen of its own accord, and that the process was
only accelerated by the family planning program
which was put in hand.

On the other hand, we seem to be confident
that there is a correlation between low educational
levels and uncontrolled population growth. There
are also general theories about the relationship
of economic advancement to fertility. It was
suggested that we ought to do some big-scale
experiments on birth control measures. I, for
one, should like to see such experiments carried
out, and I was interested to learn that Ghana is

considering such an experiment, in so far as it is about to pass a National Population Act. But in addition to deliberate experiments on massive birth control measures, I hope, as I have already said, that there will be more extensive efforts to analyze changes in fertility rates that have taken place in the past. If we knew what were the most important social factors that had made rates fall in years gone by, we should be better able to help direct future trends and accommodate to them.

But having said this, I think I should immediately add that this conference has shown that what we know about the indirect social variables that influence fertility rates is far from sufficient to allow us to take our eyes for one second off the issue of Family Planning Programs, and in particular off methods of birth control of the kind which Shelly Segal told us about yesterday. We need to encourage the more extensive use of present methods. We want better methods, better based upon knowledge we already have—on the firm knowledge we have. And once they have been devised, we want these better methods to be put into use more quickly than in a period of five years, which was the lag period which Shelly suggested applied now, and to which I added the thought that so far as basic knowledge of reproductive physiology was concerned, the period was nearer thirty years. Let us hope that the proposed use of a continuous low dose of progestin will prove as effective a method as present indications would lead one to suppose. If that does happen, and if implants of the hormone can be made available on a massive scale, it will be a major technical step forward.

We also do not want to overlook the possibility—although quite frankly I don't know how
it is going to be achieved—of a reduction in the
duration of the reproductive life of the female,
for example, a retardation of the onset of fruitful
mating habits. We heard that legalized abortion
remains a realistic means of lowering fertility
rates. And, we were told that in some countries
women are now taking this matter into their own
hands, no longer prepared to subjugate themselves
to laws made by the male of the species. There
have, for example, been minor changes in the
laws relating to abortion in the United Kingdom.
No doubt this movement will spread.

We have been persuaded that educational
levels are vitally important in the determination
of fertility levels, and that in particular we need
more focused education about reproductive
mechanisms. New educational methods are
wanted to fit the particular circumstances of different countries. What we heard from Ritchie-
Calder is enormously important here. The
people of Afghanistan and of India and of New
Guinea, to take three illustrations, do not live or
behave the way we do—and the bulk of them are
still illiterate.

I also have to consider the item in the agenda
of the meeting under the heading "Beyond Family
Planning," which I interpret to mean the measures
collateral to direct measures of birth control—
rural development schemes, problems of female
employment, and then the whole business of
incentives and deterrents, which we did not discuss in any great detail—incentives in poorer

countries to apply birth control measures, and
deterrents if they are not applied. I read in a
recent issue of a British newspaper, The Daily
Telegraph, that in Maharashtra, government employees who refuse sterilization after a third child
will be ineligible for housing or car loans. This
deterrent measure should certainly encourage
the laggards!

As I see it, the most important issue is to
press on with educational programs. They must
be encouraged as countries go in for family limitation programs. The encouraging thought was
put to us that people who have been exposed as
first generation "guinea pigs" to a family planning
program will have children who themselves will
be much more amenable to such programs.

Now I would like to make a plea for more
long-term basic research. When we were discussing Shelly Segal's contribution yesterday, we were
really discussing applications of knowledge that
has already been gained. You, Bud, reminded us
that only $25 million is spent worldwide from every
conceivable source—on basic research, applied
research, and application, in the field of birth
control. Twenty five million opposed to $200 to
$500 million, as I recall now, on cancer research.
In neither case have we got a cure. We don't yet
know how to stop cancer; world population goes
on growing.

One reason why more money is spent on
cancer research is, I think, that the problems in
that field are more easily formulated—for example, the control of cell growth by various agents.
But it is no use spending money on applied research

on fertility if the problems are not well formulated. Equally it is no use expecting great results if first-class brains are not engaged, if there aren't the people with the big ideas to follow—real ideas about how to make an area of physiology that is pretty disorderly now, orderly. The broad outline of the story of the physiology of reproduction that we have today is very much like 1935, with practically no significant change at all. It is useless, to my mind, putting big battalions to work on the difficult problems; that way one usually multiplies confusion. Bad scientific papers breed faster than does population, obscuring the real issues only too easily.

You might say that my summing-up is too complacent in tone, that my "acceptability-rate" of the present situation is too high. I want to assure you that I view the problem of unrestrained population growth with the same gravity as does, let us say, Professor Ehrlich. But I also wish to be realistic. I am impressed by statements that the average temperature of the earth will be some 3 degrees higher than it is now by the year 2000 if world population increases at its present rate, and if materials and energy go on being consumed as at present. I accept the fact that the problem of pollution is becoming more and more difficult. But, we have to ask ourselves: Who are we to decide what kind of world is going to be tolerable for the population of the world in the year 2000? Someone referred yesterday to the brontosaurus. While he was talking, I kept asking myself whether Matthew Bolton and Stevenson and his friends of the eighteenth century, the people who started the Industrial Revolution, could conceivably have projected their minds into the social situation of 1850, a situation which they helped create but to which the people of 1850 adapted, any more than the people of 1850 could have envisaged the situation we are discussing today, and a situation to which we have adapted.

The young of today are changing their habits. When we say the quality of life is being depressed, one has to ask: is that the view of the countries with which we are most concerned? do the people of Ceylon believe, for example, that the quality of their lives has been depressed over the past ten, fifteen years? who decides these things? I personally don't like the thought of the uncontrolled growth of cities, but other people appear to. I recall something which I wrote many years ago on this very subject—that we all deplore the traffic jams and polluted air and the frustrations and irritations of urban life, but that not one of us, in the satisfaction of his personal desires, would be prepared to turn his back on the material benefits of our industrial civilization.

This is how we behave as individuals. The societal pressures come later. It is only when individual actions become transformed into societal pressures that matters such as pollution and loss of amenities get dealt with, and when governments decide how much to spend to put matters right.

I myself do not believe in the concept of optimal size of population, certainly not of world population. Each country decides for itself what size of population it can support. In the United

Kingdom, for example, there are those who say
we would be far better off with a population of 30
million than the 50 million we have. But at the
same time, we are suffering from labor shortages,
and in spite of labor shortages, we introduce new
laws to cut down immigration. With these apparent inconsistencies, what could we make of the
concept of optimum population size?

Each country's idea about its optimum population size changes, too, with time. Consider the
suggestion put forward around this table that, in
order to set an example, the United States should
embark on a population policy which would be
related to an understanding of what constituted the
optimum population size for this country. This
does not strike me as being very realistic in the
face of the prevalent belief that in a competitive
world the larger the population of a highly privi-
leged society, of a highly educated industrial
society, the better.

Supposing the United Nations were encouraged
to set up a permanent commission where people
would wrangle about what should be the optimum
population size for Ceylon, for Australia, for the
United Kingdom, for Western Germany, and so
on, and once these things were agreed, the appropriate birth control programs were embarked on.
I toyed with this thought during our discussions,
but then saw, for example, the French looking
over their shoulders at the Federal Republic of
Germany and saying, "Are they really taking their
Pills? Have they got those implants? How do
we know they aren't faking the figures?" And,
what sanctions have we if they are faking? We
have none.

Short of world government, I do not see the
concept of optimal population size having any real
meaning. But I do see this: that in the whole
business of controlling population size it is individual governments that have the power. Foun-
dations, universities, people who are aware of
the situation, can give the lead. Only governments can be responsible for imposing regulations
that affect the behavior of individuals. The
Family Planning Act, which the British Government brought in this year, has helped transform
attitudes about matters that until then had been
taboo.

We were told at this meeting about an Indian
Ambassador to the United States who was keen on
promoting a national program of birth control, but
failed to get across his views when he returned to
India. As this story was told, I remembered that
a former and highly respected member of the
British Cabinet recently made a speech following
the passing of our Family Planning Act that
seemed to be absolutely in line with the terms of
the Act. The moment he had spoken, there was
uproar from people who did not want governments—Act or no Act—trying to influence family
habits, and his views had then to be qualified.

The place of women in bringing family-plan-
ning programs to bear, which was referred to
this morning, is almost as important, I think, as
that of government. Here, they are not only
propagandists for limiting the growth of population, they stand to gain by such limitation, through
the raising of their social status, in more countries than one.

But in my view government constitutes the overriding force which can bring about social change, and population control measures have to be seen in terms of what is politically feasible. In view of one or two things that have been said here I should like to remind you what we implicitly believe the processes of democratic government to be in the Western world. Before political action is possible, the views of individuals have got to be translated into a majority societal view. But, what is the view of the individual in the greater part of the world to which our discussion has been directed? It is the view of an illiterate individual whose horizon is constrained by a village life. It is that man, who lives as did his forebears in an immediate social world, who has got to be made to realize that population growth constitutes a national problem. That man has got to be made to realize that his own family habits are part of a national problem, part of its cause, that the national problem is his problem, and that is why he himself has to help solve it.

That is the simple message that has to be got across to the illiterate individual—an immensely difficult task—and his views have then to be transformed into a societal view, and a political view— and the political view to an item of governmental policy and that policy translated into action. That is what happens in most democratic societies. If we bypass any of these steps, and encourage "friendly coercion" towards birth control, to remind you of a term that has been used in our discussions, I fear that we might be endangering the political structure of the societies about which we are talking.

Instead, let us remember that one-third of
the peoples of the world, as we were told at this
meeting, is already practicing some form or
other of birth control, some means whereby it is
limiting the size of population. Let us be realistic. The one-third could soon become a half.
The better informed the world is, the more rapidly will this occur, which means that those who are
better informed, such as ourselves, have got to
help by spreading information, by carrying out
more research, by learning more facts, by encouraging the development of human skills in
societies where they are at present lacking. But
in doing these things, in spreading our wisdom,
let us beware lest we direct too much hot propaganda at some of these countries that we are trying
to influence; propaganda could boomerang.

Rome was not built in a day. Its present
population is not going to be reduced in a day,
particularly since the Vatican is quite nearby;
nor is the noise of its streets nor its air pollution,
which I dislike almost more than I do its increasing
population, going to be allayed. Spreading a knowledge of birth control is one thing; alarmist propaganda is another.

That is why, to conclude, I was disturbed at
the suggestion that the family planning movement
might be getting in the way of other and more
effective ways of limiting population. I can't see
these other more effective ways, whereas I can
see the family planning movement as a realistic
way of helping curb the growth of population.
You don't shoot the conductor if you don't particularly like the way he is conducting a piece, and

above all, you don't mow down the orchestra—in
this case, the orchestra of family planners—because you feel they aren't getting their message
across to the whole world. We can't get the whole
world into one hall to hear the message. But, we
can take heart in the thought that when Mozart
and Bach were first played, the proportion of the
then-world population to which they played was
infinitely smaller than the proportion of our
enormously increased population which today knows
their work through orchestras, gramophones, and
radio. This, I believe, is what is going to happen
with knowledge about population control.

One last word. I was provided both with a
burden and with the privilege of summing-up our
meeting. As I said, others would have done the
job a different way. But, I was also granted the
privilege of being one of this group. I would therefore like to thank the sponsors for having provided
me with an opportunity to brush up my knowledge
of population and resources, to remind myself
about some of the facts of the physiology of reproduction, and to realize the enormous number
of problems which still face us. From my point
of view, this meeting has been so successful that
I hope that in this or some other forum it will be
repeated, where people with experience of different aspects of the problem can get together to
exchange views.

Thank you very much.

SUBJECT INDEX

Abortion, 220-221; in Korea, 228, 246-247, 251-253; legalization of, 360, 444

Agriculture, 47-48, 76-86, 90-92, 100; modernization of, 108, 110, 378-379, 434-436

American Indian, 162-166

Barbados, 245

Berelson, Bernard, 25, 108, 232, 250, 375

"Beyond Family Planning," 367-368, 444-445

Biological warfare, 61

Birth control: technology of, 261 ff.; until age of 21, 388-393

Birth rate, 22, 46, 48-49; and education, 229-231; and family planning, 204; in Japan, 203-204; in Taiwan, 224-226

Bruner, Edward, 165

"Capacitation," 290

Catastrophe, 59-60, 77

Chandrasekar, 250-251

Cheap food policy, 78-79, 87-88

China, 44-45

Cities: British planning in, 193-196; control of population growth in, 197-200; growth of, 175; labor in, 183-185; movement to and from, 188-192; overcrowding in, 439-440; problems of planning in, 185-188; in the United States, 179-181

Communication: in Aisa, 385-386, 396-397; devices of, 395-400, 379-385

Continuous micro-dose progestin therapy, 271, 273-283

Contraception, 5, 21, 26, 36, 236-237, 241, 262 ff., 360, 383; antigen and, 293-295; areas for research in, 283-298; delayed conception and, 394-395; hormonal, 270-271; IUD, 266-269; legislation and, 323-324; male, 283,

Illegitimacy, 401-402

Implant, 36-37

IUD (Intrauterine device), 264, 266-269; effectiveness of, 272, 286

India, 399-400, 434-435; birth rate of, 63, 80-88, 161, 171-172, 340-343, 359; Family Planning in, 208-210, 233-234; the Pill in, 255-258; Sharda Act in, 390

Innovation, 174-175, 384

Iran, 236

Japan, 84, 162, 203-204, 230, 251

Kenya, 65, 232

Korea, 228-229

Latin America, 46, 79, 239, 254

Leprosy, 172

Malaya, 223

Marriage age, 45

Mexico, 82, 84-85

New Zealand, 46

Nuclear material: disposal of, 133-140, 142-143; (see also waste disposal)

Pakistan: birth rate in, 63, 172; Family Planning in, 208-209, 233

Pesticides, 96-98

Pill: effectiveness of, 272; in India, 255-258; in Korea, 228; side effects of, 412-415; summary of, 423; in Taiwan, 225; in United States, 256; use of as birth control technique, 265-269

Pincus, Gregory, 5, 255, 265

Plague, 48, 56, 61

Pollution, 132, 140-141, 145, 438-439

Population: acceptability of growth in, 253-254; and effects of overpopulation, 409-410; factors against control of, 379-382; and Family Planning, 201 ff.; growth of, 46, 100-105, 229, 353 ff.; 427-432; and individual rights in control of,

PARTICIPANTS INDEX

457